TRADITION AND DEVELOPMENT

TRADITION AND DEVELOPMENT

Edited by

Sachchidananda
B. B. Mandal
K. K. Verma
R.P. Sinha

CONCEPT PUBLISHING COMPANY, NEW DELHI-110015

ISBN-81-7022-072-6

First Published 1988
Reprinted 2012

Published and Printed by

Concept Publishing Company Pvt. Ltd.
A/15-16, Commercial Block, Mohan Garden
New Delhi-110059 (India)
T: 25351460, 25351794, *F*: 091-11-25357109
E: publishing@conceptpub.com, W: www.conceptpub.com
Editorial Office: H-13, Bali Nagar, New Delhi-110 015, India.

Preface

While planning for the Silver Jubilee Year Programmes for the Institute in 1984 it was decided to have an all-India seminar for each discipline represented therein. For the Division of Sociology and Anthropology 'Tradition and Development' was chosen as a theme for the seminar. The main purpose was to assess the role of tradition in the development process. It was envisaged that the role could be development promoting, development retarding, or neutral. Invitations were sent to many scholars in the country to throw light on diverse aspects of the theme. Some of them enthusiastically responded. Many of the colleagues from the Institute also volunteered to contribute papers. The seminar was held late in September, 1985. Despite a number of obstacles we were able to get together twenty one papers which were presented and discussed at the seminar. It was inaugurated by the Director of the Institute, Professor Durganand Sinha, whose illuminating address set the tone of discussions that followed. Dr. B.B. Mandal acted as the coordinator and managed the different aspects of the seminar with zeal and efficiency.

As the theme was very attractive and the papers presented were reasonably good, the Director was kind enough to promise a subsidy for the publication of the papers in book from. However, I had to leave the Institutc on having accepted assignment as the Vice-Chancellor of the Ranchi University. Dr. B.B. Mandal, Dr. K.K. Verma and Dr. R.P. Sinha, all Readers in Sociology at the Institute, however, kept on pressing the contributors for submitting their final revised version. When I came back to the Institute most of the papers had arrived and the final editing was done. I provided an introduction which briefly gives an idea of the contents of various papers.

Dr. B.B. Mandal, Dr. K.K. Verma and Dr. R.P. Sinha have collaborated in this effort from the very beginning to the final stages, in a way that merits their co-option as editors of the volume.

The Concept Publishing Company agreed to publish the book. I am grateful to Shri Naurang Rai for this.

A.N. Sinha Institute of Social Studies, Patna.
December, 1986.

Sachchidananda

Contents

Contributors

Durganand Sinha is Director, A.N. Sinha Institute of Social Studies, Patna.

A.K. Danda is Director, Anthropological Survey of India, Calcutta.

P.K. Bhowmik is Professor of Anthropology, Calcutta University, Calcutta.

Archana Sinha is Professor of Sociology, Patna University, Patna.

Sachchidananda is Professor and Head, Division of Sociology and Anthropology, A.N. Sinha Institute of Social Studies, Patna.

Sharit Bhowmik is on the Faculty of the Indian Institute of Management, Calcutta.

P.K. Nayak is Reader in Anthropology, Utkal University, Bhubaneshwar, Orissa.

S.N. Tewari is Lecturer in Sociology, L.N. Mithila University, Darbhanga.

Renu Ranjan is Lecturer in Sociology, Magadh Mahila College, Patna.

Anirudh Prasad is Research Officer, Harijan Cell, A.N. Sinha Institute of Social Studies, Patna.

R.P. Sinha is Reader in Sociology, A.N. Sinha Institute of Social Studies, Patna.

B.B. Mandal is Reader in Sociology, A.N. Sinha Institute of Social Studies, Patna.

Hetukar Jha is Reader in Sociology, Patna University, Patna.

K. Gopal Iyer is Reader in Sociology, Panjab University, Chandigarh.

Manjit Singh is Doctoral Fellow in Sociology, Panjab University, Chandigarh.

P.N. Thakur is Doctoral Fellow in Sociology, A.N. Sinha Institute of Social Studies, Patna.

Binod C. Agarwal is Scientist, DEKU-ISRO, Space Applications Centre, Ahmedabad, Gujarat.

K.K. Verma is Reader in Sociology, A.N. Sinha Institute of Social Studies, Patna.

Krishna Bala is Reader in Sociology, Patna University, Patna.

Samita Manna is Lecturer in Sociology, Kalyani University, Kalyani, West Bengal.

Manohar Lal is Lecturer in Sociology, A.N. Sinha Institute of Social Studies, Patna.

Durganand Sinha

Inaugural Address

Every society is characterised by its own system of opinions, beliefs, attitudes, values, customs and institutions. These are handed down from one generation to another and constitute a kind of accumulated experience which provide guidelines for the community and a base for its behaviour. Usually we characterise such systems as a part of the tradition of the community. In the context of development, it is taken almost as an axiom that what is traditional is an impediment in the path of modernity and progress. In fact, dichotomy between tradition and modernity is generally taken for granted, and it is widely felt that villages in India being traditional in outlook, belief systems and behaviour patterns, development there is a difficult process.

The roots of this line of thinking can be traced to Max Weber (1958) who took Hindu culture as a barrier to economic development because of certain peculiarities of its tradition, belief systems and the way of life that was inculcated. More recently, Rostov (1952) and others have talked about the interfering effects of socio-cultural features of traditional society. Focussing his attention on Hindu religion, beliefs, attitudes, family and institutions, Kapp (1963) concluded that in such a context economic planning and development in India were difficult and the national effort in this direction was doomed to failure.

Underlying all this is the domination of the West, as far as transfer of knowledge from industrialised and advanced societies to the subservient undeveloped and colonial countries of the so called Third World is concerned. Many scholars have, at least implicitly, been victims of this attitude and have indicated that for development not only the transfer of advanced technology from West is essential but it is also necessary to emulate its belief-attitude systems and life style. In other words, all that is traditional has to be cast off and emulation of the West is a **sine qua non** for development. Social scientists have, therefore, tried to abstract certain features of developed societies and have prescribed their inculcation in the developing countries. Thus, comparing data from certain developed and developing countries, Inkles and Smith (1974) have analysed what constitutes attitudinal modernity, and have prescribed it for the developing world. Harry Trinandis (1971) has also identified what he calls 'modernity syndrome' and considers it as an essential condition for development. McClelland (1961,1965) has similarly stressed the need for achievement which is so characteristic of the developed countries of the West. His study reveals that high need for achievement preceded accelerated economic development in many societies, and therefore was considered vital factor in it.

This kind of ethnocentric model of the developed man posed on the study of industrial, urban and middle class societies of the West has not gone unchallenged. People have doubted whether one has essentially to be high in achievement need, rational, individualistic with impersonal orientation and so on to show any kind of development. The universality of such a model of the developed man has been questioned and the vital role of culture-specific factors operating in the process has been high-lighted. The unique case of Japan which has shown socio-economic development its traditions, belief systems and way of life has often been cited. The model of development based largely on economic and technological terms has also not gone unchallenged. Not only the concept of development in such narrow terms has been criticised but a more expanded view in the shape of total development of man or human development has been substituted as an alternative. Further, the negative aspects of development as witnessed in the industrialised-urbanised societies of the West have forced people to give a second look at development itself. The problems of pollution, alienation, delinquency, stress, mental health, to mention only a few, that seem to be associated with development have shaken our belief in the kind of development that has taken place in the West. At this point, people have begun to view the relevance of traditional belief systems, values and life style which is in congruence with the "culture of the country". In fact, a second look at tradition as a whole is being given to analyse its functional components and those which are dysfunctional and inimical to development. There is controversy about the functional utility of certain belief systems and orientations. If one takes for granted the features of western societies which are developed, then personal autonomy rather than interdependence or dependency on others, individualistic orientation rather than collectivism and concern for others, impersonal orientation rather than valuing personal relationships are significant conditions for development. But looking at the recent studies conducted in some eastern societies it has been found that there are no such dichotomies. It all depends upon the way these values and behaviour patterns operate in the context of work and organisational behaviour in a particular society. In my own studies of the nature of motivational pattern associated with development of certain villages, there was clear indication that greater community participation and stronger collective orientation rather than individualism were factors associated with villages that had shown all-round development in recent years. Udai Pareek in his paradigm of development has also taken need for extension and concern for others as one of the vital factors for development which has to operate along side of striving for personal excellence and lower need for dependency. It is also to be noted that in the West the distance between the individual and the community seems to have become a little too wide and striving for personal achievement is so acute that its impact on mental health is not quite conducive. Our tradition prescribes individual excellence but at the same time emphasizes harmony with the community and the environment generally. Traditional model of developed man that we get from our religious and philosophical texts is certainly not the mad chaser of achievement but an individual who attains personal excellence but at the same time remains an integral part of society and the community. In fact, there is nothing like conquering or subduing the environment/nature. A developed man is one who is in tune with his environment which includes physical as well as social environment. He need not follow the western ideal of conquest of nature.

I have hinted at these points to indicate that one need not throw away the tradition altogether. In this context, I would refer to the concept of endogenous development as outlined and emphasized by the UNESCO in its publication **Thinking Ahead: UNESCO and the Challenge of Today and Tomorrow**(1977). It emphasizes the model of endogenous development for countries of the Third World: "Different societies must retain their individual character, drawing their strength from their own community, made of thought and action and adopting the goals keeping with these values with perceived needs and with resources at their disposal". Thus, development implies a socio-cultural context of which the tradition is an integral part.

There is always the danger, however, of going to the other extreme and eulogising everything that is traditional. Such an uncritical attitude is as harmful as emulation of the West and condemning everything that is indigenous and traditional. What is required is a careful examination and analysis of tradition to find out what is functional and dysfunctional to development and utilise those in the process rather than try to transplant such characteristics that have been found associated with development in societies that are alien to our own socio-cultural milieu. If the goals and strategies are rooted in the soil, quick development with least amount of negative fallout is possible. In this sphere, understanding and utilising the tradition and the indigenous systems is essential. Here sociologists and other social scientists have an important role to play.

REFERENCES

Inkeles, A and D.H. Smith 1974 Becoming modern; Harvard University Press, Cambridge.

Kapp, W.K. 1963 Hindu culture, economic development and economic planning in India; Asia Publishing House, Bombay.

McClelland, D.C. 1961 The achieving society; Van Nostrand, Princeton.

McClelland, D.C. 1965 Towards a theory of motive acquisition; American Psychologist, 321-333.

Rostow, W.W. 1952 The process of economic growth; Norton, New York.

Triandis. H.C. 1971 Some psychological dimensions of modernization; Proceedings of the 17th International Congress of Applied Psychology, Bruxelles, Vol.2(12),57-65.

UNESCO 1977 Thinking ahead: UNESCO and the challenge of today and tomorrow; Paris, Unesco.

Weber, M. 1958 The religion of India-the sociology of Hinduism and Buddhism; trans. and edit. by H.H. Gerth and D. Martindale, Free Press, Glencoe.

ONE

INTRODUCTION

The two terms tradition and development have loomed large in the conceptual baggage of sociologists in the context of social transformation in the countries of the third world. This has been so in view of the fact that tradition and development infiltrate and transform each other. Earlier Marx had characterised tradition as a great retarding force, the inertia of history. In his survey of the Asian scene Gunnar Myrdal corroborated this view and held that traditional values, beliefs and orientation slowed down the process of development. Even if overtly they scarcely meet the eye, they affect the implementation of development programmes since they dominate the psyche of the people in those areas.

Tradition is characterised by relatively unchanging techniques, limited economic opportunity, age old conventional understanding, attachment to authority, respect for the pastness of things, dependence on routine and exaggerated respect for precedent. It is realised that tradition is not something removed from oneself. It is created and shaped to present needs and aspirations in a given historical situation. Sometimes tradition provides legitimation for present action. It is in this way that tradition is metamorphosed into an ideology.

In the third world countries development has been accepted as a goal and an aspiration towards which society is expected to approximate. It is most desirable form of social change as through it people seek ends of their choice. They apply their skills and talents to these ends. Sometimes it has been found that traditional means are employed to achieve modern ends. On the other hand, sometimes modern means made available through science and technology are used to further traditional goals. In this process sometimes tradition is itself modernised. As a matter of fact, traditions are not immutable and have changed from age to age. Changing tradition appears like jetsam on the sands of time.

The interaction between tradition and development offers a vast field for study. It has three broad dimensions. Tradition may retard development or it may promote it. In some cases tradition itself may be neutral. It would be useful to illustrate these different dimensions from the widely varying Indian Social scene. For this purpose A.N.Sinha Institute of Social Studies organised a seminar in October, 1985 as part of its Silver Jubilee Celebration programme. A large number of scholars from different parts of India took part in the deliberations and presented papers. This volume is a collection of some of the papers presented at the seminar. The papers have been revised by their authors in the light of the discussions in the seminar. There are altogether twenty papers. Some of them fall into broad themes but a few others illuminate a different aspect in each case.

Three papers deal with changes in the village as a unit of study. A.K. Danda has discussed the implementation of directed change initiated through programmes of community development and Panchayati Raj in West Bengal village. Implementation of Community Development programmes brought about certain immediate material changes which, to a limited extent, are reflected in the social, economic, political and cultural life of the people. However, no significant change is found in the set pattern of dyadic relationships like landlord-tenant, workman-customer etc. Changes in authority structure and control of economic resources were also not much to be seen. On the other hand, positive changes were found in the rules of commensality, untouchability, caste order and social distance. The introduction of Panchayati Raj gave a serious jolt to the locus of power, economy and socio-ritual status. This has generated rivalries based on caste, lineage and religion leading to dismemberment of traditional authority structure and the value system.

P.K. Bhowmick presents a study of continuity and change in a village in Midnapur district of West Bengal. Before the onset of fast moving changes since the sixties, people were psychologically and emotionally united in ceremonial ties inspite of wide ranging economic disparities and exploitation of one class by another. On account of the work of modern forces represented by communication facilities, media exposure, growth of literacy and changing political scene, the village is now a house divided against itself. It is full of disharmony and the sense of belongingness is fast disappearing. The village festivals which give psychic unity to the village have also declined in their popularity. The traditional power structure has ceased to function.

In her paper Archana Sinha has made a study of changes taking place in a village close to Bhagalpur of Bihar. It is a longitudinal study based on observation over a span of more than two decades. In her experience, in regard to this particular village, tradition has not worked as a deterrent to development. She finds that people have better inter-caste relation, are more tolerant and work together. Their quality of life has changed for the better. There is a sharp decline in indebtedness and epedemics have been controlled to a large extent. The intermediate castes have become affluent and assumed leadership roles.

Three papers deal with tradition and development in the context of tribal societies in Arunachal Pradesh, West Bengal, Orissa. The basic assumption in the paper on Arunachal experience is that tradition does not always create an insurmountable problem in ushering in development. Sachchidananda has demonstrated this with reference to his studies among the Apatani, Wancho, and the Digaru Mishmi. The Apatani have adopted with enthusiasm the innovations in economy and agriculture. Their earlier tradition of capital formations, labour management and handling intricate transaction had promoted trade and business in that community. They have taken advantage of education and have entered government employment in a big way. Ritual practices like scarification of women's faces and marriages between boys and girls with wide age disparity are being discouraged. However, the traditional dual class division and domestic rites and festivals continue as before. Their traditional practices have not prevented them in adopting new measures. Among the Wancho despite concerted efforts made towards control of swiddening, the practice still continues as it is closely integrated with their political and social systems. There is no private property in land which is under the control of powerful chiefs. The greatest obstacle in this, however, is the lack of availability of plain land on which settled cultivation could be carried out. The limitations are as much ecological as cultural. The Digaru Mishmi, on other hand, have in some areas adopted a new way of life giving up swiddening for settled cultivation. Success was achieved in this effort through enlightened leadership and constant monitoring of the project by district officials. In times of transition, therefore, tradition, both entrenched and emergent, coexist. In course of time, the emergent tradition wins over the entrenched.

Sharit Bhowmik analyses the impact of development programme on the lives of the tribals who have migrated from Chotanagpur and Santhal Parganas in Bihar and are now settled as cultivators in Jalpaiguri district of West Bengal. They had originally gone as tea garden labourers but now have taken to agriculture. The tribal development project has not been functioning properly. The cultivators were given improved implements which are lying unused as the tribals did not know how to use them. Handlooms have been given but due to lack of resources for buying raw materials and the difficulty of marketing, the scheme failed. A proper assesment of the needs of the beneficiaries and preparation of the people for making use of the innovations was not done. Beside this, the prevalence of corruption in administration led to failure. Thus such a failure may be attributed not to the tradition but to administrative shortcomings.

P.K.Nayak has studied the functioning of Dongria Kondh Development Agency in Orissa in the background of tribal situation in the State. The author shows that the development measures which are in congruence with the tradition of people has greater chances of success as it facilitates the participation of the people. A flexible approach, confidence in the people and the orientation of development personnel in tribal culture are pre- requisites for success. It has also to be borne in mind that development of tribal communities alone in a mixed area is likely to affect the socio-economic balance and adequate measure must be taken to offset the problems created on account of this. The author makes a plea for understanding tribal tradition before introducing development measures in a particular area. The change agents would thus know which elements of tradition could be used to promote development and which others have to be avoided.

Three papers deal with the theme with special reference to two scheduled castes, the Musahar and the Bhangi. S.N. Tiwari has examined the socio- economic conditions of the Musahar in a village in the Bhojpur districts of Bihar during the period of emergency and the Janata Rule. On account of the Panchayat election, the Musahars were politicised and mobilised by certain Communist workers. This led to frequent conflicts between the Musahars and the landlords as a result of which agricultural wages and other facilities were increased. During the Janata Rule, although several measures for their betterment were initiated, their fruits could not reach them. The Musahar leader lost the election and there was great deal of frustration. The author concludes that besides implementing radical measures for the uplift of the Musahars, effort should also be made to change the attitude and behaviour of the higher castes towards them. The traditional position of the Musahar in society is a great stumbling block in their over all development.

Renu Ranjan delineates the changes in the pattern of life of the Musahar and the Bhangi living in both rural and urban areas. Both the communities are getting out of their own traditions and adopting the traditions of the higher castes. Instead of bride-price, dowry had become more common. Widow remarriage and divorce which were common in earlier days now receive social disapproval. Thus the contention that a community giving up its traditions adopts norms associated with modernity, is not wholly true.

The Musahars of the Bodh Gaya region have, in recent years, been in the vortex of change on account of voluntary work done by Samanvaya Ashram and other agencies as well as agrarian struggle against the Mahanth of Bodh Gaya. Anirudh Prasad has studied the changes in their life styles after their liberation from bondage. Even the women in that area have undergone a radical transformation in their attitudes and orientation. People's drinking habit has been reduced, a new leadership has emerged. Consciousness of their rights has dawned upon them and they are making concerted efforts to raise their standard of living. Their daily wages have gone up, they have opted for new technology and send their children to the school.

Changes are to be seen only in such pockets were voluntary workers have been active for a long time. The Musahars have reached a stage when they can absorb change.

There are two papers which throw light on women and children in the context of tradition and development. R.P.Sinha deals with restrictions on the participation and role of women in decision making in the villages of Bhojpur district in Bihar. The study covered 120 married women in the age range of 18 to 49 in three villages situated at a distance of 20 kms. from any urban centre. Traditionally women are subservient to their husbands who place many restriction on their social and political activities. Upper caste women particularly suffer from more stringent restrictions. The wife has almost no say in the family decision making. The traditional role of women is considered to be inside the home and not outside it. They are regarded as weak and dependent requiring constant protection. This makes for male dominance. Tradition provides the ideological and moral basis for this state of affairs. Although certain efforts have been made since Independence towards the legal emancipation of women, the hold of tradition is still very strong both on men and women. It not only effects the awareness of their rights but stifles any attempts towards the liberation of women.

B.B.Mandal has identified a set of norms as developmental in the welfare programmes in Bihar. Some of these norms will be institutionalised easily as they reinforce the traditional norms. Those norms which do not necessitate change in structural relations will also be institutionalised as they provide better alternative to the traditional norms. But those which necessitate structural change will not easily be institutionalised. They will be incompatible with the traditional norms and the incompatibility can be resolved only with the passage of time and with the growing awareness about the inadequacy of traditional norms in achieving the concept of development.

Two papers deal with education. In his paper on colonial legacy and higher education in Bihar Hetukar Jha examines the role of the elite in colonial education in Bihar. Before 1820 education was being spread by the government without any distinction of caste or creed. After the introduction of western education, the elite came to control educational administration. Education was the medium for the formation and sustenance of caste associations. All centers of higher learning were monopolized by the higher castes. The colonial legacy still continues to have a dominant influence on present day educational policy. Thus education which is the vehicle of development has been used to strengthen the position of higher castes; thus enhancing hierarchal structure of the system.

In another paper C.S.P.Sinha shows why with the best of effort in the part of the government, education has failed to deliver the goods. He shows how habits die hard and more so when the road to development has not been clearly defined, We have not made the best use of our tradition. Education should be made more participatory in order to be an effective instrument for development.

Two papers are devoted to migration. In a perceptive paper on the Subaltern in Bihar, K.Gopal Iyer and Manjit Singh have shown that there has been no change in the pattern of their exploitation during the colonial era and after independence. This class is constituted by the scheduled castes and tribes. The emergence of the intermediate castes as dominant peasantry has accentuated repression against the subaltern. Migration which was one of the avenues of escape from the feudal oppression continues to be so even at present. While the migration of labourers from north Bihar was voluntary in nature in the past and continues to be so to-day, for the tribals it is forced as well as accompanied by bondage. Conditions for migration are embedded in the agrarian conditions in Bihar. Those who migrate are drawn from the agricultural labourer and poor peasant categories.

P.N.Thakur discusses the impact of migration of Bihari labourers in Gauhati at the place of the origin of the migrants. The migrants remit money every month to their family and visit their village once or twice every year. Income saved by the migrants has been able to improve their socio- economic status at home. They have become some what well-to-do and the quality of life at home has definitely improved. Traditionally the prestige of the family is defined in terms of land holding, the kind of housing and the level of expenditure on social occasions. Thus migration has made it possible for them to conserve and promote the traditional values. Of course, some new ideas are also brought by the migrants as they have been exposed to outside influence. Their visits reinforce traditional family ties and customs.

One paper is devoted to changes in communication media in recent time. Studies indicate that there exists an information gap between males and females due to unequal access to information. Binod Agarwal re-analysing the data of the survey, conducted to evaluate the impact of Satellite Instructional TV Experiment (SITE), examines whether during SITE, there was an increase in the information gap between information-poor (i.e. women) and information-rich (i.e. men). He shows that TV exposure in community situation has led in bridging the information gap between women and men. In this perspective, a plea has been made to conceive communication as modernizing force of the tradition in which the information gap is consciously maintained so that the position of men and women remain unequal.

K.K.Verma views tradition interposed between developmental efforts and the end result of such efforts as a "screen". In one situation developmental efforts are neturalised by the traditional forces that strive for maintaining the status quo. In the other, efforts are diluted and in third situation the efforts go undisturbed. Verma calls the differential effects of tradition as "screen effect" of tradition. On the basis of observations drawn from the studies of the impact of agricultural development programmes, introduction of micro-technologies, functioning of non-formal education, health and family welfare measures and impact of development communication, he says that the screen effect of tradition is nearly absent in the area of agricultural development. It is the financial and technical constraints which come in a big way. In case of social development tradition comes in a big way and change takes place in this area at a slower pace. In this process of interaction of tradition with developmental efforts, traditions sometimes themselves get changed or modified.

Krishna Bala discusses disease etiology and the mode of treatment in the context of secular and sacred. She equates secular with modern and sacred with tradition. The majority of patients perceived disease in secular terms although a sizable section viewed it as part of the sacred. The mode of treatment of different diseases depends to a great extent on how disease etiology is perceived. Although patients accept the secular mode of treatment, the sacred mode is not outrigtly rejected. In fact, a sizeable section of the people want to adopt both the secular and the sacred methods of treatment simultaneously in cases of serious ailments. The study shows that tradition and modernity are not incompatible, rather they are adapted to each other. Such adaptation reduces social and psychological tension.

Samifa Manna examines the extent of development orientation among people of a small town in the district of Midnapur in West Bengal. The town originally comprised six villages and is still to shake off its rural characteristics. She finds that the people of this town suffer from anomie. They are politically aware and have a preference for communism. They want to move ahead, prefer the small family, aspire for higher education for their children, accept new technology and secular ideas and are generally aware of varied problems that the country faces.

Manohar Lal unfolds the story of the impact of road improvement in some tribal pockets in Ranchi districts in Bihar. Roads provide greater access to educational, health, employment and marketing facilities in the area. They also make the people aware of social and political changes taking place in the country. Opening up of new communication affects traditional norms and values. He shows that road improvement has influenced the family, kinship and marriage, economic relations, distribution of power and level of aspiration.

TWO

Ajit K. Danda

Tradition and Change in an Indian Village

The study of change has, during the past few decades, be come a matter of central concern for all branches of social sciences. In the field of anthropology, an increasing number of studies has focussed on rural societies in transition. Peasant culture represents a local expression of the civi lization of which it forms a part (Redfield, 1961 : 41) and thus provides a useful modal for the study of cultural change in the larger system. The manner by which any item in a programme of directed change affects the sensitive areas can be clearly seen in villages than in cities. In the In dian context the villages, being the sustainers of her civi lizational edifice, approximate the ideal unit of observa tion for such study. Information gathered from a village of the Gangetic plain, Gandhar, furnishes the principal basis for the present analysis dealing with the processes of development and change in rural india.[1] There has been par ticular reference to directed change introduced through the programmes of community development and panchayati raj or peoples' government.

1. The data from Gandhar were gathered in phases during the past three decades. Due to ethical and practical reasons the village has been named ficitiously.

II

As envisaged, the programmes of community development was responsible for integrated development of India's village communities and the panchayati raj was intended to have provided the structural basis for such change. To what ex tent these objectives could be approximated through im plementation of programmes is the special highlight of the present discussion.[2]

When India achieved II independence in August, 1947, here national leaders found themselves facing many urgent problems which demanded immediate attention. The job of socio-cultural and economic reconstruction was one such problem. There were 558,000 villages in the country at that time where 82.7 per cent of her population lived. Agricul ture, engaging 73 per cent of all gainfully employed people, was the mainstay of the economy which provided nearly half the value of India's total production.[3] Mainly because of ancient methods of cultivation the average farm output was very low. Occasional natural calamities further auggravated the situation. Consequently, during the first few years after independence India had to import, on an average, three million tons of food grains every year.

India has been undergoing slow industrialization for the previous few decades. This process has done little to im prove the lot of India's rural population. On the contrary, competition with the industries brought a serious decline in rural cottage industries, depriving many village craftsmen of their main sources of livelihood. As there were not enough industries to absorb the surplus rural labourers, villagers suffered from chronic underemployment and low in come. Neale observed in this connection, "Though Western elements were introduced to disrupt the old society, but not enough to bring the rapid economic advance enjoyed by the West" (1962 : 4). At that time the per capita annual income in India was 255 rupees,

---

2. For the purpose of generalizations some references will be made to observations from a number of other villages belonging to different parts of the country studied by the researchers of the Anthropological Survey of India during 1973-75 as part of the project, "Study of Socio-economic Changes among the Weaker Sections of the Indian Population since Independence."

3. Comparative figures from the United States and Japan are 9 per cent and 18 per cent respectively.

which was far below the bare mini mum necessary to supply two meals a day. Uneven distribution of wealth helped the few rich people to become more wealthy, while the vast majority remained unfed or half-fed. Those who had wealth, had monopolised power and the socio-ritual status.[4]

In the sphere of literacy the picture was grim. Even by the most modest criterion only 14.4 per cent of India's population qualified as literate.[5] Nineteen per cent of the children of school-age were attending school and only half of them reached the fourth grade. Public health and sanita tion facilities were not very satisfactory either. In 1951, there were 154.6 deaths per thousand live births. The general death rate of the country was 25.9 per thousand, and the average life expectancy was only 29 years. On an average, there were 6,300 people per physician. But in rural areas there were 25,000 people for every physician.

In addition, there was the problem of India's millions of underprivilaged groups, the so-called Scheduled Castes and Scheduled Tribes who, when India attained independence, num bered 50,000,000 and 17,900,000 respectively.

The proportions and the urgency of these problems of the newly independent country was so vast that putting into operation of some massive plans was considered essential and immediate for survival and prosperity of the nation.

III

The Indian National Congress had set up a National Plan ning Committee in 1938, to examine the resources of the country and to prepare plans for India's economic reconstruction. There were two major objectives. The com mittee was to explore the means of attaining self suf ficiency for the country as a whole and of doubling the present standard of living of the people within a prescribed time limit. The findings of the National Planning Committee, though did not spell out the social goal of the country very precisely, were

---

4. Most of pre-independent India was under the over- lordship of 562 kings and innumerable zamindars. For details see Lamb, Beatrice Pitney, 1966 : 218-251.

5. One who could write and read one's name was counted as literate.

utilised to a considerable extent in the formulation of post-independent India's First Five Year Plan.

The Planning Commission was appointed by the Government of India in March 1950, to assess the resources of the country and to formulate a plan for their most affective and balanced utilization. Increased productivity and reduction of inequalities were the two main objectives of the plan. Agricultural programmes along with irrigation and community development received the highest priority in this respect and the scheme envisaged a gradual transformation of the so cial and economic life of the villages through cooperation of the villagers for their own betterment.

The Planning Commission divided the whole country into 5,223 blocks and programme had been implemented in 5,195 of them. The remaining 28 had been kept for a marginal adjust ment. As already indicated, the Community Development Project was evolved as a scheme for integrated area develop ment, though the main thrust of the programme was on agriculture and allied items.

IV

Gandhar with its population of 1018 is a moderate size village according to the regional standard. The village is situated in Saharanpur, a district in the North-Western part of Utter Pradesh. Because of its situation between two rivers, the Gangas and the Jamuna, the area is known as Doab, a Persian expression meaning two waters. The ap proximate latitude and longitude of the village are 90°40' north and 77°37.5' east respectively.

The climate of the area is monsoonal. Between June and September the percentage of humidity is very high and the area experiences occasional rainfall. If temperatures are not moderated by rain during this period, day temperatures often reach 100°F or even more. Nights are comparatively cool. November to February is the winter season. The summer months between April and June, are the agriculturally slack season.

The communication system of the area is fairly developed. A broad-gauge track of the Northern Railway passess through the area and connects the region with Punjab, Haryana, and Delhi. The nearest railway station from Gandhar is situated three miles north-west of the village. An asphalt road con nects the village with the railhead. An inter-state high way runs parallel to the railroad.

Gandhar has a total area of 1331.66 acres, nearly 15 acres of which are inhabited and other 37 acres are under water. The rest are agricultural fields. One hundred per cent of the cultivable lands are irrigated. Approximately 500 acres are irrigated by the upper Ganges Canal System and the rest are irrigated by privately owned tube wells. Canal irrigated areas have abundant supply of water only during rainy months. Tube well irrigated areas have ready supply of water throughout the year. Fragmentation of cultivable land poses some problems for irrigation and tractor operation, al though, in comparison with other regions of India, the situation here is somewhat relaxed.

The village is inhabited by sixteen caste groups, ten of whom belong to Hinduism, the remaining six are Muslim. The distribution pattern of land by caste of Gandhar can be seen from Table 1. More than 97 per cent of the village lands are owned by the Tiyagi, who are traditionally agriculturists.[6] Average size of land-holdings per family and per head of the village are 7.357 acres and 1.308 acres respectively. Non- agriculturist castes like Brahman, Chamar, and Kumhar have some cultivable land, although both the amount of land owned by them and the extent of their involvement in farming are relatively meagre. Some of the service castes like Bhangi, Jhiuar, Joogi, Muslim, Lohar, Nai, Sakka, and Teli have no farm land.

There are about 1000 heads of cattle in the village in cluding bullocks, buffaloes, cows and calves. Bullocks and male-buffaloes are used as draft animals by the villagers. Some lend bullock carts and thus supplement their income.

About 28 per cent of the village population is literate. This is above the district and state average but below the national average. Forty-two per cent of the males and 22 per cent of the females are literate. Most of the literates are from Tiyagi (Hindu and Muslim) and Chamar castes. Whereas both male and female are preponderantly literate among the Tiyagi, in case of the Chamar only one out of the 33 literates is female. At present the Chamar

6. The Tiyagis claim Brahmin ancestry, though there is no record of their having any linkage with priestly profession.

among all castes are taking maximum interest in sending their male children to school. As the proportion of land owned by them is relatively low, they are striving to achieve a breakthrough by attaining literacy.

Table 1 : Distribution of Land (in acres) in Gandhar by Caste, Family and Person

Caste	Amount of land owned	Percentage of land owned	No. of families owing the land	Average landholding per family	No. of persons owing the land	Average landholding per head
Bhangi	0.00	0.00	5	0.00	17	0.00
Brahman	2.33	0.17	1	2.33	9	0.26
Chamar	1.67	0.12	29	0.06	148	0.01
Dhiman	18.33	1.38	2	9.16	12	1.53
Jhiuar	0.00	0.00	2	0.00	12	0.00
Kumhar	0.33	0.02	3	0.11	30	0.01
Lohar (Hindu)	11.00	0.83	8	1.38	37	0.29
Lohar (Muslim)	0.00	0.00	2	0.00	9	0.00
Nai (Hindu)	0.00	0.00	1	0.00	6	0.00
Nai (Muslim)	0.00	0.00	2	0.00	12	0.00
Phakir (Muslim)	5.00	0.38	6	0.83	24	0.20
Sakka (Muslim)	0.00	0.00	7	0.00	36	0.00
Saini	1.00	0.07	3	0.33	16	0.06
Teli (Muslim)	0.00	0.00	8	0.00	36	0.00
Tiyagi (Hindu)	663.33	49.81	19	34.91	165	4.02
Tiyagi (Muslim)	628.67	47.21	81	7.76	443	1.42
Total	1331.66		181	7.357	1018	1.308

Although a majority of the village craftsmen and menals live on the income derived from their specialized jobs, most of the Chamar and to a certain extent the Jhiuar, Lohar (both Hindu and Muslim), and Saini live on income derived through extension of wage labour or on money earned as farm- servants.

V

Choice of an individual's profession in rural India is traditionally circumscribed, as is his position in the political set up and social hierarchy. In general, one who has money, has power, as well as socio-ritual status. Quasitotal superimposition of these three factors makes any mobility almost impossible and results in stagnation of society. For a country, where the line of division between those who have and those who do not is so sharply defined and socio-culturally approved that to effect any change be comes a stupendous job.[7] Analysis of information from Gandhar gathered through intensive studies may contribute to our understanding and clarity of the situation.

Gandhar came under the community development programmes as early as on October 2, 1953. The major areas covered by the programmes are : (1) agriculture, irrigation and allied fields; (11) education and social welfare; (111) industries and housing; (1V) health and sanitation; (V) transportation and communication.

Through community development programmes and introduction of the panchayati raj system a three-pronged attack was designed against stagnation and the perpetuation mechanism of Indian society. For a quick but steady economic recovery, agricultural and industrial programmes were initiated. Hous ing, transportation and communication, health and sanitation programmes were designed to promote a better way of life, and education and social welfare programmes were intended to level up the society. In other words, community development schemes in conjunction with the panchayati raj were designed to make frontal attacks against the stagnation of society by planning economic take-off and elemination of socio-economic disparities. The panchayati raj system in particular was made responsible for bringing about change in the locus of power in rural India and thus affecting

---

7. Observations from 26 other villages from different part of the country studied by the investigators of the Anthropological Survey of India as part of the project "Study of Socio-economic Changes among the Weaker Sections of the Indian Population since Independence" corroborate the fact that in rural India in general those who have money also have control over economic resources, power structure, and socio-ritual status. The poor are characterized by the absence of all these qualities and thus the line of division between the 'haves' and 'haves not' is sharp and unam biguous.

redistribution of control over resources and for stabilisting such changes. Most of the programmes of community development were con sidered favorable by the villagers of Gandhar. Intensive probing revealed that, the extent of coverage, both in terms of number of adopters and intensity of programmes, increased with the passage of years.

VI

Introduction of community development programmes ushered in a series of transformation, although changes in rural In dia did not begin with the community development. Transfor mations to a limited extent, in the form of incorporation of new ideas and traits with or without rejection of the old, took place even earlier. Contact with outside world, in creased exposure to urban traits, growing literacy, and pressure of various reform movements and other factors helped to create new ways of thinking. But, as they were un directed and spontaneous in nature, various forces of change often acted at cross-purposes and with little resulting im provement in the existing system. Community development and the introduction of the panchayati raj were the first large scale nation-wide state-sponsored programmes of directed change in India. Due to implementation of these programmes, although on the surface certain immediate material changes become conspicuous and these, to a limited extent, have reflected upon the social, economic, political, and cultural behaviour of the people, no significant change in the set- pattern of dyadic relationship of rural India like landlord- tenant, master-servant, workmen-customer, and so on could be noticed and the intended breakthrough in the set-pattern of relationship in rural India by and large turned out to be illusory.[8]

Specific changes in rules of commensality, untouchability, caste order, and social distance were observed at Gandhar. The high caste Hindu Tiyagi there not only dined with the untouchable Chamar who occupy a very humble position in the village hierachy, they were also instrumental in initiating a campaign to propagate a similar practice. But the intended changes in the authority structure and control over economic resources were not that conspicuously visible.

8. Observations from 26 other villages from different part of the country indicate that except in some limited areas, no significant change in the set-pattern of struc tural relationships has yet taken place in rural India (c.f. footnotes 7).

Initially, because of demographic imbalance, the creation of new professions, and various other reasons, some occupa tional mobility was already in evidence in rural India (Bose 1958 : 73-97). The age-old supremacy of caste sanction lost much of its significance in this respect when mass literacy programme had equipped people for non-traditional occupa tions. Informal discussion circles, participation in which was limited to members of the same caste, changed their character when they became less exclusive in nature. The emergence of pragmatic ways of thinking, the extension of caste affiliation outside the village, and intrafamily relationships are the other areas that experienced change in Gandhar. Marginal changes were also observed in the lagdar kirsan or workmen-customer relationship particularly with reference to mode of payment.[9]

Because of the establishment of sugar mills and other in dustrial undertakings in the vicinity of Gandhar there has been an expansion of non-traditional employment oppor tunities. Landless job-seakers, who used to hire themselves out as auxiliary farmhands during planting and harvesting seasons became interested in regular employment in in dustrial undertakings. The literate section was already apathetic towards farming. As a result of these new employ ment opportunities and consequent economic independence, the people did not pretend to be as obliging to their tradi tional employers as they used to be. Changes also have taken place in many other areas: views about women's education, recreational pattern, germ theory of diseases are to mention a few. But neither of them could create sufficient thrust for initiating any perceptible change in the set-pattern of socio-economic relationships. Perhaps the single factor to have maximum impact in this respect was the introduction of the panchayati raj system.

9. According to tradition, the service castes, locally known as lagdar, get a fixed proportion of the cereal product of the kirsan. With the expansion of areas under crash crop, which is sugarcane, there has been a propor tionate decline in the cereal output of the village. This has reduced the amount of grains that workman used to get as their share from the farmers.

VII

According to Panchayati raj rules, powers were vested in the village government elected by all adult members of the community and they were made responsible for executing cer tain planned programmes. After a period of brief apathy, as becomes evident from the case of Gandhar, there emerged a tendency among people for capturing power. Apparently, this has generated inter-caste, inter-lineage, inter-religious rivalry and resulted in the dismembering of traditional authority structure, the value system to some extent, and the emergance of cummunal tension and ill feeling to a large extent.[10] But there could be altogether a different inter pretation of the development. People, who had little say in the affairs of the village got their due share of recogni tion or at least tried to assert their rights.

On the basis of the nature of right over land, the vil lagers can be divided into landlord and tenant groups. the land-lords, because of close contact with and favour from the supralocal political authorities, used to enjoy absolute rights over lands in their respective territories. It was left entirely to their discretion to formulate rules for renting out lands to tenants. Tenants, in contrast, had no or very limited rights over land. Further, a set of cir cumstantial obligations were also imposed upon them by the landlords. Because of their extremely precarious economic condition, tenants often sell their labour to the landlords in advance. They also receive food-grains on loan during the lean seasons. As their economy hardly permits total repay ment of all their borrowings plus interest, the tenants get caught up into a semi-bonded existence. Naturally they were brooding over age-old grievances and were seeking an outlet.

Villages where there were no landlords, had landowners and farm-hands. These categories are based on the quantity of land possessed under right of usufruct. Based on their share in the labour management mechanism, the people could also be recategorised in a number of other ways. A landlord of land owner, however, always enjoyed the lion's share of what was produced even though that product was mostly the result of the tenants' or farmhands' labour.

10. For a detailed discussion of emergence of factional rivalry in Basudha see Danda, Ajit K. and Dipali G.Danda, 1970:63-7.

The latter categories of people were economically so tiedup with the former that they could hardly venture a comment even if they had genuine grievances. Over-centralization of power, super-imposition of socio-cultural sanctions, and mass illiteracy helped per petuate this set-pattern of relationships. Thus, with the shift of locus of power, expansion of literacy, and economic independence, a major breakthrough could became imminent in rural India.

As indicated earlier, until the introduction of panchayati raj system the locii of power, economy, and socio-ritual status were more or less unicentered. Interplay of these three systems created a hard-top equilibrium that no small force could possibly crush. With the introduction of the in stitution of democratic decentralization of power, one of the strong pillars supporting the perpetuation of set-pattern of relationships was removed. Growing literacy and expansion of employment opportunities emancipated at least partly the hitherto subjugated people of Gandhar. In socio- ritual sphereas also there were definite strides in a major break-through from the old order of life. These together made the whole situation apparently disquiet.

VIII

Representative institutions did not immediately bear the desired fruits. Even partial release of human resources from their age-old bonds created a condition in many parts of the country that was apparently unfavourable for the dissemina tion of induced programmes. Yet it became evident that, by and large, the process was irreversible.

The material progress recorded at Gandhar did not lead to any significant change in the set-pattern of relationships in the village. Most of such benefits flowed to the Tiyagi who were substantial land-owners and economically well-off. The 'have nots' like the Bhangi, Jhiuar, Joogi, Sakka, Saini, and most of the Chamar being landless had very little to gain from the programme of economic development through agriculture and allied schemes. As a result, the village failed to achieve one of the two major objectives of the community development, that is, removal of economic dis parity. In reality, the situation has further aggravated due to the over-absorption of inputs by one section of the vil lagers at the deprivation of another.

In Gandhar, as already indicated, the'haves' at the begin ning ignored the political developments that arose due to initiation of the democratic decentralization process. But when the 'have nots' organised themselves for dislodging the former from the village authority, they consolidated their strength and applied all pressure under their command, in cluding economic, for repelling any change in the political sphere. What should be the proportion of benefits of the 'haves' and 'have nots', particularly when it is intended to remove the disparity? When we evaluate the situation taking the whole village as an unit, Gandhar recorded a creditable success. But a more intimate look within the village indi cates that emotional gratification apart as fellow villagers of a successful village, the 'have nots' there had very little direct gain. All benefits from the agricultural and allied programmes went to those who possess control over resources. Introduction of the "panchayati raj" system did not allow the 'have nots' any access to the village authority. Gandhar thus recorded no major change in the basic structure of set-pattern of relationships of the vil lage. This suggests the need for a sharper and clearer un derstanding of the primary aims and objectives of the rural reconstruction programme.

There cannot be any denial of the fact that economic development, as part of the rural reconstruction programme is a must and should seriously be taken up. But economic development alone, without well-specified social direction, instead of solving problems may further intensify them. In spite of specific mention in the objectives of the programme from the illustrations of Gandhar, no very clear picture of any social direction emerges. It seems necessary that while evaluating a programme, the economic and socio-cultural goals are thoroughly understood and distinctly reviewed for an objective assessment of the over-all situation.

REFERENCES

Bose,Nirmal Kumar 1958 some aspects of Caste in Bengal; Man in India, 38 : 73-93.

Danda, Ajit K. 1966 Planned Development and Leadership in an Indian village; Unpublished Ph. D. dissertation, Department of Anthropology, Cornell University, New York.

Danda, Ajit K. 1970 Changing Authority Structure in a Bengal Village; Man in India, 50 : 63-77. 1973

Dańda, Ajit K. 1973 Development and Change in Basudha: Na tional Institute of Community Development, Hyderabad.

Dube, S.C. 1958 India's Changing Villages; Cornell Univer sity Press, New York.

Lamb, Beatrice Pitney 1966 India : A World in Transition; Fredrick A Praeger Publishers, New York.

Neale, Walter C. 1962 Economic Change in Rural India; Yale University Press; New Heaven.

Redfield, Robert 1961 The Little Community and Peasant Society and Culture; The University of Chicago Press; Chicago.

THREE

P.K. Bhowmick

Continuity and Change in a Bengal Village

Village are basically aggregated of some homesteads oc cupied by many castes and communities and they sometimes have well demarcated boundaries among themselves. At times, these might be coterminus with the revenue units or Mouzas. Dependency on agriculture or traditional cottage industries has been the main economic pursuits of the villagers. They have close relationship among themselves and this relation ship brings in its wake duties and privileges among them in a systematic way. Sharing of common background in geo- physical, psycho-emotional involvement and participation in socio-political and religious activities develop a common feeling of local patriotism which reflects itself in many of their action pattern and concerted group life. Villages are not isolated, but are related to larger social and economic systems around and thus become part of a greater regional socio-economic and politico-religious system.

Establishment of villages dates back to pre-historic civilisation period when a section of mankind identified the fertile land with new agricultural technology in the global context. Since hoary past, experiences of mankind have been added to it. With the change of the ways of life, specially in villages, these have widened their views and ideas and slowly but surely tinged their rituals and performances into colourful ones, appropriate in the thickly woven fabric of the entire system. As a result, villages have survived with their basic values through many historical upheavals by mutual adjustment and assimilation.

India, in particular, is a land of villages and about 80% of her population live in rural areas, though the background or geophysical conditions of ruralism differ from place to place, allowing the scope of adjustment in varied degrees. Study of the villages was, in general, stepped up with elaboration after the second global war, specially, from the mid fifties and attempts were made to note facts about vil lage life with a view to depicting the real social and cul tural life of diverse groups living in the villages. There were also some problem-oriented studies. After independence, many more researches on rural life were and are being spon sored by various institutions like Banks, Government agencies. viz., Rural Development Department, planning com mission to ascertain the economic changes of the rural people, to locate the nature of constraints hindering their growth, and thereby to examine the social transformation through modernisation. At the same time, some selected aspects of social life of the villagers, e.g., the inter- relationships between diverse individuals or groups and to record the dynamics of changing processes, were also studied. In consequence, in India we have many valuable data on villages. The village-India has been portrayed and projected with innumerable and colourful facts which so long enveloped the people, their mind, imagination and their world view.

Background

This paper aims at recording the nature of changes that took place in a West Bengal village, which was studied by the writer about twenty years age.[1] This particular village named Daharpur (J.L. 233), is situated about 18 KM to the south of the Kharagpur Railway Junction in the Police Sta tion is about 2 KM to the south of this village and this Railway track bifurcates the village into two. Orissa Trunk Road, which is a metalled road, is running parallel on the Eastern side of this railway track in which innumerable buses and automobiles ply to Digha, a coastal health resort in Southern Bengal, to Balassore and other places in Orissa. This village is important in

1. Caste and Service in a Bengal village : Man in India :1963; subsequently reprinted in the District Census Hand Book, Midnapore Vol. 11, 1961, captioned' Four Midnapore Villages'

many respects, specially to the social scientists. It has diverse ethnic groups, castes and communities, for example Brahmans or priests, at the top as found in conventional Hindu Society, and then Kayasthas to which the scribe belongs, Sadgop/the land-owning caste, Napits/the barbers, Kamars/the blacksmiths, Bagdis/the Bagra Kshatriyas (a Lower and scheduled caste), Dhopaṣ/the washer men (a lower as well as Scheduled caste), Bagals/a cattle herding community (a hierarchically low but unscheduled caste and possibly, a migrant community), Hadis/the sweepers (an untouchable caste), Jugis/Naths (a Saiva sect-definitely of a low status), along with Lodhas, Scheduled de-notified tribe and the Mundas, another Scheduled tribe of Chotanagpur origin. The two tribes probably migrated to this village within this century or a bit early from the Western tract and have settled on the banks of some big silted tanks, which were treated as Khas, i.e., Government lands. These silted tanks in and around the village bear signs of excava tion for the purpose of using them as permanent water reser voirs. Possibly, this work was done during the reign of Sasanka (606-638), the king of greater Bengal, who attempted to supply water to the local people of this perennially drought-prone area during his rule. Ruins of an abandoned Darga (a sacred place for prayer of the Muslims) in one cor ner of one of the silted tanks and the annual sacrifice (Korbani) of a cow there on the last day of Paush (December- January) by the Muslims of nearby villages signify that there was once the habitation of Muslims in this village and it also dates back to the Governorship of Shah Suza (1639- 1659) who had his administrative headquarters at Midnapore town proper for about 20 years during the Mughal period. The Orissa Trunk Road also runs parallel to the derelict un metalled road which is considered to be holy, as it was reportedly traversed by the Lord Srichaitanya on his pilgrimage to Puri. Even in recent times, i.e., during the British Rule (1906), an attempt was made to murder the then Governor of Bengal-Bihar-Orissa by the late revolutionary, Barin Ghose, on the Railway track, which passed through this village, while the Governor was travelling by a train from Cuttack to Calcutta. Thus, the village has its long and mosaic historical past which possibly has slipped into oblivion now due to long sufference of the local people from influenza in an epidemic form that almost depopulated the village bringing the original castes-conglomerates into a thin body, allowing the Muslims to leave permanently to some other nearby villages predominated by the Muslim and sub sequently resettling the migratory tribal groups, Lodhas and the Mundas, more or less in a permanent way.

The village will appear to a casual traveller having dis proportionately dusty roads bearing the marks of erosion due to constant movements of the bullock carts during the fair weather. During the rains, they become muddy, sometimes waters drain off on the roads themselves. Mud-built thatched huts of the caste villagers are situated on both sides of the roads. Thorny bamboo bushes and thickets enmeshed with some haphazardly grown native variety of cactus define the boundaries of the huts from one another and also the village roads. Of course, a few well commodious mud built houses with tiled roofs or thatched with corrugated iron sheets can also be seen with an open courtyards, possibly used for stacking paddy stalks and as the threshing ground during the harvest. The courtyard of each these houses is again fenced with uncut bamboo twigs very neatly tied with long bamboo slips. After a few minutes walk a play-ground is found in one corner of it. There is a shrine of goddess Sitala, a tutelary village deity, where **Jathal** festival is celebrated on the first transplantation day in the month of Sravan (July-August). The Siva shrine of the village is topped with corrugated iron-sheet roof having a phallic (Lingam) symbol in it. A little away on a raised ground, the devotees and the visitors attending the Gajan festival on the last day of the year are accommodated on a wide space on the ground. Then there on the periphery of the bank of a tank on the North-Western side the S.E. Railway main Railway track which has been stretched to Madras from Howrah via Kharagpur, live a few Lodha families.

A cross-way has been created by bringing the Railway track to the ground level to afford a through pass to the bullock carts in continuity of the village path. There, the begra Kshatriyas (lower caste) live along with the Jugi/Nath families. A little distance away another silted tank (popularly known as Mesak) is situated. The Darga stands on one corner of it and the dotted thatched huts of the Lodhas on another. There is yet another tank known as Jalapaddy. On its banks the Mundas live. The road is blocked just in front of a dry canal, which however rattles off during the rainy season to drain out the excess water. There are a few Munda hamlets on the banks of the silted tanks in this Mauza, un connected with any distinct road, but the ridges of the paddy-field serve the purpose of a village path. Strikingly enough, the Welfare Centre, popularly known as Bidisa Ash ram, has been separately linked with an approach road made of moorum from the metalled G.T. Road, which has very recently been constructed by the Organisers. This growth Centre has attracted many people for varied purposes, namely, sightseeing, seeing vegetables and flowers raised in the field and gardens, the functioning of the gobar (Cowdung) gas plant and the deer park, running of Schools, Library, Seminar Halls and Industrial Centre including car pentry, weaving, tailoring, printing press, etc. This road is communicable by all types of vehicles, in season and out of season, that carry the intending visitors to the campus of the Centre day in and day out.

In all seasonal phases, the villages have their usual shares of light and darkness, according to the appearance of day and night.

But the prevailing nocturnal darkness associated with the rural life of drudgery has vanished from the Bidisa Campus for its dazzling electric street-lights and intermittant ringing of the gong to announce the receding phase of the night.

Changes began at varied degrees

After independence, massive drives for development through Community Development Project were initiated all over the country and, as such, administrative infra-structure was slowly built up all over the State of which Narayangarh is a part. Electrification in the rural area, widening of the metalled road and double-lining (1967) of the Railway track, have been accomplished in a relatively short span of time. Electrification in this area opened up the possibilities of sinking deep tubewells (1966) in the vicinity and ushered in a new promise to the agriculturists. Tribal Welfare Programme, especially for the ex-criminal Lodhas heralded many development projects through establishment of land colonization schemes and educational facilities through Ash ram hostel (1964) of the Lodhas in this village. Estab lishment of many educational institutes from pre-Basic, Bal wadi to high School along with craft/vocational training for many with carpentry, tailoring, weaving, press and printing technology along with dairy farming and improved agricul tural system, 'Gobar' gas plant etc. changed the cultural landscape of the entire village. Regular bus stop at the entrance of the village as well as at the top of Bidisa ap proach road craddled many shops of varied nature to cater to the needs of the passersby and the villagers. And, last but not the least, the massive investment by the Central Govern ment through the State Government has definitely created ripples, or rather small waves, in the placid waters of vil lage life. If it is difficult to ascertain its effect on village life, it has doubtlessly exacerbated factional fights in the village and given birth to new elements of corruption. But at the bottom of all this is flowing the current of slow change of the rural mind imbued with conser vation and traditionalism through magico-religious rituals and festival cycles which vibrated in their worships, celebrations and annual fairs, reflecting their collective participation and forging in the process of integration, which suffers, of course, occasional disruption through fac tional fights and of late the political bickerings fanned by the political parties, especially during the agricultural season, with their respective fire-brand slogans and hollow assurances for their supporters.

Thus the villagers have traversed a long distance from its initial situation. It would be interesting to consider the accounts of life in the village, recorded some twenty years ago and examine the changes that have taken place through development, what is being claimed to be development, and the attendant anxiety and tension and also the consequent disintegration of community life in the village. To the anthropologists it may appear to be a useful exercise to identify the change-factors, define their nature and assess how these brought about the transformation, and also ascer tain the direction of the same.

Two decades back : A look in retrospect

There were altogether 46 families of castes and com munities, 49 of Lodhas and 83 of Mundas in this particular village.

The Brahmans and all other castes were practising their traditional calling, except one Bagdi, a Bagra Kshatriya and another Nath/Jugi, who accepted carpentry as the means of livelihood. This was because carpentry was in demand in this area. The agricultural activities were limited by seasonal rains, because people had to depend on rains for their agricultural activities. This agricultural activity demanded labourers which were supplied by the local Bagra Kshatriya, Lodha and the Munda communities, and sometimes by seasonal migratory labourers (Pachchiali Munish), both male and female,belonging to Begal, Kora, Munda and Bhumij com munities of West Midnapore. All sorts of craft services were rendered by the carpenters and the blacksmiths, who were paid in cash and kind. Ritual assistance in respect of agricultural festivals was offered by the Brahman priests and the Napits/barbers. Of course, there was also a kind of division of labour depending on sex, in the activities con nected with agriculture. The rate of payment to them was low at that time,but the prices of the essential commodities also were low. For a whole time agricultural labourer, a landowning family used to pay Rs. 18/- per month, in addi tion to free board and lodging and one pair of napkins and the required number of clothings during a year. For cattle herding purposes, a cow-boy was paid Rs. 5/- only per month plus other fringe benefits as above. It is to be noted that the Brahmans, Kayasthas or a few Sadgops claimed higher status than that of other castes and communities in the vil lage and did not take part in any manual labour.

The borrowing and lending of paddy and money were governed by certain customs. Some well-to-do families used to advance loan on pawning, ornaments, metal utensils, etc., against land as security, at an exhorbitant rate of interest. Then, there were also others, like the Mahajans or money-lenders, who used to advance loans with security and the rate of in terest charged by them was equally high, e.g., 75 percent in a year, if not higher. Besides, there was a local Kalipuja Committee. The surplus collection of this Committee was spent in advancing loans to the villagers. It too charges 75 per cent interest per annum. The system of advancing paddy was there at the rate of 50 per cent as interest, i.e., per 40 kg. of paddy the borrowers had to pay 20 kg. as interest plus 40 kg. as principal within six months after the har vest. Beside these, there were some other types of money lenders who were the Mohammedans of the Orissa State. They demanded 75 per cent of interest, but no document or security was obtained from the loanees. They used to write down the names of the loanees and the amount of money lent out in their books and then advance the loans. They advanced money during the agricultural activities and realised the loan after the harvest. In case some body failed or showed reluctance in paying off the loan in time, they chastised him rudely, shouting at the top of their voice, and as such they were known as 'Khakha' Mahajans, i.e., 'shouting money-lenders'. In addition, some Kabuliwallas or the moneylenders from Kabul used to come and lend money during the Puja fes tivals against articles. This amount was to be paid back in 10 instalments, i.e., one instalment in every week after the Paush Sankranti. Only one village Cooperative was also functioning, but the rate of interest was 7.50 per cent at the minimum. Such loans were confined within the members only. Also, some money-lenders from Gujarat used to come and they advanced money in the lean period, i.e., September-October in cash approximately with the interest rate of 75 per cent and simultaneously pushed the sale of some local spices to the loanees, the price of which was added to the principal to make it a round figure. The loan was paid in ten instalments, i.e., in one instalment a week from the Ist Magh (15th January) onwards. Thus if an amount of say, Rs.10/- as principal loan was repaid in 10 instalments with 25 paisa weekly interest, altogether it came to Rs.12.50. This was very common and almost all the villagers used to take loan. Terms of advancing paddy were the same for the share-croppers and the others. For one maund of paddy bor rowed during the agricultural operation by a family, it had to pay half a maund as interest along with the capital, after the harvest. This was very common to the villagers and the rich and affluent section specially the Sadgops and Kayasthas had this privilege of lending paddy and earning interest on it in this way. The high caste people who did not indulge in manual labour for agricultural purposes req uisitioned all types of people as labour, who used to be paid in cash generally with one full meal, breakfast, Re. 1/- in cash and one seer of rice as remuneration. The per sons rendering craft services also used to get the remunera tion in cash and kind from their respective employers.

In respect of educational institutions, there was only one Primary School manned by two teachers. At that time only higher caste people used to send their wards to the School. There was not then a single person in the village who passed the Matriculation or School Final Examination. But Club named Hitarthi Sangh, having library facilities, was started in 1961. The members of the club were all high caste people. They organised soccer (or, as they would describe it, football) teams, the members of which were recruited from all castes and communities including the tribals. This 'Hitarthi Sangh' at that time organised a soccer tournament with the benevolent donation from one Mrs. Amodini Pal, an affluent widow in the village.

In 1962, a local Panchayat Board was duly constituted with 9 members, of which Shri Atul Krishna Pal, a rich Sadgop was the president. There were three Munda members in it and the other members were from the other communities. This Pan chayat Board used to deal with a variety of affairs con nected with development of the village. Besides, there were some traditional local caste Panchayats, especially among the Lodhas and the Mundas, to deal with all local problems, like petty thefts, adultary cases, breach of traditional customs when the offender was to be punished by the Pan chayat, who were empowered to impose fine.

The villagers used to perform many worship and festivals in which all castes were involved in accordance with tradi tional customs. They celebrated Pujas and other festivals with joy and revelry. Among the common festivals and wor ships were the worship of goddess Sitala (performed twice in the year), one grand worship of goddess Kali, worship of Chandi (Jathel on the first transplanting day) and the famous 'Gajan', i.e., celebration of worship of Lord Siva, on the closing days of Chaitra or the last month of the Ben gali calender. The Gajan used to continue for 10 days and it ended on the last day of the year. Besides, there were some individual and family worships and rituals related to the welfare of the family, agricultural prosperity, individual success, and so on. The 'Gajan' demanded sixteen Bhaktas, i.e., devotees, who were used to be recruited from the various caste groups. This team was headed by one Sadgop, who was known as Raja Bhakta and his assistants were known as Deulia Bhakta. These Bhaktas, i.e., devotees, used to lead a somewhat secluded life for the entire period. They used to wear a dhuti (one-piece unsewn clothing), and one Uttari (uttariya). They used to perform some rituals, viz., walking on the white-hot burning charcoal barefooted, swing ing on a rope tied to a bar, etc. Some Mundas also were recruited as manat Bhaktas, i.e., oath-bound devotees, but they constituted a body which was outside the team. Their involvement was very important, specially on the last day of the Charak. The Munda devotees used to pierce their tongue with iron pins, penetrating a twisted rope on the skin of the upper arm as feats of physical torture to appease god. This penetration of the skin is called Rajnafonrd.

Festivals, rituals and many other inter-caste/community involvements were so strong that villagers were psycho- emotionally forged in ceremonial ties in spite of disparity and exploitation. Despite all these, it was found that the headman along with Chaukidar, the official village watchman, used to demand some fowls from the local Lodha families, the denial of which was taken serious notice of. This led to their arrest in collusion with the police for alleged thefts etc.

People, in general, had no other source of medical help and treatment than some local Aurvedic practioners, spe cially Shri Atul Krishna Pal, and there were also some sorcerers/witch finders who used to diagnose the various causes of diseases as well as their remedial measures. The Brahmans had a role to play through propitiation and wor ships, just to overcome not only the crises of life through diseases and mishaps, but also through Prayaschitta rituals, i.e., expiation or atonement by performing rituals and sacrifices/gifts. This undoubtedly reinforced Brahman's status and position in the society and interlaced the group into bigger local Hindu belief system which was never to be questioned.

The intercaste social disparities were to be redressed by ceremonial kin ties when different caste groups forged a relation, on some occasions, and this was considered to be a strong institution through establishment of ritual kinship with mutual privileges and obligations.

In the village, there were some concubinal relationships, of which two might be within the caste members and only one across the caste boundaries. There was no question of think ing of inter-caste marriage in the village at that time.

It is to be noted that almost all the life-cycle rituals were performed in the traditional way in which various castes and communities used to participate. They were also remunerated traditionally, sometimes in cash but mostly in kind or with the presentation of new cloths, etc.

Thus, the village life was marked with all its hierarchy, disparity, poverty and exploitation in which caste and com munity had their respective traditional roles. There was very little scope for violation or even deviation from the norms. High castes with better economic position were in power to dictate the situation and enjoy the benefits out of it.

The Changing Scene

The area including the village itself witnessed many changes during the past few years. Long established Congress rule ultimately lost its ground in West Bengal, though in the earlier days of independence, opposition parties were tardily making their existence felt in different areas of this State. People's so-called left leaning got adequate vent in many spheres of life and these have been reflected later in many ways. The political propaganda offered many hollow promises to the exploited section of the masses and this ultimately dealt a severe blow on the existing social and political arrangements. This practically helped the in tensification of factional rivalry among the villagers, one alienating and being alienated from another.

Rural electrification and broadening up of metalled road, double lining of the railway track brought physical changes and these had their impact on the village as a whole.

A deep tube-well at Siara (Daharpur) was sunk in 1966. This helped a good number of villagers of Daharpur in enjoy ing the command area benefits to the extent of approximately 40 acres of land of this village. The V.L.W. of the Block was posted (1964) in the village. He showed the village by practice new type of agriculture and H.Y.V. of paddy cul tivation which depended only on perennial water supply without dependence on the seasonal rains. Slowly, the vil lagers began to be accustomed with this new type of paddy as well as vegetable cultivation. The vegetable surpluses went to the daily market which had grown at Nayayangarh within a short period of time.

During these years, many changes took place in the economic life of the people. One Sadgop gentleman of this village purchased a power tiller for his personal use as well as for lending the same to others on rent. A good num ber of families acquired pump sets of their own in addition to many other improved agricultural implements. These were made available to the villagers through Government loan on easy instalments from Block Development Office. Traditional ploughs had been removed, rather replaced, by one type curved broad-blade 'Bose-Plough'. The Black Smith of the village was not in a position to repair or mend agricultural appliances. Tata-made spades and hoes were and are very com mon in use in the village even now. Fertilisers, pesiticides and many other things are available not only in the urban centre of Narayangarh but even in the village.

The rate of wage of daily labour has changed. The Left Front Ministry has scheduled Rs. 13.06 paise per day per in dividual labour.

Labourers were organised under the banner of C.P.I.(M) or C.P.I. and had to work as per direction of the local party leaders. Even for the work under the 'food for work scheme' a list of bonafide labours was to be sent to the Block Development Office to recruit labourers through it. In this way, agricultural activities came under the control of the political parties. Land owning persons having less coopera tion with the ruling political party faced serious trouble in the form of non-participation of labour and thus their land remained uncultivated. Of course, personal rivalry and jealous allowed some local leaders to misuse this newly achieved political power, sometimes by boycotting the agricultural activities through the labourers or claiming false right of land cultivation as Barga-cultivators, i.e., share-croppers which has been regularised by the Government under the programme, 'Cooperation Berga'. This caused ten sion, counter-tension and anxiety among some groups and ul timately forced them to change their political loyalty through alternative defence strategy, alienation and new alighment.

The money lenders from outside are non-existent now. This is due to the tact that most of the people wilfully avoided repayment of loans under the changed political conditions and the distortion of the values. Contrarily, Government loan, Bank loan, dole, relief, subsidy, etc., have been made available to some villagers. Political considerations and favouritism have come to replace the considerations of sym pathy or personal obligation or neighbourly feelings that existed earlier. It has become relatively difficult to get loans from those who can afford to advance the same. Even a well-to-do man avoids today helping a needy person.

The poor have lost the old sources of succour, however, imperfect they might be, but do not find any better alterna tive. It has resulted into their sufferings.

Some monocrop area has turned into multicrop areas demand ing semipermanent engagement of labour and practically the rate of wages for the labour, nature of payment, etc. are to be settled by the dominant C.P.I.(M), the most powerful party in the State Government. Opposite political camps in itiated by the C.P.I., Congress have been started in the village. The villagers changed, as a result, their political views and slowly nucleated in three unequal power blocks.

A good number of Munda tribal men were employed during the laying of the second (double) line on the railway track of which 8 persons are now permanently engaged by the Railway authorities as gangmen and in some other railway services. They earn a sum of Rs. 500/- to Rs. 700/- approximately per mensem. In consequence, a section of the Mundas is prosper ing well. For other caste-service or craft service, the af fluent villagers go regularly to the market where they get also laundry and saloon facilities. One Primary Health Centre has been established at Mokrampur about 2 KM. away and most of the people take its advantage. Besides, family planning has been accepted by many and the poorer Lodha and the Munda offered vasectomy as they were allured to have Rs. 100/- in cash.

Through educational facilities, 6 persons of this village have graduated and all of them are now employed in different sectors, like teaching in school or office work. More than 14 persons have now passed Madhyamik standard, of which 2 are from the Lodha community and 2 are from the Munda com munity. All of them are also employed now. The tribal stu dents have passed from the Bidisa Ashram. Naturally, these groups of people earn from outside and as a consequence they have improved their economic condition and have come to en joy comforts like better housing and possess bi-cycles, wrist-watches and radio or transitor-sets. As an illustra tion, 4 Lodha families possess transistor sets and 2 persons have bi-cycles. One Lodha girl having education upto Mad hyamik standard is also engaged in teaching.

Side by side, there is evidence of sale of land. One Brah man family had to sell out his six acres of land and six Sadgops also had to sell their land. According to them, due to successive droughts, non-availability of agricultural labour in time and the exhorbitant rate of their wages, in sincere agricultural activities were the factors which prompted them to sell out their lands. As they had to main tain a distinctive life-style and perform their social obligations, which necessitated money, there was no alterna tive left to them than to sell the land which they possessed. Besides, some of them had to spend money for defraying the cost of litigation to affirm their claim on the land against illegal or false 'barga' claim. With all these hindrances, some well-to-do families are getting poor and the poor have become poorer. The latter have little land but no money for cultivation. So, either the land is given to others or it is left uncultivated. Worse still, the quan tum of minimum wages, fixed by the Left Front Government, is not operating in numerous local situations. A labour gets after mutual settlement, during agricultural operation a cash of Rs. 5/-, one kg. of rice, its price being Rs. 3/-, 250 grams of perchased rice as breakfast, amounting to Re. 1/-,i.e., Rs. 9/- in all. This employment is only for 2 to 3 months. As a result, they have to go outside in search of employment and this has caused a kind of semi-nomadism among the lowest economic strata of the society where a sense of belongingness including many of the good human qualities is fast disappearing.

Hitarthi Sangha, the old Club organised by the affluent Sodgop caste people of the village, is now defunct. The structure that housed the Club was a tiled roof house, which was constructed long ago. It has been abandoned now.. Three Clubs, however, have been established in its place, viz., 'New Star' led by one Begal boy, 'Agragami' led by some Sodgop boys and 'Sramik Sangha' organised by the Mundas. They subscribe to daily newspapers and other periodicals and magazines and they have radio sets of their own which were donated by the Government. Bidisa Ashram has their own big library and newspapers, journals, radios and T.V. too. The three village Clubs organise football (soccer) tournaments every year and this has been continuing in the village for quite some time. Beside, three adult education centres have been started in the village also.

Individual or family worships are performed by the people with the assistance of the Brahmans. The village festivals have declined to some extent due to intervention of the political party. The old Kalipuja Committee and the 'Gajan' Committees are no longer constituted by the older generation or the dominant caste people. New emerging political sup porters dictate in all matters and, as a result, for the last few yeas there was no annual Sitala worship in this village.

This was previously used to be performed twice a year. 'Chandi" worship or Jethal is just observed in a poor way. It has lost its previous glamour. It was associated with the first transplantation day. Due to deep tube-well and pumping facilities,cultivation process continues uninterruptedly. So, very few people are now interested in 'Jathel' or 'Chandi' worship. Annual 'Gajan' festival has lost its ear lier grandeur. Last year, only 9 **Bhaktas** or devotees were available.

Of course, the Mundas are involving themselves as usual. The annual Kalipuja is also continuing with new leadership and a new Committee. Though annual fair with braying loud-speaker music etc. adds to its glamour to some extent, this is not participated in by the older generation. The ceremonial or ritual kinship is not well forged, except only in one case which took place outside the village.

The traditional political organisation is almost defunct now. The new leaders suported by CPI(M), have been in power since the coming of the Left Front Ministry into power in the State. Prior to the general election of 1977 and sub sequent to the Panchayat election in this State, this vil lage had only Congress as the Political Party supported by the local people, irrespective of rich or poor, caste or community or tribe. CPI(M) encouraged one Sadgop youngman, who won the Panchyat seat and ultimately he was elected as the Chairman of the Gram Sabha. This youngman is a half-educated, affluent person. Within two years, he began to misuse his power,i.e., just provoked a man against an other with his supporters, who are landless tribals. These land less tribals got some vested land and other lands claiming as share-croppers.

He along with his supporters also boycotted some other rich neighbours and in course of time he was alleged to have misused government money. CPI(M) ultimately suspended him from the party and, as such, he is associating himself with C.P.I., the party directly rival to the C.P.I.(M) in many matters. There are a few Munda and Lodha supporters in his favour. Beside this, there are some Congress men also. They have a few supporters from the poorer section. But the party constellation was newly nucleated with new alienation and alignment on the basis of personal and familial rivalry. Shri Atul Krishna Pal, who was a staunch Congressite and a leader of all the activities in the village, was boycotted by the CPI(M) labourers for a few years, has turned into an active supporter of CPI(M) and, strangely enough, the deth roned Chairman has been boycotted by all the supporters of CPI(M) in all agricultural activities. These are the events of the day; a poor man is pitted againist another poor man in the name of political party affiliation. In this connec tion it can be said that two representatives of the Gram Sabha are of tribal origin and they have to work as per the direction of the local affluent CPI(M) leaders of the area.

Inter-caste and inter-tribal as well as intracaste and tribe marriage has been accepted by a few of the villagers. One Lodha married a Munda widow without any resistance from any side. One Bagrakshatriya youngman married a Lodha girl who read in Bidisa School. Both of them have been accepted by the society. The couple also got a job in a Cold Storage establishment at Garbeta.

One Lodha boy very recently married a Brahman girl, Again Lodha girl married a Munda boy. They were reading in the School. One Sadgop boy married a Kayastha girl by registra tion. This is the first instance of marriage by registration in which CPI(M) party mambers took the initiative. Of course, these two were working at Bidisa Printing Project.

In this connection, it may be noted that once West Bengal Government's Publicity Division wanted to do a film in which a Santal girl wanted to marry a caste Hindu boy and ul timately it was accepted by the Society. The film was to be taken from Belpahari Tribal Girls' School at Jhargram. Strangely enough, none of the Santal girls reading in the School wanted the theme to be filmed. Ultimately it was dis carded. It is important to note here that 3 Santal girls reading and residing at Bidisa Ashram wanted to marry one Lodha Madhyamik passed boy and two other caste Hindu boys. They have shaken off the prejudice, but things did not materialise because the authority remained silent to this issue in order to avoid the unwanted situation. Thus, the village as a whole has changed in many ways and in many directions due to changing political climate and man-land relations, which have their impact in other spheres of life.

Bidisa : The Establishment For Diffusing Light

Bidisa Ashram itself contributed substantially in many ways to cause this change, to bring in a 'culture' in this region, though its main thrust is to enculturate the downtrodden, who are lagging behind for centuries together. It helped the Government in rehabilitating the Lodhas with land. It established many schools from pre-basic, Balwadi to High School with all vocational training schemes to utilise the waste land, surplus man-power with input of new tool and technology. Above all, it tries to develop the human resources by which they can utilise all developmental plans properly. Here, more than 300 inmates live and they belong to varied ethnic or community groups. In a disciplined way, all the inmates including the teachers, social workers and the students disseminate new technology to raise the aspira tions of the people. In an evaluation report by the N.C.E.R.T., Delhi (1976) we find;

> The development in the Ashram attracted the attention of scholars and it is now the field station of the Institute of Social Research and Applied Anthropology .... The management of the Ashram have not taken any evaluation of their work. According to them, there cannot be a terminal stage in so cial transformation. But the changing environment, replace ment of wild bushes by sheaves of wheat and paddy, shedding of superstition and sluggishness, admission of more and more children to the School, increase in the number of cattle and above all the smiles on the faces of all people, young and old, are an index of their increasing success. They have to enculturate a tribe that had never known progress with the progress of mankind after thousands of years of effort. They are on their way.

Thus Bidisa Ashram opened up new vistas of development, new ideology, an assuring prosperity through active par ticipation in all matters of life. Bidisa causes culture, continues culture and vibrates it in many forms through early morning Upanishad recitals to the tune of the tribal folk dance and music. Many cooperative and concerted group- life activities ripple with waves, generate vibrations in the locality in which modernization and attempt in develop ing human resources are significant. In order to develop the aspirations, capability and control are emphasised in the Bidisa Project. Naturally, this Ashram is in a position to suggest many solutions to the problem-ridden, superstitious human enclaves, to bring them to a certain level needed for a better living in modern time.

Continuity and Change

Society is a continuous process, subject to change from time to time, from one direction to another. This particular village, once a back-drop of rural aggregates, almost un touched by any wave of change, had been found to respond in many immediate situations. Daily newspapers, radios, a good number of regularly plying service buses with two stoppages at the two corners of the village indicate its importance and people's participation outside the village environs.

Lo cal trains and super-fast trains whistle around and alert all the villagers, young and old. Announcements from the All India Radio are heard by most of the villagers having radio sets and the availability of almost all types of newspaper and a T. V. set in the village definitely establishes its relationship with the outside world-with Calcutta and abroad.

People are now aware with the honking of the automobiles about their destinations. Thus, speed has widened their out look, delineated the limitations. The village in a few decades has advanced more than any other villages around. Population has increased, families have split up and land has been fragmented creating more problems in their day to day life. Many articles useful to their daily life are now available in the village or nearabout which has improved material life. Their style of living has either penetrated in the humble thatched cottages or the knowledge of their availability has been acquired by the villagers. But in majority of cases the villagers can not afford to have them, because of the bad economic position. This has created a hiatus in their mind bringing dissatisfaction and discon tent.

With all these possibilities, wider world views, imagina tion and attitudes, the poverty continues to stare them in the face. It has circumstantially compelled some groups together in their struggle for existence and at the cost of poverty, power has been acquired by some affluent people of the village. Politics of distrust, bitterness and violence has brought a social fragmentation in the village, new alienation and alignment with new caste and community con stellations have started through factional rivalry.

REFERENCES

Bhowmick,*TH* P.K.1963 Caste and Service in a Bengal Village; Man in India, Vol. 43 no. 4, Ranchi.

Bhowmich, P.K. 1967 Four Midnapur villages; in District Cen sus Hand Book, Midnapur, Calcutta.

Bhowmick, P.K. 1973 Caste and conflict in a Bengal Village; Bulletin of the Socio-economic Research Institute, Vol. 4, no.1, Calcutta.

Bhattacharya, N.C. and Natesan L.A. 1932 Some Bengal villages; University of Calcutta, Calcutta.

Dube, S.C. 1954 Indian Village; Routledge & Kegan Paul Ltd., London.

Marriott, Mekim, 1955 Village India; Studies in the little community; The University of Chicage Press, Chicago.

Srinivas, M.N.(ed) 1955 India's village; West Bengal Govern ment Press, Calcutta.

FOUR

Archana Sinha

Tradition and Development in a Bihar Village

A study of tradition and development in any Indian Village reveals various facets of social change. One can witness such changes in every sphere of a villager's life. While the country-side is in such a state of flux, it is fruitful to watch the change and continuity going together. The charm of modernity captivates a young boy and girl in dress, sports, recreation and food, whereas the old ones cling to what is old and traditional and stubbornly reject modern methods of sanitation, hygiene, and hold on to caste taboos and religious superstitions. A breakaway from tradition and wel come to new development in thought and living, requires a community's whole-hearted participation. Education and en lightenment through various media help to prepare people psychologically for a change, but in the case of villagers, the process is quite slow. Villagers resist abrupt change. They prefer to give fight even while the new changes make for socio-economic gains. On the one hand, they see metalled roads and buses running across their villages, and they are happy; on the other, they still cling to their bullock carts to go to their Hatia (weekly markets) and sell their produce or bring their requirements. Above all, the village belles travel in bullock-carts singing folk songs, while thc vil lage youths travel on bus-roofs and sing a Lata Mangeshkar or a Kishore Kumar tune. These two aspects of change in vil lage life impelled the researcher to visit village, 'Gaura Chowki', which is close to the divisional town of Bhagalpur in Bihar.

Method

The writer has been visiting and observing changes in the life-patterns of 'Gaura Chowki' for the last two and a half decades beginning 1957. The study is based on a keen and continuous observation made by the researcher, as she used to visit the village three to four times every year. Obser vations, recording of conversation and analysis of the in formation collected, have been made for this study. The ob jective of the study was to record the variations, the withering away of traditions, approach to fresh developments and progress, and finally the swinging of the scale in favour of changes coming in by the efforts of the government and voluntary organisations.

The Local

The village, Gaurachowki is 7 Km south from Bhagalpur on the Bhagalpur-Kajraili road which connect Amarpur and Banka. Gaura (a synonym for Parvati) is the deity of the village. It derives its name from the deity which used to be wor shipped and then immersed in a pond owned by Late Shree Muk teshwar Prasad, formerly a rich zamindar and a Treasurer of Bhagalpur University. The village is in Nathnagar Anchal. The Block Development Office is situated 2 Km from Nath nagar. Formerly the Bhagalpur-Kajraili road was a 'Kachcha' one but in the year 1972 the road was metelled. According to the Census of 1971, the village has 94.29 hectares of land with 217 residential houses and a population of 1513.

Population

In the population Koeris are numerically dominant while Yadavas come next. Harijans like Pasi, Dusadh are in a large number, but there are no higher castes. On all counts the village can be called poor and backward but it is free from feuds. The Panchayat is quite strong and decisive. There is only one family of Bania who runs a shop selling paddy, Wheat, Kerosene oil, grams, pulses and sugar. He seems to be affluent from the village standard, and is helpful and cooperative. Closely live a few families of Doms and Chamars, doing business in bamboos and pigs. They are very backward and untouched by any kind of development. Poverty and squalor dominate their lives.

Land of the village was previously owned mostly by Mar waris and Bengalis and Muslims of Bhagalpur town. Now the Marwaris and Bengalis have sold their land to the local people at a throw away price. Now the two big land owners of the village are Rammu Marar and the family of the Late Babu Ram Khelawan Lal. The former resides in the village and the later has two sons, who are highly educated, well placed, and live in the town. But they visit the village regularly and are always helpful to the villagers. The remaining lands are owned by the villagers.

Social life

The people of Gaurachowki can be divided into three groups - middle income, low income and below the poverty line. The least income group is not numerous; both men and women mem bers constitute the agricultural labour force. There is no industry, small or medium. The closeness between the agricultural land holder and his labour force makes life homogenous and cordial and without conflict. Consequently, the life pattern among the three groups is the same, viz, they worship the same village deity, celebrate Ramnavami, Holi, Dusserah, Gitia (for children), Teej (for husbands), Shivaratri, Kalipuja, and all the rest. The children sit together in the primary school unmindful of caste and socio- economic status. This is a great gift of modern thinking ushered by radio, cinema, and movement for eradication of untouchability. There is no T.V. in the village. But make- shift theatrical performances take place on the occasion of of Saraswati Puja and Durga Puja. There is no temple or mosque in the village; what exists in its name is just some village dieties symbolised by raised platforms where Vaish nava or Sakta worship takes place. Music on such occasions is either the Loud - Speaker blaring cinema songs or the Chamars playing their Tuthi. Young brides are offered silver ornaments; bridegroms go in for thick soled shoes, terelyne Hawai Shirts, trousers, watch and transistors. Silk clothes or gold ornaments are not available to them. What is really encouraging is that they turn to medical experts for advice in sickness and thus they have reduced maternity and infant mortality. Quackery persists, but witchcraft is not heard any more.

The most striking feature of the village, at the first glance, is that although extremely poor by the standard of Haryana and Punjab or Maharashtra, it is noticeably more prosperous than it was two and a half decades ago. Against only two brick houses then, every sixth house is now 'pacca'. The 'Kachcha' road that linked the village with the main road is now a 'pacca' one. Moreover, just at the road terminus there are facilities for Tamtam, Rickshaw, private buses against the bullock-cart or mules which were the only means of transport formerly. There are two motor-cycle in the village owned by prosperous and educated Koeri boys. Formerly there was only one cycle in the village owned by a man working as a lab-boy in T.B.B. College before 1970. Nor are the landless worse any more. Two decades ago many of the Harijans could wear nothing but a loincloth. Today they are clothed, particularly the young women and children are bet ter clothed than ever. Young boys wear terrylene while the middle aged and the old use thick cotton.

The wind of change blowing through the countryside has not made much difference to the poor so far. But it has brought some hope of a change for the better even in their drab lives. The village, sunk in traditions is fast awakening to the warm breath of new ideas. Thanks to the green revolu tion, the growth of new welfare services, increasing literacy rate and a steady increase in the number of people who read newspapers, listen to radio or have a change of viewing T.V. programmes in the towns or gather information in the office of the political parties. The villagers are gradually growing conscious of their participation in the government.

It will be wrong to assess the changing village scene solely in terms of haves and haves-not. The economic gain of development may have gone mostly to large and middle farmers, but social and political changes are affecting the entire village. Increasing politicisation of the well-to-do backward castes and the poor Harijans have taken remarkable shape in day to day life. Though the Harijans still live in well demarcated hutments away from the rich backward castes, ideas of total purity of the rich and pollution by the poor are no longer as pervasive as they were even ten years ago. Any family in the village does not mind a visit of a Harijan or a Muslim doctor or of a nurse, midwife or any health visitor of any caste or creed.

Gaurachowki is still in the category of a backward vil lage, when it is considered in terms of economic progress, per capita income, standard of living, education, hygienic sense of living and social set-up; but it is a developing village, when considered in terms of political conscious ness, health facilities and other economic programmes in itiated by the government.

Economic Situation

Agriculture

Agricultu: is the mainstay of Gaurachowki People. Organic fertilisers like 'Gobar' and household refuge are used as manure. 'Bataidari'or share cropping is in danger due to Naxalite and other land-grab movements, but it continues. The methods of cultivation are the same but the farmers have been quick to see the uses of chemical fertilisers, improved varieties of seeds and pesticides. There is a growing con sciousness to produce green vegetables and other cash-crops like sugercane etc. Pesticides are used in orchards of mangoes and guavas and vegetable fields. Use of pumps for spray is now a common sight after 1970. One of the important hurdles formerly in agricultural output was the absantee landlord. But now the domination is not the same as prevailed during the days of zamindari.

Irrigation

For irrigation the villagers still have to depend on na ture, they perform certain rituals for proper rainfall. A seasonal rivulet 'Andheri' passes through the village. It is being harnessed for irrigation purposes. The Minor Irriga tion Department has provided a channel from 'Chandan' and 'Mahmuda' rivers which serves the village. There is a government tube-well installed in the village in 1977 but it does not function. The incharge of the tube-well is often on leave or away from the site. 'Latha' and 'Kuri', the old ir rigation system, still helps the villagers. This is because power-supply in Bhagalpur is erratic and more erratic is the tube-well management. Hence the ancient system of 'Latha' and 'Kuri' comes handy. Even now much of the soil is sandy and is ravaged by white ants and other pests and deserves soil treatment.

Cattlewealth

Cattle like cows, buffaloes and goats contribute to the economic wealth of the local people. The breed has changed. Buffaloes are in large number but goats outnumber these. Dogs keep watch and keep jackals and other predators away but they are lanky and ill-fed, still they are loved by children. Asses and donkeys are rare because there is no washerman in the village. Potters are few but they carry their day ware themselves. Formerly the villagers were not having poultry but as a result of interaction with town the schedule castes are having their own small poultry. The young generation enjoy eating eggs and chickens.

Indebtedness

There has been a decline in the ratio of indebtedness even among the landless, but the system of 'Mahajani' still per sists. This system is prefered more than banks. Of course wherever and whenever possible loans from Banks are applied for through middleman or agent who enjoys a share or a heavy rate of commission. Mortgaging land or paying high interest to Mahajan is preferred to transactions with nationalised banks. In times of dire needs such as illness, death, mar riage and birth, the mahajans come to their rescue.

A shortage of male labour force seems to be overtaking many villages in Bihar so also Gaurachowki. Young boys run to towns to become rickshaw pullers and powerloom operators while their agriculture suffers for want of manpower. They also work in hotels, garages, shops, and a few are employed as domestic servants.

Education

There is an ill-managed primary School in the village with a corrugated iron roof and broken floor. The school attracts young boys and girls of the village. Girls read upto the age of ten in the school. Boys continue to go ahead and some of them go up to High School which is situated at 'Baijani' only 3 Km. away from Gaurachowki. A matriculate girl is still a dream, a college going boy is rare, but there is a clamour for government jobs among the boys, especially among the newly classified Backwards and scheduled castes youngmen. Women do their household chores, sell vegetables and work as agriculture labour.

Health

Epidemics have been controlled; Measles, enteric diar rohea, sometimes cholera, do take place, but the health workers are readly available. People are now more interested in allopathic treatment. Two decades back they used to rely on ojhas and on indigenous medicines but now they rush to hospital at Bhagalpur. They also visit private prac titioners. They now understand the usefulness of triple-antigen and polio medicine. Nobody prefers a big family in the village; rather those who tend to be careless in this regard are indirectly slighted and looked with derision. Man power is indeed required, but not for swelling poverty as food from land is limited. This is their new awareness. We can call it a departure from traditions and read therein a sure sign of essential development or a march towards gradual welfare. Poor and conservative people still depend on 'Ojha and Bhagats'. 'Tabij' and other kinds of black magic - 'tonas' etc. are still in practice when problems in regard to marital adjustment and child birth arise. To have more sons is the cherished desire.

Nearby is a Leprosy centre which is managed by philanthropic doctors working under a committee and food grains and money are collected by their volunteers. Late Babu Ram Khelawan Lall had opened a homoeopathic dispensary after retirement from Railway service in 1948, but after his death a few compounders and quacks meet the local needs of the villagers. Strongly enough, they are quite a good help, as for example during rains and nights, but lately a few doctors have chosen to stay within a vicinity of 2 miles and they are a god-send.

Mosquito nets are used by well-to-do farmers. Garbages are burnt in cattle-shed to drive away mosquitoes and save their animals from mosquitoes and other pests. Veterinary com pounder and Doctors visit on call to treat diseases of animals.

Social and Cultural

Majority of the people are Hindus, there are only four houses of Muslims. They celebrate all the festivals and ob serve the rituals. 'Nag-Panchami' and 'Behula Puja' are celebrated with great enthusiasm and they visit 'Champanagar', a Mohalla of Bhagalpur town, where snakes are worshiped in the temple and procession of

Bhagats with images of Behula, Chand Saudagar, and one demoness is taken out with elaborate arrangement. There is a fair on this oc casion. Durga puja is also celebrated with all pomp and show. Most of the villagers visit 'Mahasaya-Deori' in Cham panagar with their family. Formerly on 'Veerastarui' day they were visiting Chand Babu's 'Vyayamshala' to see physi cal feats.

The villagers also organise Yatra-party, Bhajan-Mandali and boys visit cinema houses at Bhagalpur and Nathnagar. There is a sharp change in dress habits. One can notice most of the growing girls wearing Salwar-Kurta and Dupatta, and ladies wearing synthetic saris. Young boys wear fullpants and shirts of terricotton and polyester fabrics. Use of electric bulbs on special occasion for decorating the house is also increasing. Even the new brides have certainly made some march towards modernity or better say, towards develop ment of new tastes imitating the affluent brides of the towns. The brides of Gaurachowki use 'Mehndi;'alta' nail- polish, talcum powder and use a good mirror for facial make- ups. Gone are the days when they used soft, whitish soil for their hair-wash; 'Lux', 'Rexona' and 'Hamam' appear in most houses. Even the time of marriage songs are on the line of popular film songs. Tatooing is fast vanishing. Bata's Hawaii is the main foot-wear. This is, indeed, development. But they still drink unfiltered water, wash hands and uten sils with clay that are full of harmful bacteria, use cow dung during worship, keep their food open to the invasions of flies and dust. This is, indeed the persistence of tradi tion.

Political awareness

Without doubt, people have become politically conscious. Conscious of what ? Power, prestige and self. They are to tally oblivious of duties and responsibilities to the country or the society. Recurrent elections, political speeches, centralisation of power, benefits from joining the ruling party are indeed the influencing factors. Only once, during the Janta wave, the people of Gaurachouwki decided to move away from the congress (I). The slogan of 'Total Revolution' led by Shree Jaya Prakash Narayan in 1974 had reached this village too. Bhagalpur town and its suburbs had played very active role in this upsurge. Some of the young boys are involved in the working of Yuva-Sangharsha-Vahini and some are members of Youth Congress. After the failure of the Janata Government, people have swung back to Congress (I). The

Pramukh, the Mukhia are minor symbols of power, the Block Development Officer and Circle Officer are middle class power-elites, and the Minister is the supreme - these are very clear in the mind of the villagers. But power pyramid is built like that and the people are pleased to worship the modern Pharoah. The people are far more con scious of their rights and their bargaining power. The caste tyranny still persists and often takes a nasty turn but the fear of a dominant caste is threatened: Increasing reliance on musclemen and on one's own kinship group appears to be one of the reasons why cases of atrocities easily tend to acquire the colour of caste conflict.

Emerging affluent middle class among the backward classes and its sensitiveness to changing values shows the new pat tern of change. But social evils can rarely be eradicated through legislation alone. How difficult the task is to check child-marriage among the Harijans and conservative communities, marked by illiteracy, ignorance and poverty. Among backward castes child-marriage is now replaced by early marriage because it is less expensive in comparison to marriages performed in higher age group. Besides this, the villagers believe that parents who do not marry their daugh ters at early age will not get a suitable boy. Even boys' father want to marry their sons between the age of 15-17 years otherwise they would not get a suitable bride and the groom-price. Surprisingly the fact is that most of the people are aware of the law against child-marriage and early marriage. Benefit of late marriage is also known to them. Still it is not practised.

To sum up, Gaurachowki presents a beautiful case study about traditions and development in a Bihar Village. One thing is evident like a fresh morning flower: Villages are on the march to new way of life, scientific, national, and useful. No doubt, very slowly - but surely enough, a poor and backward village like Gaurachowki shows unmistakable signs of progress in irrigation and cultivation, education and sanitation, social and national outlook, apart from health and hygiene, production and sale, in short, of a rich subsistence born out of a zeal to see a better dawn and a bright future for their children.

REFERENCES

Carstairs, G. Morris *TH*1952 A village in Rajasthan; Economic weekly Vol IV, Nos. 3 and 4

Dubey, S.C. 1954 A Deccan Village; Economic weekly Vol. VI,Nos. 19 and 20.

Dubey, S.C. 1958 India's Changing Villages; Routledge and Kegan Paul Ltd., London.

Dubey, S.C. 1965 Indian Village; Routledge & Kegan Paul Ltd.

Dubey, S.C. 1975 EK Bhartiya Gram; Translated by Dr. Yogesh Atal; National Publishing House, Delhi.

Desai A.R. 1961 Rural India In Transition; popular Book Depot., Bombay.

Gough, Kathleen 1952 The Social structure of a Tanjore Village; economic weekly, Vol. IV, No. 21.

Ishwaran, K. 1968 Shivapur, A South Indian Village; Rout ledge & Kegan Paul, London.

Joshi Pooranchandra 1966 Bhartiya Gram: Sansthani Parivartan Aur Arthic Vikas; Raj Kamal Prakashan, Delhi.

K.M. Kapadia (Ed) 1954 Prof. Ghurye Felicitation Volume. popular Book Depot., Bombay.

Mckim Marriolt (Ed) 1955 village India; Chicago University Press Chicago.

Majumdar D.N. 1958 Caste and Communication in an Indian Village; Asia Publishing House, Bombay.

Milton Singer (Ed) 1958 Traditional India; Structure and Change; Special Number, Journal of American Folkore, Vol. 68. No.. 281.

Srinivas, M.N. 1962 Caste in Modern India and other essays; Asia Publishing House, . Bombay.

Vidyarthi, L.P. 1964 Cultural Contours of Tribal Bihar; Pun thi Pustak, Calcutta.

FIVE

Sachchidananda

Tradition and Development in Arunachal

In the context of fast moving changes in the third World the terms tradition and development have loomed large in the conceptual baggage of sociologists. It is necessary to define these terms clearly. A traditional system is charac terised as "a series of agrarian villages in setting rela tively unchanging technique, limited economic opportunity and age old conventional understanding, attachment to the authority, respect for the pastness of things, dependence upon routine and an exaggerated respect for precedent" (Nash, 1965, 3.). However, it is realised that tradition is not something far removed from ourself. It is created and shaped to present needs and aspirations in a given historical situation. People referred to aspects of the past as tradi tion in an effort to find legitimation for the present ac tion. It is in this way that tradition is metamorphosed into an ideology. Similarly in the third world countries develop ment has been accepted as a goal, an aspiration towards which society is expected to approximate. It is a desirable form of social change. Through it people seek the ends of their choice. They apply their skills and talents to these ends. Thus, the desire to develop and the desire to preserve tradition, both exist side by side and function as ideology. They do not stand face to face but shoulder to shoulder. Sometimes the effort for development finds support in the ideological side of traditionalism. In this process tradi tion itself may be changed, modified or structured in the face of challenges of the time. Thus changing traditions ap pear like jetsam on the sands of time.

In tribal areas in India tradition has two more functions. It is a cloak for socio-economic compulsion rising from en vironmental shortcomings. An excellent example of this is Jhum cultivation in north eastern India. The other function of tradition is to underline the identity and exclusiveness of particular tribal groups. They take extra care to preserve some of their tradition both in social structure as well as in dress, so that their identity is not eclipsed by the growing tide of mass culture.

In this paper an attempt has been made to examine the in teraction between tradition and development in Arunachal. This is a region where cultural influence from Tibet and Burma have mingled with those from India. For a long time it was outside the purview of Indian culture. It is only after 1962 that fast changes have gripped this region. Along with the spreading arms of Indian administration, there has been a fast inflow of new ideas, norms and values which are basi cally derived from the mainstream of Indian culture. These have produced a great impact on people and society in Arunachal. The concern for promoting people's well being and putting them on the road to development has produced response, some favourable and some unfavourable from the people. The response has generally been favourable in the case of such induced changes which do not go against the grain of the existing tradition in that sphere of activity. Thus some traditions have promoted desired changes, some have remained neutral while some others have produced nega tive reactions. This is but natural as in all societies change is selective.

This process has been analysed with reference to one tribe and one cultural practice in Arunachal. The tribe chosen for discussion is the Apatani and the cultural practice is Jhum cultivation. The Apatani are a small but influential and ar ticulate tribe concentrated in a small plateau at the hight of 5,000 feet in the lower Subansiri district. They have a long tradition of settled wet rice cultivation which enables many families to accumulate a sizeable surplus. The prevalence of slavery in the region gave them access to cheap labour. Along with this they had a well established system for the maintainence of order in society. Besides agriculture and animal husbandary which were their mainstay, they engaged in trade not only with neighbouring tribes but also with the plain people in Assam. This gave them good ex perience for making money through business.

Arunachal Pradesh has been the traditional home of Jhum cultivation. 70% of its arable land is under Jhum cultiva tion. This, however, is not so by choice. The lie of the land is such that it cannot permit permanent cultivation. Thus, Jhuming is the cultural mechanism for adjustment to an environment. In the different areas of Arunachal Pradesh different tribal communities practise Jhuming with slight differences and make a living. Jhuming, however cannot sup port a population higher than 22 persons per square kilometer, at the subsistence level. Sociologists have come to consider Swidden cultivation as a way of life. We will see the differential response of some tribes of Arunachal in respect of the induced change over from swiddening to settled cultivation.

II

The Apatani have been experts in growing several varieties of rice on terrace fields irrigated by a complicated system of channels and ducts fed by streams and rivulets. They plant both early and late repening variety of rice and use the highlands for cultivation of millet, maze and potatoes. Recently they have begun growing vegetables introduced by the administration. They plant fruit trees and carefully tend bamboo groves and pine trees which they use for build ing materials. Every bit of land is intensively cultivated. They have readily accepted innovations in the field of agriculture which held a promise of increasing their yield. However there has not been any substantial change in their agricultural techniques. Attempt to introduce ploughing has not met with much of positive response, although they possess bullocks. But they have eagerly accepted fish farm ing in their flooded rice fields as it provides them with considerable cash income. Similarly fruit farming initially subsidised by the government has been developed more successfully. Some far sighted people have planted several thousand fruit trees and derived large profits from the sale of their produce. It is thus clear that Apatanis have ac cepted only such changes which are congruent with their ab sorbing interest in agriculture and horticulture.

In Apatani society a man's status and influence depended on the extent of land holding. Although this notion has diminished to some extent on account of the emergence of new sources of wealth, land is still a cherished possession and the surplus is usually invested in land though the return in monetory terms, is less then the interest one could earn through bank deposits. Many Apatanis have entered government service and are serving outside the area. The result is that the land belonging to these are leased out or given on share cropping basis to their landless brethren. To meet the shortage of family labour some people now employ labourer for cash wages. Previously most of work on the field was done by labour gangs whose member worked on the fields by rotation on reciprocal terms. Some wealthy landowners spend about Rs. 5000/- a year on payment to agricultural labourers.

In earlier days wealth among the Apatanis was started in the shape of cattle. The value of cattle has gone up. Mithan was earlier valued as a sacrificial animal a medium of ex change and a store of value. Now a days it is valued largely as a sacrificial animal, the other two values having disap peared with the large scale use of cash. The Apatanis also keep cows and bullocks, mostly for beef. These are also sold at a large profit to neighbouring tribal communities. There is also a flourishing trade in small pigs which are reared to full size in Apatanis household and other sold or eaten up.

The Apatani penchent for trade has led to their large scale involvement in commercial exchanges with the people of the plains. They also make good money by supplying provi sions to government employees posted in the hills and by working as contractors in various other capacities for government agencies. They were fortunate that the district headquarters came to be established in one of their villages and it was linked by an all-weather road with North Lakhim pur in the plains of Assam. Hapoli, which houses the dif ferent district offices has grown into a township with a large bazar offering a choice of goods herdly inferior to that found in any average Indian district headquarters. The bulk of the shops are owned by the Apatanis and run by men and women shopkeepers who are fluent in many languages. Hundred of Apatanis have earned cash wages in the road building projects and other public enterprise. They have in vested their savings for putting up these shops. The Apatani contractors could supply and control labour and make sub stantial profits on account of the experience of wealthy clan heads in directing the work of numerous slaves and hired labourers in their agricultural operations. The money earned by the local people led to the emergence of an adequate number of buyers from these shops. Of course, in this process the government helped by prohibiting outside merchants from engaging in trade in the hills. They were thus saved from keen competition from Marwaris or other more aggressive businessmen. Their success in business en terprises is reflected in the large number of current ac counts in Hapoli branch of the State Bank of India. Some of the balance in these accounts were over Rs. 1,00,000/-. This process was facilitated by the rapid spread of education which has been made possible by the growth of a class of business men who were capable of handling intricate transac tions involving a good deal of paper work, both in English and other languages.

The Apatani have advanced through the rapid spread of education. They took advantage of the newly established government schools. In more recent years affluent parents have also sent their children to public schools outside Arunachal Pradesh. The literacy rate is relatively high and in the early Eighties there were 45 Apatani graduates with university degrees, and many more were studying in univer sities in Gauhati, Dibrugarh, Shillong and Delhi. Education provided an avenue to government employment. In 1980 there were 15 Apatanis in gazetted posts and 342 in non-gazetted posts and Government employment not only bestows upon in dividuals prestige, but also gives them opportunities for throwing about their influence in various spheres of ac tivities and also provides funds for enlarging their capital assets.

Despite their change-prone outlook their social structure has remained more or less the same. The dual class division, *Guth* and *Guchi* which corresponds to patricians and com moners, still obtains. These two classes are traditionally endogamous but under two influence of education and new op portunities for commoners in trade and government employ ment, this endogamy seems to be breaking down. However, it is still looked down upon. Although slavery was abolished in 1962, most of the former slaves are still employed with their masters as wage labourers. The patricians received compensation for the loss of slaves, which they have in vested in business.

The Apatani youth Association which is a non-political body for social reform has taken some measures such as decrying scarification of women's faces, marriage between persons with large age disparity etc. Inter class and inter tribal marriage is being encouraged but there has been no demand to stop polygyny. There are many exmaples of success ful businessmen and politicians maintaining two houses one in the village and other in the town and each being managed by a separate wife.

In the sphere of rituals the Apatanis continue to perform public as well as domestic rites in the traditional manner. Even public servants and students temporarily residing out side Arunachal make every effort to return home when their village performs the triannual celebration of Mloko, the greatest of the seasonal feasts. They hold firmly to their traditional faith of Donyi-Polo and do not seem to be at tracted either to Christianity or to Hinduism.

III

The Wancho are a small tribe with a population of nearly 28,000. They are concentrated in the Longding Subdivision of the Tirap district whose border touches Nagaland and Burma. The density of the population in the areas is about 12 per sons per sq. Km. The entire area is covered by hills, some of which reach a hight of 5,000 ft. The area is largely forested. However, on the hill slope Jhuming has been carried on for a long time. As the pressure of population is little, the Jhum cycle is eleven years long.

Wancho society is highly stratified. Order is maintained by a hereditary autocratic chief in each village. He is the foundation of all honour and the only dispenser of justice. He enjoys a number of prerogatives such as free labour for cultivation of his land and construction of houses. He receives gift from villagers who also contribute to its gra nary. He is responsible for the safety and well being of all his villagers. He used to lead hunting expedition in earlier days and could inflict punishment or a person found guilty of any offense. At present he is also incharge of organising developmental activities.

All land in the village and around is owned by the com munity. A person has the right of using the land alloted to him by the Chief but he has no right of ownership. The only right he has is on the homestead land. The Jhum cultivation keeps people busy all the year round except for two months i.e. May and June. During these months those who have a surplus take it for sale. Alternatively they take up wage labour wherever available. Most of the shifting cultivation is extremely arduous particularly for the women. Despite the hard labour the produce is scanty. They raise a poor variety of paddy besides millet, maize, arum, tapioca and a number of vegetables through a system of mixed farming.

In recent years efforts have been made by the Forest Department to control swiddening. Under this programme similar schemes were started at four places with the concur rence of village Chief and the local leaders. A number of cash crops have been planted in the demonstration area. These are cardamom, coffee, ginger, medicinal plants, pepper and fruit trees. In selected areas turmeric could also be grown. Local people were provided employment in the demonstration area so that they would be acquainted with the agricultural operations involved. Besides providing them a fixed income, care was taken to make available food grains, firewood, housing, education and health and nutrition serv ices to them.

The experience of working this programme for three years showed that it had not evoked any positive response from the Wancho. The people regarded it only as an employment scheme. None of them has planted any of the cash crops or fruit trees on his own lands. The chief reason for this is that the land is communally owned and its working is decided by the entire village. No person can take initiative on his own. Moreover, these cash crops have a gestation period of three years. During that period it is not known how the tribal will maintain himself. The bulk of the tribals in this area is not aware of evils of shifting cultivation. However, they know that the yield is much more in settled cultivation. They cannot do much in this matter because plain land for wet rice cultivation is very scarce in this area. Whereever it is available the tribals have gone for it. It is thus been that it is not the cultural barriers that prevent the Wancho from taking up settled cultivation.

In the Lohit district successful attempts have been made to relocate shifting cultivators in newly settled villages where they have been provided with flat land. The tribe in this case is the Digaru Mishmi. They have been engaged in shifting cultivation for a long time on hill slopes, on heights between 2000 to 3000 feet. Unlike the Wancho, they do not have the village chiefs or tribal council and can af ford to be more faxible. In 1972 a detailed survey of one of the Jhum villages was made just above the foot hills about 10 Km. from the district headquarters. It was decided to bring together people living in seven traditional villages. Development workers used to visit these villages and impressed upon their leaders the desirability of settling at one place on the plains. One advantage that the people per ceived in having a settlement colony close to their tradi tional villages was that they were not required to break off their links with these villages. The government employed the people from these villages to clear the forest at the foot hills and to reclaim about 1200 acres of land on both sides of the roads. The reclaimed area also included homestead land. Each person was given a subsidy of Rs.2000/- for building a house. The allotment of land was according to the size of family and the working capacity of the members of the household, with a minimum of 2 acres and the maximum of 30 acres. In a short time, with the help of agricultural ex tension agents, the tribals were acquainted with the methods of settled cultivation. At first only dry crops were grown. In course of time, when irrigation facilities were made available, wet rice cultivation was adopted by many families. Besides agricultural inputs, the new settlers were given support through animal husbandary programmes. The new settlement was known after one of the villages in the hills from which the people had migrated. Now there are 85 households in this village with a total population of 508.

The main reason for the success of this scheme is the close supervision and guidance of government officers over a number of years. The tribals in this case had some notion of private property and they maintained their links with their older villagers. They saw the advantages of increased yield with less effort. They had also the advantage of forward looking leaders among them.

IV

The discussion above amply brings out the fact that tradi tion and development, both in the context of a society or of an institution, do not exist as bipolar opposites. Human mind is so ingenius that in the face of urgent demands tradition may be relegated to the background and new ideas and innovations begin to influence human action. In the realm of religion, particularly in the area of ritual, tradition still holds its sway. It is also strong so far as social structure is concerned. But, in this also, through slow processes, imperceptibly new ideas do produce impact. Among the Apatani this is visible so far as the dual divi sion in the society and tribal endogamy are concerned. Similarly, the endogamous character of the two social classes is also losing its legitimacy. None of the tradi tions has stood in the way of their traditional skills in business have given them a distinct advantage as is shown by their emergence is highly successful trading and business community. Similarly, their tradition for a highly ordered and disciplined society has stood them in good stead in making advances on the path of development.

It may also be noted that in many areas of developmental activity, there is absence of traditional norms. In these areas, changes take place much faster than in those in which traditions may run counter to the ideas put forth through development messages.

Shifting cultivation cannot be viewed only as an economic activity since all economic relations are set in a social framework. The entire social life of the community may re volve round the practice of swiddening. But each case of swiddening has to be studied in its specific historical physiographic and socio-political contexts. Among the Wancho it is closely integrated with their political and social systems. The Chief holds absolute power over land commonly owned and distributes land to heads of households according to their needs as well as their capacity to cultivate the land. Since no private ownership of land is acknowledged, there is no incentive among the people to development of their land as they would like to enhance their own income. Endemic wars and rains in the past increased the powers of the Chief. If people had to supplement their income, it was only their working as casual daily labourers in road con struction work or in various plantations. In some cases even in the Wancho area, people are aware of the soil erosion and they have devised mechanisms to reduce it to the minimum. Lastly, there is the question of availability of plain upon which people can be resettled. In view of these factors it has not been possible to reduce the coverage of swiddening in the Wancho areas. But it is not the faith in traditional practices and rituals that are responsible for this.

The experience with the Digaru Mishmi clearly reveals that people may be willing to adopt a way of life if in exchange they are assured of a better living. Their leaders co- operated with the Government officials in persuading their friends in the seven villages to come down and settle at the new location on the foothills. Success was achieved in this endeavour due to enlightened leadership in the community it self, some idea of private property in land and the constant monitoring of the project by higher officials at the dis trict level. In this case, their traditional beliefs and rituals did not prove an insurmountable barrier when they cast in their lot for settled cultivation. Moreover their tribal identity was not in danger. In times of transition like this, traditions, entrenched and emerging, co-exist for some time. In course of a generation, the emerging tradition triumphs over the entrenched.

The Indian tribes and for that matter, the whole country faces both directions. Like Janus they stand halfway between the past and the future. Dr. Zakir Hussain echoed this sen timent some time back as follows:- To survive we need a revolution in our thought and outlook. From the altar of the past we should take the living fire and not the dead ashes. Let us remember the past, be alive in the present and create the future with courage in our heart and faith in ourselves. Indian genius can operate at the same time in the tradi tional world as well as in the modern. Thus on the Indian scene, there is no confrontation between tradition and development and traditional structures have always adopted themselves to new situation.

REFERENCES

Furer-Haimendorf, C.Von 1982 Highlanders of Arunachal Pradesh; Vikas Publishing, New Delhi.

Nash, M. 1985 The Golden Road to Modernity; John Wiley and Sons, New York.

Sachchidananda 1985 Swiddening Among the Wancho of Arunachal; UNESCO, Bangkok.

——1985 Economic Development, Education and Social Change in Arunachal; Man in India, March.

SIX

Sharit K. Bhowmik

Development Problems of Chotanagpur Tribals in North Bengal

The paper deals with the problems of the Chotanagpur tribals who are engaged in agriculture in Jalpaiguri dis trict of West Bengal. The district is situated in the north ern part of the State and is the larger of the two tea grow ing districts in the State (the other being Darjeeling). The tea growing area in this district is known as Dooars and it lies in the foothills of Bhutan. This area was originally a part of Bhutan till it was annexed by the British in 1864. A distinctive feature of Jalpaiguri is that its proportion of scheduled tribes to the total population is the highest in the State. The district's population in 1981 was 2,214,871 of which 491, 791, i.e., a little over twenty two per cent, were scheduled tribes (Ghosh 1982:4). Moreover, an over whelming majority of these scheduled tribes comprise tribals migrated from the Chotanagpur Santhal Pargana region of Bihar, who are called Adivasis. The autochthonous tribes such as Mech, Rabha and Tota, form a small minority.[1] The Adivasis had been originally recruited as tea garden labour and they emmigrated soon after the tea gardens came up in 1874. The district has 152 tea gardens which employ around 1,40,000 permanent workers, a majority of whom are Adivasis. Those Adivasis who are not engaged

1. Of the three main indegenious tribes, the Totos have a population of around 700. The population of the Mechs is the largest of the three. It was 10,387 in the 1971 census while the Rabhas numbered only 343. On the other hand, the population of Draons was 159,619, Mundas 71,685, Santhal 71,539, Mahali 24,320 and Kharia 14,120 (see Ghosh 1971 B : 578,503).

in the tea industry have taken to cultivation and have settled in villages bordering the tea gardens. As mentioned earlier, the focus of this paper is on the development problems of these Adivasis. The paper is divided into four parts. The first part forms the background and it deals with the settlement of Adivasis in agriculture. The second part deals with their conditions in the post independence period and the third part appraises the role of the Integrated Tribal Development Programme (ITDP) and its impact on the lives of the Adivasis. The final part discusses the trends in tribal development and what could be its likely outcome. The data presented in the first part is based on secondary sources and in the sub sequent parts, on my fieldwork in this area.

Settlement of Adivasis in Agriculture

Migration of Adivasis for work ranging from tea planta tions to cultivation in the nearby agricultural areas has been going on almost since the inception of the tea industry in the district. Workers after retiring from tea garden work would invariably settle in agricultural work. The lure for land is very strong among the Adivasis and they often take to cultivation even before retirement. J.P. Gruning,author of the 1911 district gazetteer, observed "many tea garden coolies after working for a time and saving a little money settle down permanently in the district. Oraons are hardworking and make excellent cultivators; they are good settlers, giving little trouble and paying their rent regularly"(1911 : 31).

There were basically three types of land in Jalpaiguri district during the British period. Firstly, tea-grant land, which was divided into 180 grants of temporarily settled es tates, and which were primarily meant for tea cultivation. Secondly, reserved forests and lastly, the land meant for agriculture. This was divided into five government estates (**tehsils**), three of which were in Dooars. The tehsils were divided into lots (known as **Jotes**) and were leased out. The leases were known as **Jotedars** and they paid their rents to the treasury (Ibid: 86).

The first comprehensive settlement of agricultural land in Dooars was done in 1895 and the lands which were not in pos session at that time were regulated by the Waste Lands Manual. Asok Mitra, author of the 1951 district census hand book, noted that under this manual government found it con venient to lease out large tracts of waste lands to a few leases. So "inevitably all arable land... in the district has been cornered by a handful of **jotedars** (Mitra 1953 B : LXXV).

The **Jotedars** were mainly Rajbanshis, Hindu and Muslim (Sunder 1895 : 45). Rajbanshs are indegeneous community of North Bengal and they have been declared as a scheduled caste in the post-independence period. Most of these **Jotedars**, including the Rajbanshis, had started settling in Dooars since the Bhutan regime from the neighbouring State of Coochbehar and the districts of Rangpur, Dinajour (Both in Bangladesh Now) and Purnea (Bihar) (Ibid : 46).

There were a few Adivasi **Jotedars** too. These people were mainly the Sardars or their descendents. The Sardars were gang-leaders in the tea gardens and they were also engaged in recruiting new workers from the recruiting districts for which they got a fee. In addition, workers recruited by a Sardar were put under his charge and he got a small part of their wage as a commission. These people were therefore in a position to some wealth which they could invest in possess ing land and becoming **Jotedars**. D.H.E. Sunder, Settlement Officer of the 1895 land settlement in Dooars, noted in his report that some of the **Jotedars** in Dooars were Oraons (Ibid : 47).

Some tea garden workers also settled in forest lands. The Forest Department needed labour for its new plantations and it lured tea garden workers by granting them land in ex change of their labour. The planters often protested against this "unfair" practice as it meant loss of their labour. For instance, in a letter to the Conservator of Forests, Bengal, dated 26 January 1920, the Chairman of the Dooars Planters, Association (S.P.A.), which was the most influential body of the European Planters, wrote that workers were leaving the tea gardens to work in the forests because "they had been promised land rent free in return for work on sal seedling plantations, and in other directions". He further stated, "I have to remind you that tea garden coolies are recruited at great expense, and my committee (viz. Executive Committee) considers that it is most unjust and unfair that such people should be enticed and employed by means of land at nominal rent" (DPA 1920 : 29). Attraction to work on land provided the main incentive for the workers to leave the tea gardens for forest work. The D.P.A. frankly admitted that "tea es tates cannot compete with the Forest Department, if the lat ter offers land rent free or at a nominal cost" (Ibid). This practice did not last for long as the planters used their political influence to prevent the Forest Department from recruiting its labour from tea gardens.

Apart from the few **Jotedars,** Adivasis were hardly able to cultivate land under their own possession as there was very little scope to do so. The government insisted on distribut ing large tracts of lands, which the Adivasis could not af ford to lease. Moreover, by the beginning of this century practically all cultivable land in Dooars was leased out. Gruning noted in 1911 that in Mainaguri **tahsil,** which was the largest of the three **tehsils** in Dooars, "nearly all available land...has been leased out and there is keen com petition for any land fit for cultivation" (Gruning 1911 : 86). J.A. Milligan, Settlement Officer for the 1906-16 land settlement in Dooars, noted that in 1910, **adhiars** (sharecroppers) who were ex-tea garden tribal workers cul tivated 64,281 acres of **Jote** lands (Milligan 1919:14). This is quite a significant amount as the total area cultivated by adhiars during that settlement was 148, 602.84 acres (Ibid : Appendix 2, p. iii).

The **adhiars** had no security of tenure on the lands that were sub-let to them. Initially they were not recognized as tenants or even under-tenants. In fact, Sunder refers to them as tenants with no rights (1895 : 119). He also noted that the **adhiar** is in a chronic state of debt (Ibid). Mil ligan tried to point out the injustice of this system in his settlement report. He remarked that **adhiars** were being frequently shifted from plot to plot so that they could not claim tenancy rights in future (Milligan 1909 : 91) as the Board of Revenue conceded that an **adhiar** who had been in possession of a piece of land for 12 years could get tenancy rights (Ibid : 92). His appeals did have some effect as the government granted some occupancy rights to the **adhiars** but, as Asok Mitra (1953 B : Lxxvi)observed, "such a system, based essentially on private oppression which the long arm of the law cannot reach by virtue of limitations imposed by itself, is liable to slide back unless held in check". Since the **adhiars** were unorganized, they were unable to impose any such checks.

Mitra also pointed out that the **Jotedari** system had resulted in the backwardness of agriculture in the region. He wrote that this system "has amounted to an enormous con centration of land and agricultural wealth in the hands of a very few landlords, some of whom outwardly of mean ap pearance, are fabulously rich .... Inspite of the enormous concentration of wealth in his hands the **Jotedar** has sig nally failed. He does not spend enough to improve his land or obtain improved seeds and manures or in acquiring machi nary for improved cultivation, so that the land may yield more prosperity. Instead he parcels out almost all that he has to **adhiars** or agricultural serfs, who hold from him for a share of the crop which is often undefined". (Ibid : Lxxv).

It is fairly clear from the preceding discussion that the **Jotedari** system had contributed to the backwardness of agriculture and consequently impoverishment of the Adivasi Peasantry. The Adivasis were all the more helpless because they were unorganized and hence unable to fight for their rights. During the pre-independence period, Dooars was an isolated area having little contacts with the outside world. The Adivasis, both in tea gardens and in agriculture, were practically unaffected by trade union or peasant organiza tions. It was only in early 1946 that trade union organizers of the Bengal Dooars Railway extended their activities to the tea gardens. This union was controlled by the Communist Party of India (CPI) and most of its whole time organizers were communists. The railway gangmen, who were also Adi vasis, helped the Union organizers in establishing contacts with the tribal tea workers. These organizers formed the first trade union for tea garden workers in 1946 and were able to stir up unrest in a few tea gardens. They came in contact with the Adivasi **adhiars** through the railway workers and tea workers.

In late 1946, when the **tebhage** movement,[2] which was in itiated by the CPI, started in other parts of Bengal, the railway workers publicised it among the tea garden workers and the **adhiars** through leaflets and clandestine meetings. The All India Kisan Subha, which was the peasants' wing of the CPI, sent some of its organizers to Dooars to assist and guide the union organizers. By early 1947, Adivasi **adhiars** started the movement in Dooars. Soon, the entire

2. This section is a Summary of a more detailed work in chapter 5 of my book (Bhowmik 1981). The tebhaga movement was an agitation by sharecroppers in defferent parts of Bengal in late 1946. The word tebhaga means 'three parts' and the share-croppers demanded that instead of the customary half, the produce should be divided into three parts of which two parts should be given to the share- cropper and one part to the rentier. For a detailed account of this movement see, Sen 1976.

western part of Dooars (mainly Mainaguri **tehsil**) was engulfed in the movement. Tea garden workers too participated in it. They left their work and joined the **adhiars** in their agitation. They also used this movement to focus on their own grievances against their employers. One significant feature of this movement in Dooars was that it comprised exclusively of Adivasis. Adhiars belonging to other communities such as Rajbanshi and Muslim did not participate in it.

The **tebhaga** movement happens to be the only major uprising of the Adivasi cultivators in Dooars. However, though it was primarily a movement of share-croppers, it benefited tea garden workers more because it became the foundation of the trade union movement in the area. This was for the first time that workers of different tea gardens unitedly par ticipated in a mass movement. These lessons in unity were carried over to the garden level when workers united to fight against the management. The trade union movement gained momentum after this.

Post-Independence Developments

An unfortunate development after this stage was that the major political parties in this areas, such as the CPI,Revolutionary Socialist Party and the Congress, which had so far been concentrating on organizing the tribal peasantry, shifted their attention to tea plantation labour. Hence, after the initial spurt in organizing the tribal peasantry to fight for their rights, they were again neglected and left to fend for themselves. It would almost appear as if the political parties had started working among the tribal peasants in order to have an access to the tea garden labour through their kinship links. Once this was achieved, the political parties got more in the problems of tea garden labour than in the peasantry. This point is rein forced when one notes a similar trend in another section of the working class, namely, the railway workers. As noted earlier, communist organizers had gained a foothold in this area through work among railway workers. In fact, the CPI and RSP trade union leaders among the tea gardens workers were drawn almost exclusively from the whole time organizers of railway workers. However, since the early 1950s the com munists seemed to have lost interest in retaining their in fluence over them.

Growth of the trade union movement in the tea gardens brought substantial benefits to the workers. These people were not only poorly paid but their managements ruled over them with an iron hand. The entry of trade unions altered the nature of industrial relations in this industry. The workers gradually gave up their passive submission to the dictates of the management and they learnt to organize struggles to fight for their rights. Hence, when compared to the pre-trade union stage, tea garden workers were able to substantially improve their living and working conditions. There were laws in the pre-independence period granting some protection to workers, such as the Trade Union Act, In dustrial Disputes Act and Minimum Wages Act, which were ap plicable to tea plantation workers. However, the government did not provide the adequate machinery in these areas to en sure their enforcement and as the employers were not too keen to implement them, the laws remained only on paper. Un der the leadership of trade unions, the workers were able to unitedly force their managements to recognize their rights.

The tribal peasantry, on the other hand, remained unor ganized and helpless because the political parties were con centrating more on the trade union movement in tea. Their problems were further increased due to the partition which resulted in a large influx of migrants from across the bor der. This phenomenon resulted in a high growth rate of the district's population during the post - 1947 period which was well above the national growth rate of 13 percent per annum. The district's population increased by 8.13 percent during the decade 1941-51 which appears to be fairly low. However, three police stations in the district were trans fered to East Pakistan (Bangladesh) in 1947 and this should have actually resulted in a decrease in population. The in crease in population shows that immigration off-set the decrease caused by a reduction in the size of the district. During the next decade of 1951-61 population increased by 48.27 per cent (Ray 1969 : 25) as compared to the national growth rate of 13 percent. Growth rates in the next two decades, 1961-71 and 1971-81 were lower, i.e. 28.76 percent and 26.11 percent respectively (Ghosh 1971 A : 90, Ghosh 1982 : 4), when compared to 1951-61 they were higher than the national growth rate of 25 percent.

The decennial growth rates during the period 1901-41 was erratic, but it never exceeded the 1901-11 figure of 21.30 percent. During the three decades of 1911-21, 1921-31, population increased by 4.92 percent, 6.47 percent and 14.42 percent respectively (Ray 1969 : 25).

The high growth rate during the post - 1951 period would indicate that it is not accounted solely through natural in crease in population but through migration. In fact the 1961 census noted that there were 218,341 persons in the district who were born in Pakistan (Bangladesh, in the present context). According to the 1981 census, 86 percent of the district's population resided in the rural areas (Ghosh 1982 : 4), Hence, this population increase was absorded by this sector. For instance, the 1961 census recorded that 171,617 of the persons born in Pakistan were enumerated in the rural areas (Ray 1969 :64). All these data indicate that firstly, immigrants caused a high growth rate of the population and, secondly, these immigrants were spread mainly over the rural areas. This also implies that the pressure on land increased as the immigrants were vying for land. The Adivasi cul tivator had to contend with this competition though it in creased his problems.

At the same time, another phenomenon was taking place. The tea planters, under the pretext of increase in costs, started decreasing the number of workers. The plantations employed 176,196 permanent workers in 1951 (Mitra 1953A : 263) and this was reduced to 143,022 in 1980 (Tea Board 1983 :119). These surplus workers too had to be accommodated in agriculture.

Under these circumstances the Adivasi cultivators were hardly able to improve their condition of existence. In the post-independence period, the government abolished the Zamindari and Jotedari systems under the West Bengal Estates Acquisition Act of 1954. The tenants were expected to benefit by these actions. However, competition for posses sion of land due to the immigrants and the unemployed tea workers, eroded whatever benefits the Adivasi cultivators could accrue.

The new Panchayat system introduced by the State Govern ment in 1978 was expected to give a fillip to people's par ticipation in development activities. This three tier system has the Zilla Parishad (Z.P.) at the district level, the Panchayat Samity (P.S.) at the block level and the Gram Pan chayat (G.P.) at the local level. Members to these three bodies are directly elected by rural voters. Rural Develop ment activities are carried out by these bodies as it is felt that elected members will be more sensitive to the needs of the rural poor.

There are a few cases of Adivasis being elected as Pradhan (Chairperson) of GPs but as the subsequent study shows, they are not always able to conduct their activities to the required level of satisfaction because of their low level of awareness. This reflects firstly, the backwardness of this community and secondly, its helplessness because its elected leaders have not been trained for this process. The findings of the study of the ITDP in the next section will illustrate these points more clearly and will also provide an insight into the prevailing situation.

ITDP and the Tribals

The Integrated Tribal Development Project came into opera tion in Jalpaiguri District in 1979. This scheme functions at two levels. Firstly, on the community level, by providing amenities, such as drinking water facilities, road, adult education, minor irrigation etc., in selected tribal vil lages. Secondly, on the individual level, where tribal beneficiaries are provided facilities for improving their economic conditions. These include agricultural aid, schemes for providing cattle, pigs, poultry, fish cultivation, vil lage industries etc.

The beneficiaries are selected by the CPs and the schemes are processed by the Panchayat Samitis. Schemes for in dividual beneficiaries are subsidies by the government upto 50 percent or more, 10 percent is given as interest free margin money and the rest as bank loan at a low rate of in terest. The entire amount, i.e., loans plus subsidy is dis bursed through banks.

A survey[3] conducted in the four development Blocks of the district revealed a number of discrepencies in the implemen tation of the project. The records available at the Block Office show beneficiaries. In most cases, the beneficiaries were supplied the imputs in kind and not in cash so as to prevent them from misusing the money sanctioned. Hence, in the case of animal husbandary, the beneficiaries were sup plied the specified number of cows, pigs, goats as the case may be. However,out of the 111 beneficiaries interviewed un der the animal husbandary scheme, we could identify only 5 persons who had actually benefited. There were two ways in which beneficiaries were being deprived. Firstly, they received less than the sanctioned amount and secondly, the animals supplied were of inferior stock as they were either diseased or too old to be of any productive use.

The discrepency between the sanctioned amount and the dis bursed amount was found in mainly there of the four blocks. For instance, we covered 33 beneficiaries who had been given milch cows and we found that 22 of them had been given the sanctioned amount of two cows each, eight had been given only one cow each and three had been paid the cash equiv alent for two cows but they had each received Rs.300/- less than the sanctioned amount. The cows had been distributed a year earlier and we found that of the 52 cows actually dis tributed only 19 were in possession of the beneficiaries. The three beneficiaries who were paid in cash, did not pur chase their cows. We also found that the depletion in stock was in some cases due to sale of the cows for economic reasons, but in most cases it was due to death as the animals supplied were either too old or were diseased. We found almost the same situation in the case of

---

3. The following section contains a summary of the main findings of an evaluatory study on the functioning of the ITDP in Jalpaiguri district. This study, titled "Evaluation of the Integrated Tribal Development Project in Jalpaiguri District" was sponsored by the Department of Tribal Welfare, Government of West Bengal and was Supervised by Prof. N.C. Choudhury, Department of Sociology and Social Anthropology, University of North Bengal and myself. We were assisted by Mahabub-ul-Alam and Amal Dutta in the data col lection. A survey of the beneficiaries of the ITDP residing in 13 villages situated in four of the twelve Development Blocks in the district where the ITDP is in operation was taken. The field work was conducted in February-March 1984. The survey covered 300 beneficiaries residing in these 13 villages. The objective of the survey was to assess the role of the ITDP in improving the socio-economic conditions of the tribal population in the district. An attempt was made to find out the loopholes in the scheme and remedial measures were suggested.

goats and pigs. In some cases the animals were so diseased that they died before the beneficiary could reach his home. In two cases beneficiaries told us that not only were the goats supplied diseased, they had even spread it to their own healthy goats which also died. Hence their economic condi tion had deteriorated. In the case of pigs we found that suckling piglets were supplied and they died of starvation as they could not get their mothers' milk. Some of the pigs supplied were of exotic varieties and the beneficiaries were not in a position to tend to them properly as they required special feed which the tribals could not afford. Of the five cases where this scheme had helped the beneficiaries, three of them had been supplied good quality cows and the other two had been given female calves (instead of cows) and we can hope that in future these will yield milk and benefit their owners.

The same depressing picture was found in the case of the other schemes, such as agricultural aid, improved agricul tural implements, village industries, and dwelling houses. In the agricultural aid scheme, Rs.250/- was distributed to each beneficiary for purchase of seeds and manure. None of the beneficiaries covered received the money before the sowing season and they had all spent it on food and clothes. Had they received the money on time, they may have been able to utilize it for agriculture. However, it is also notewor thy that all these beneficiaries had repaid the loans.

Under the improved agricultural implements scheme, the beneficiaries were given implements like a hand compression sprayers, seed drills, wheel hoes, paddy weeders and mould- bolt ploughs. Most of these implements were lying unused (except for seed drills and sprayers) as the tribal cul tivators were unawars of how to use them. The mould-bolt ploughs were very large in size and were possibly designed for large sized plough cattle as in Haryana and Rajasthan. They were hence of no use in this region.

The village industry scheme had been implemented in only one of the four blocks and here too in only one case. Eigh teen women belonging to the Mech tribe had been given looms with 75 percent subsidy and were also supplied thread. The women sold enough cloth to repay the 25 percent loan and utilized the rest of the cloth for their personal use. Had they sold more cloth they would have been able to invest the money in buying more raw materials. Instead, the scheme folded up because the beneficiaries could not purchase raw materials. We found that the women did not know where to market the cloth. Had marketing facilities been provided, they would have sold all the cloth and purchased raw material for continuing the scheme.

The village industry scheme could have proved helpful to some of the tribals. Several tribal beneficiaries belonging to Turi and Mahali tribes told us that they had asked their Panchayat representatives for assistance in basket weaving or making of musical instruments, which were their respec tive traditional occupations. They were given pigs or goats instead. The money damarcated for this scheme was lying unused or had lapsed in the three other blocks.

There are some points which arise while assessing the per formance of the ITDP. Firstly, it appears that a proper assessment of the needs of the beneficiaries had not been done and the inputs were without being consulted. Many of them told us that they had asked for something other than what was given to them. This becomes all the more surprising because the names of the beneficiaries for each scheme is supplied by the GP whose members are expected to know the needs of their people.

Secondly, we found that several names of beneficiaries which had been passed by the GP and the Panchayat Samity had been dropped by the banks because they were not economically viable. In other words, the bank found these people too poor and hence they may not be able to repay the loans. This brings up a contradiction in the objectives of the project. On the one hand, the government started this project to help the tribal poor to improve their level of living as these people may be unable to do so through their own resources. On the other hand, the financial implementation of the schemes is done through the commercial banks which are in terested in ensuring that their loans are repaid. Hence, it is likely that the very people this project tries to help will be disqualified by the banks.

Thirdly, interviews with the beneficiaries revealed that their awareness about the project was very poor. They were not clear about what the project's aim was and what benefits they could get from it. This was one of the reasons why the tribals could not assert their actual needs and the GP rep resentatives took decisions on their own. Awareness about the project and their own rights as tribals is an important factor for the success of rural development programmes as only then can the tribal beneficiaries actively participate in development programmes. The only exception we found, in this respect, was in the Mech village which we covered in one of the blocks. There were a number of educated tribals in this village who helped the others in demanding the req uisite facilities. We found that the animal husbandry, agricultural aid, implements and minor irrigation schemes benefited them as these had been implemented after assessing the needs of the people. This example to some extent proves that awareness does play a role in the success of a scheme, otherwise, the scheme will appear as charity.

A low level of awareness was found even among the Pan chayat members who were Adivasis. The thirteen villages covered were situated in eight GP areas and the majority of the population in seven of them was Adivasi. However only three of these GPs had tribal Pradhans. Two of them were Adivasis and third was a Mech. It should be mentioned here that there are no reserved constituencies in the Panchayats. Hence non-tribals can be elected from tribal majority areas. The non-tribal members of the Panchayats tend to dominate because they are more articulate. The three tribal Panchayat Pradhans were also beneficiaries and when asked how they got to know about the particular scheme (a question asked to all beneficiaries), the Mech Pradhan replied that he was in formed by the block office while the Adivasi Pradhans each named a non-tribal member of their respective GPs as their informants. This response is quite significant because the GP Pradhans are expected to disseminate information regard ing development programmes in their areas through the mem bers of the GP. The process seems to be reversed here as members have conveyed information to the Pradhans.

An Assessment

It is quite evident that in spite of the attempts of the government there have not been any substantive changes among the Adivasi peasantry in the district. Development cannot be the one-sided exercise where the government or other exter nal agencies assume the role of the benefactor and the people play the passive receivers. Policies for development can be fruitful only when the benefactor can effectively en sure that the facilities reach the people concerned and, if necessary, have them suitably altered to meet the prevailing needs. Hence, an active interaction between the government and the beneficiaries is a necessary condition for success. The people have to organize themselves so that they are able to articulate their problems in a collective manner. This is woefully lacking in the case of the Adivasis. Indifference of political parties and peasant organizations in organizing them to assert their rights is largely responsible for this state of affairs. The Adivasis therefore are unable to develop any collective consciousness through which they could focus their backwardness to the authorities. In the absence of such consciousness, they tend to accept the crumbs bestowed on them as charity and they feel grateful for these.

The backwardness of the tribals in the district is reflected in the literacy rates of the tribal and non-tribal population. In the 1961 only 7.47 percent of the scheduled tribe population was literate as compared to 19.22 percent of the district's population (Ray 1969 : 84) and in 1971 the respective figures were 9.29 percent and 25 percent (Ghosh 1971 : 794,816). Literacy rates in 1981 : 12.10 percent for tribals and 30 percent for the district (Ghosh 1981 : 1). Though Jalpaiguri is a backward district and its level of literacy has been substantially lower than that of West Ben gal, the level of literacy among the scheduled tribes has been a little more than one-third of the district's level of literacy.

The low level of literacy of the tribals and their rela tive isolation from the development process place them in a position where they are rarely able to manage the complex requirements of the new schemes of rural development even if they are given the responsibility. The performance of Adivasi Pradhans of the GPs are clear indications of this. Such instance may lead one to conclude, though wrongly, that Adivasis are incapable of handling their own affairs. In reality, isolation of this group as a result of their il literacy and the indifference of peasant organizations in helping to train them, have checked the growth of their awareness, and consequently, participation in issues relat ing to development.

The present situation clearly indicates that dependence on others, whether it is on the government bureaucracy or on peasant organizations, has not been an affective means of easing their problems. The few instances of successful im plementation of the ITDP among the Mech tribe were due to the fact that these people have a higher level of literacy and they were able to articulate their problems effectively. This would indicate that, given the present situation, the Adivasis too have to develop leadership from within them selves which will be able to organize the people so as to evolve a collective consciousness on their problems and the solutions. In this respect, the only ray of hope appears in the new generation of educated Adivasi Youth. Many of these people are trying to understand the problems of their com munity and they also have the potential of emerging as leaders. One may be optimistic in expecting that when this generation takes up the leadership of their community, as the present trend indicates that they will, the pace of development among the Adivasis will improve.

REFERENCES

Bhowmik,Sharit*TH* 1981 Class Formation in the plantation system; People's Publishing House, Delhi.

D.P.A. (Dooars Planters Association 1920) Report of the General Committee for the year 1920; Calcutta.

Ghosh, Bhaskar 1971A Census of India 1971, Series 22, West Bengal, PT. IIA, General Population Tables, Government of West Bengal, Calcutta.

Ghosh, Bhaskar 1971B Census of India 1971, Series 23 West Bengal, Paper I of 1982, Final population tables, government of West Bengal, Calcutta.

Gruning, J.F. 1971 Eastern Bengal and Assam District Gazet teers (Jalpaiguri); Government of India, Allahabad.

Milligan, J.A. 1919 Final Report on the Survey and Settle ment operations in Jalpaiguri District 1906-16; Bengal Secretariat Book Depot, Calcutta.

Mitra, Asok 1953A Census of India 1951, Vol. VI, PT IA,(West Bengal, sikkim and Chandernagors), Report, Government of West Bengal, Calcutta.

Mitra, Asok 1953B Census of India 1951 Vol. VI, (West Bengal Sikkim and Chandernagors), District Census Handbook; Jal paiguri, Government of West Bengal, Calcutta.

Tea Board, 1983 Tea Statistics 1981-82; Tea Board of India, Calcutta.

Sen, Suinil, 1976 Agrarian Unrest in Bengal 1946-47; People's Publishing House, Delhi.

Sunder, D.H.E. 1895 Survey and Settlement of Western Duars in the District of Jalpaiguri 1889-95; Bengal Secretariat Press, Calcutta.

SEVEN

P. K. Nayak

Tradition and Development in Tribal Orissa: A Case Study of Dongria Kondh Development Agency

In 1964 the Orissa Government started the Dongria Kondh Development Agency (DKDA) for launching development programmes among the Dongria Kondh, one of the primitive tribes of the State. Curbing exploitation by the local traders and the Domb (the scheduled caste neighbour of the Dongria Kondh) and checking liquor vending in the hills were felt to be the cardinal measures for undertaking development activities among the Dongria Kondh. It started with the PSFS (Purchase and Sale Fair-price Shops) scheme through which the indigenous produce of the Dongria Kondh (Dongria Kondh basically being the horticulturists produce huge quantities of pine apples, oranges, banana and turmeric etc.) were being purchased by the Agency at a reasonable rate and the daily necessities like salt, kerosene, tobacco, match box and cheap garments etc. were being provided to the people at a fair price. In order to make the scheme more effective 23 hill-top villages were selected by the Development Agency and one PSFS shop was opened in the heart of the Dongria Kondh area to cater to the needs of the people. One senior state level officer was put in charge of the Agency as its Special Officer. The officer himself evinced a lot of inter est in the people firstly being deeply impressed by the serenity of the nature pervading all through the habita tional area of the Dongria Kondh (the pictureseque Niamgiri hills of 4500 feet with the perennial streams flowing down) and by the queer customs and proud cultural styles of the people (the officer being one of the

Gyanapitha awardees in Oriya literature). Secondly he was impelled by the humanis tic drive of sympathising with the miseries of the people and promoting their welfare in the interior.

During his tenure of four years (1964 to 1968) the P.S.F.S. scheme had one positive impact.It promoted the awareness of the metric system of weights and measures among the Dongria Kondh as a result of their frequent direct transaction with the Government shop. But the negative impacts were many even though during the operation of the scheme the local traders and Domb neighbours were disallowed to deal in the produce of the Dongria Kondh (infact it was checked publicly) and all types of family loans of the Dongria Kondh from the Domb neighbours were repaid by the Agency. In consequence the Domb were estranged because the Agency gave everything to the Dongria and nothing to the Domb. They were apprehensive of the talk in the plains that they would be removed from the Niamgiri hills. They reacted to undo the development measures of the Agency. They succeeded in creating dissen sion and producing factionalism among the Dongria Kondh clans which were traditionally feud ridden. They manipulated to exploit this weakness of the Dongria Kondh and plied their trade and business vigorously inside the hill country as they had a stake in the social-cultural and economic life of the Dongria Kondh which the Development Agency could not tackle. Thus, all the development measures were undone. Even the plantation programmes of the Agency met an unfortunate end. Besides their belief in their indigenous products and aversion for exogenous ones, the Domb impressed on their mind that the plantation plot in course of time would be taken possession of by the Government. In addition, both the Dongria and the Domb contrasted their own plantation with the government sponsored plantation and categorically decried the latter's skill in growing plants in the hill slopes and lost faith in the plantation efforts of the Agency.

The consequence became still worse when the P.S.F.S. scheme was taken over and manned by the Marketing Officer and the Branch Manager of the TDCS (Tribal Development Cooperative Society). The scheme functioned more as a business organiza tion than a development institution. There was no strict vigilance on the procurement of the produce of the Dongria Kondh, and as usual the Domb played their business tactics and trapped the Dongria Kondh producer. Exploitation was rampant. It so happened that the benefits given to the Dongria through the PSFS scheme could not be enjoyed by them as a large portion of it was appropriated by the Domb.Traditionally the Dongria Kondh are producers and landholders and the Domb are the landless middlemen,the petty businessmen who deal in the formers' produce to main tain their livelihood. The Dongria Kondh after repaying their loans indulged more in liquor drinking and the Domb exploited them further. The Dongria realized the halfhearted interest of the Government in their welfare and prized in their traditional mode of socio-economic interaction with the Domb who had been providing them help and support at the time of need and difficulty. By acting as subservient to the Kondh the Domb served the purpose of the people better. This tradition of Domb-Kondh interaction was so deep rooted in their sentiment that some individual Dongria Kondh who have gone against the Domb and welcomed the government measures and introduction of modern socio-political attributes have gone back on their words. However, from 1968 onwards it was observed that individual Domb families from the neighbouring districts of Kalahandi and Phulbani infiltrated into the area and there was rise in the Domb population. Gradually they captured the Dongria Kondh Market.

With the emergence of the sub-plan concept, the Dongria Kondh Development Agency was revived in 1975 and functioned as a micro project covering 52 hill villages. A Senior Re search Officer from the Harijan and Tribal Welfare Depart ment was deputed there as the Special Officer of the Agency. He pursued the plantation programmes in a few villages but it was of no effect as by then the situation was so dif ficult that the officer failed to win their confidence and consequently became indifferent towards their development and continued on the job for three years only.

As the plantation target could not be achieved in 1978 the Government decided to depute an agricultural scientist as the Special Officer of the Agency to pursue vigorously the plantations through which it was hoped that the people's lot could be improved. The agricultural scientist did not con sider the people' involvement as a factor for their economic development and indiscriminately went on preparing planta tion plots in the areas having road communication which he could reach by jeep and by motor cycle (on his initiative the bullet motor cycle was purchased for the purpose of su pervising the field). The road side areas far away from the villages were preferred for plantation as higher officers could visit them daily. He continued till 1982 but neither the plantations nor any other development activity could be successful. The Domb traders became very active during the period, for the officer himself wanted to use them for doing anything in the area as he did not have faith on the Dongria Kondh people nor on their development. The agricultural scientist behaved more as an officer than a development agent. This had dangerous consequences. The Dongria Kondh were scared of the officer himself and this Domb agents and this unhealthy trend affected the Dongria Kondh so much that after a house-fire incident the people of one of the prosperous Dongria Kondh villages wanted to shift their vil lage to another area but some how or other they were recon ciled by the intervention and persuasion of a Gandhian lady worker who had been pursuing social welfare work since 1965 in the area.

However, in 1982 an enthusistic young anthropologist of the Tribal and Harijan Welfare Department was deputed to the area as the Special Officer.Basically being a student of ac tion anthropology and having experiénce of fieldwork in many tribal areas of Orissa, Bihar and Andaman Islands and being the right kind of person he has been pursuing development activities among the Dongria Kondh in full swing and has set an example in the State.

The techniques and methods adopted by the anthropologist for the development of the Dongria Kondh have been evolved by him after gathering knowledge about the beliefs and ac tivities of the people. To start with he visited all the 52 villages of the project areas on foot and made personal con tact with the Dongria Kondh villagers. He even made it a point to spend several nights in the interior villages to win the confidence of the people. He also persuaded the sub ordinate welfare personnel to make regular visits to the villages. In this way he prepared the ground for implement ing the development programmes.

A short review of the development activities undertaken by him will highlight the strategy of development in tribal areas.

He continues to hold regular meetings in the hill villages as many times as possible in order to assess people's mind, their problems and their desire for undertaking development activities by themselves and also discerning the types of elements among them. In the beginning he stumbled as he did not take into confidence the Domb neighbours. But later he realized their role in that area and patted them and put on moral pressure on the Domb Barikas, the traditional mes senger of the villages to look after the development ac tivities and to inform him directly the other socio-cultural problems and developments in the villages and also in the region. He pacified them by getting them loans through the Banks for plying their business.

He introduced plantations of all varieties including growing vegetables like potato, tomato, cabbage, brinjal, chilli and ginger, preparing turmeric plots, terrace plots mainly for paddy cultivation and cultivation of seasonal cereals and pulses with irrigation channels from the main streams in the interior most villages. People adopted plantation plots in vast tracts. He made it possible by engaging the people themselves in line with the functioning of the traditional labour cooperatives in which all the villagers irrespective of the Kondh and the Domb participated in clearing the bush, bunding the swidden and plantation plots in lieu of a buf falo, and the required quantities of rice towards the com munal feast.

He has been successful in resolving their traditional feuds over trifles and in getting support of women by paying at tention to their cultural issues for he knew that unless these were solved he could not pursue his development ac tivities (Nayak : 1984). He has even helped people in get ting loans from the Bank for paying the bride-price which facilitated them in acquiring their desired women. This measure has further been helpful in checking their tradi tional practice of working in the father-in-law's house for 2-3 years. By this both the landless and the landowner in dividual Kondhs have been benefited and have felt secured in their social life which resulted in bringing about economic stability in the family. In 1984 he succeeded in getting wives negotiated earlier by 57 youngmen but not acquired due to non-payment of bride-price.

At one level he observed that the Kondhs were still the vic tims of the Domb and exploitation continued in some measure. He decided to allow the Domb to procure the produce of the Kondh at the rate fixed by him and asked them to sell them to the society of the Agency at a marketable price keeping their own profit. This has thoroughly checked the tradi tional mode of exploitative business transaction of the Domb with the Kondh and the monopoly of the latter. The village school teachers, the Welfare Extension Officer of the Agency have been instructed to be vigilant about individual trans actions between the Kondh and the Domb and the cases of deviation are being reported from time to time to the Spe cial Officer who puts it in the village council meeting and the culprits are reprimanded publicly. This method of con trol of deviant cases in line with their traditional method of social control has solved the problem better and the Kondh and the Domb alike are aware of the stringent con sequences.

The delineation of the foregoing case material depicts the activities of the Development Agency, its failure and success from time to time and suggests the elemental fea tures of pursuing development which could be broadly concep tualized as the basic propositions which have their bearing on carrying out developing activities specifically among the primitive tribal communities.

The basic propositions could be stated as follows:

1. Economic development determines socio-cultural development : they are the two sides of the same coin;
2. pursuance of development measures in line with the tradi tion of a primitive community is easier and results in greater success where in lies the feasibility of par ticipatory development, the highest goal of development success;
3. Confidence in the people, confidence in oneself (the development practitioner) and confidence in the success of the development measures are the basic requirements to go ahead with the development activities provided the bureaucratic machinery and political interference do not act as barriers;
4. Pragmatic rather than mere humanistic approach helps solve the problem of development and for the scientific develop ment of tribal societies in particular regions. Orientation of the development personnel in fieldwork in tribal societies with a research zeal ought to be the first con sideration for it smoothes undertaking development activities;
5. Personality of the development scientists counts in the development process. 'The right kind of person' can only tackle the problems of development in tribal areas; and
6. Development of exclusive tribal communities has a bearing on the development of the neighbouring non-tribal com munities

which historically used to have a stake in the socio-economic life of the former.

This is so far as the empirical observations made among the Dongria Kondh with respect to development but as regards the development experience in other tribal communities of Orissa, the following discussion will throw light with specific reference to tradition and development in the back- ground of the tribal situation in Orissa.

Tribal situation in Orissa : Development and Change

The total tribal population of Orissa is 5,915,067, the second highest in the country, next to Madhya Pradesh (11,987,031). Tribal population of Bihar (5,810,867) is com parable to that of Orissa. However, tribals in Orissa con stitute 22.43% of the total population of the State whereas in Madhya Pradesh and Bihar they constitute 22.97% and 8.31% respectively. The total population of tribes in the country is 51,628,638 (7.76% of the total population), whereas the percentage of tribal population of Orissa is 11.46, of Bihar is 11.25 and of Madhya Pradesh is 23.22 of the total tribal population of the country. This shows that in respect of tribal population, Orissa has got the second priority be sides the North Eastern tribes of Nagaland, Meghalaya and Mizoram.

Orissa has as many as 62 distinct tribal communities,the highest number in the country. From among the 62 tribes, a few still subsist on food gathering and hunting, some others depend chiefly on Swidden cultivation and the rest on low land paddy cultivation. In each of these categories there are further variations and the cultural variation is more pronounced than the economic variation. Moreover, some of the major tribes like the Kondh and the Saora have as many as 9 and 13 distinct sub groups or subtribes whereas the other tribes have subgroups or subtribes ranging from 2 to 5.

The tribal situation in Orissa in particular is such that most of the culturally prominent primitive tribes like, the Bonda, the Koya, the Gadaba, the Saora, the Kondh, the Juang, the Bhuiyan and a few others are distributed in two distinct ecological niche. While one section lives in the hills(high-landers), the other sections lives in the foot hills or in the undulating plains (low-landers). This dif ferential ecological situation has made the tribes vul nerable to differential acceptance of development pro grammes. While the hill dwellers are culturally more primi tive, the low landers are relatively more acculturated. Com munication plays an important role in the development process. Where there is better communication the oppor tunities for pursuing development programmes are more and where communication is less developed the development effort is less and so also the development response. Professor Mohapatra has reflected this in his paper (1981) on the basis of his study of two contrasting tribal situations in Orissa.

Most of the major primitive tribes of Orissa are observed to have lived in the hills and forests since ages, having dis tinct groups of scheduled caste people as their neighbours. In some areas these scheduled caste neighbours claim the **khunt-kati** right on par with the tribes. Both the groups traditionally have been bound up with strong socio-economic ties and even today in most of the tribal areas of the state the scheduled caste neighbours someway or other play dicisive roles in the economic development and change of the tribals. The situation is more acute in the isolated and in terior regions. Particularly, understanding of this inter ethnic interactional situation is very significant from the point of view of pursuing development activities among the tribes so that the development efforts are not deflected.

Development activities in tribal areas of Orissa are being pursued through as many as 21 ITDPs, in the Santal, Munda, Ho, Kolha, Bathudi, Oraon, Kisan, Bhuiyan, Juang, Gond, Kondh, Paraja, Gadaba, Koya, Bonda and Saora concentrated and 9 Micro Projects in Pauri Bhuiyan, Bonda, Dongria Kondh, Saora, Lanjia Saora, Kuttia Kondh and Juan areas. The ITDPs and Micro Projects cover 68.13% of the tribal population of Orissa. In order to cater to the needs of the tribals of lesser concentrated areas outside the Sub-Plan, 6.38% of the tribal population are being covered under the Modified Area Development Approach (MADA) and there are as many as 30 MADA areas looking after the development of these tribals.

At this point a summary discussion on some of the findings from the Bonda Development Agency in comparison with the Dongria Kondh Development Agency will highlight the dif ferential course of development taken place in these two communities because of their differential traditions.

The development activities pursued among the Bonda (the Bondo highlanders of Elwin), through the Bonda Development Agency and the direction of change and development marked among them present a striking contrast with the Dongria Kondh although both the tribes are equally primitive and have the same hill dwelling habit. It is largely due to the prevailing differential ecology and cultural potential (tradition). Bonda hills are lacking perennial streams having scanty vegetational growth. Hill slopes are steep which allows Swidden cultivation only in the lower slopes whereas in the Dongria hills people prepare the swidden plots even on the top of the hills. Shifting is less frequent in the Bonda hills than in Dongria hills. Due to rich ecological potential and horticultural adaptation the subsistence level of the Dongria is higher than that of the Bonda. Thus, scope for the exploitation of the natural resources is more in the Bongria hills than in the Bonda hills. Yet in the recent years the level of economic development achieved among the Bonda is comparable to that of the Dongria Kondh. Here lies in the traditions of Bonda which have prompted them for making positive advancements stimulated by the efforts of the Bonda Development Agency and manned by one of the Senior Research Officer of the Harijan and Tribal Welfare Department (the officer being a student of economics has orientation in anthropology since the beginning of his profession career).

The Bonda have been depicted as the aggressive people. The Pano,the scheduled caste neighbour of the Bonda were serving the Bonda as subservient to them. In the socio-cultural life of the people they had less role to play and so far as the economic life of the Bonda is concerned the Pano sometimes were working as labourers in their fields and as the busi ness prospect was bleak they had minor roles to play as mid dlemen. Moreover, their number was less. With the introduc tion of the development programmes in the area atleast no such hindrances were encountered on account of the Pano. Whereas in Dongria Kondh area the Domb-Kondh relationship was analogically equivalent to mothers' brother and sisters' son relationship (**Mama-bhanja**). That is to say that at the socio-cultural level they were intimately interacting and at the level of economic life of the Kondh, the Domb had a decisive role. Therefore, the hindrances of the Domb were encountered in the Dongria Kondh area.

The Bonda social structure is strikingly different from that of the Dongria Kondh. While the Bonda have as few as 6 clans and 23 villages in the hills where feuds were ordained to be less frequent, the Dongria Kondh have as many as 33 clans and 110 villages and hamlets in the hills where inter clan and intraclan feuds were more frequent. Thus communal unity is more expressed in the Bonda tradition than in the Dongria kondh tradition. In addition to this, the Bonda have the **Charu Bhai** corporate group in which members of different clan groups interact and perform the **Pat-Khanda** ritual together and which at the same time binds the villagers of 10-12 villages together in such a way that they never inter marry. This group also in its meetings takes important deci sions and the knowledge of functioning of this group has been utilized by the Special Officer of the Agency in such a way that the people themselves have been alert to their developmental prospects and all development programmes are being channelized accordingly. Among the Dongria Kondh there is no such forum in which the different clan groups could unify, rather there are forums in which each clan group is segregated from the other. Attempts in the direction of unifying Dongria Kondhs across clan distinctions have been also made by the Special Officer DKDA which have been par tially proved successful.

The Juang of pallahara of Dhenkanal District present a situation where in their villages some households are land owners and the other households are landless. Some of the landless households cultivate the land of the landowning households as tenants and some others as labourers in their field. Thus, traditionally the landowning group hold control over the landless group and it is to be mentioned here that the traditional leaders are hailed from among the landowning group. However, when the individual household benefit scheme was introduced through the ITDP the traditional leaders (hailed from the landowning group) dissuaded the families accepting the Government aid and allegedly harassed them in their village council meetings. Some disgruntled Juang in dividuals wanted the agents of the ITDP to interfere in their cases but they were helpless since the Juang leaders explained that it was their traditional socio-cultural af fair and they (the officials) had no business to interfere and decide cases about which they had no knowledge.

Among most of the tribes of north Orissa, particularly among the Juang and Bhuiyan of Keonjhar and Santal,Munda, Ho, Bathudi, Khadia and Oraon of Mayurbhanj, problem of land alienation has been conspicuous. This is because Muthadary of land ownership has been less in vogue and individual rights over land have been granted to the tribes since long. Moreover, as there is predominance of caste population in the tribal villages probability of land alienation has been obviously prominent. This is in contract to South Orissan situation. Thus, the historical tradition is held respon sible for the land alienation and exploitation in the tribal areas of Orissa. However, in the recent years there has been growing alienation of Saora land in Chandragiri area by the Tibetan refugees and of Koya land in Malkangiri area by the Bangaladesh refugees. The benefits given to the Koya and the Saora in these two areas are appropriated by the respective group of refugees. The present demographic situation (proportion of tribals/refugees) in these two areas along with the big difference in the functioning of the Central Government Scheme for the development of refugees and the State Government Schemes for the development of the tribals produces a disproportionate social and developmental situa tion (the refugees are progressive and the tribals retrogressive, and lavishness of Central Government Scheme and poor show of the State Government Scheme) that the tribals who were once the master of their land have become subservient to the refugees. There is growing dissatisfac tion among the tribes in the wake of the changing situation. Therefore, the present tradition of development approach in these two areas needs to be revamped.

In the recent years many Santal, Munda, Ho and Kolha tribesmen have been attracted towards working as labourers in the iron ore mines and as daily wage earners in in dustrial and urban building complexes and some of them have also taken to rickshaw-pulling in the towns and cities of Orissa. Their fortunes are precarious for now they are be having as errand boys. At home they are job-less, at outside they are restless. Their future is limited to the present only. The Santal have developed their own script and have formed their cultural associations through which they have been determined to stabilize their tradition. The educated Santals are more after this. Political consciousness of the Santal has further divided them along different political lines, the impact of which is acute among the agriculturist Santals living in the villages among whom economic develop ment is taking place 'at the same rate'.

Consequent upon the construction of river dams, installa tion of factories in different tribal areas of Orissa some of the Pengo Paraja, Jharia Paraja, Bhatara villages border ing Kalahandi and Koraput districts and a few other tribes of Koraput, Sundargarh and Sambalpur districts are facing the problem of displacement and rehabilitation. So far no government effort has been made to study the problems of the people in order that their miseries will be alleviated in right earnest. A group of Post-Graduate students of the Department of Anthropology, Utkal University under the stew ardship of Professor L.K. Mohapatra, studied the foreseeable socio-cultural, economic and psychological problems of the denizens of the Dam Project area. The study shows that very casual attention is being given by the government towards their present problems and people on their own are leaving their home and hearth to settle in the non-project area. Un less something in very concerete terms is done for the rehabilitation of these people with proper planning, the fu ture of the people will be dark. One prosperous Jharia Paraja burst into tears when he was interviewed by one of the students on the problems of their future displacement; he came all the way from his village to see this student off in the field camp with all the hopes that on his return to Bhubneswar he would ventilate their worry and agony, to the Government. This warrants immediate attention of the deputa tion of a development Scientist to alleviate their problems.

The problems of the tribes of Orissa are many. Everybody realizes that Development efforts are being made to al leviate them, specifically poverty among them. But it is to no effect. This is due to lack of sufficient understanding of their socio-cultural and economic problems and want of scientific perspective in the development plans and programmes. Among the state government officers who are being deputed to the tribal areas for undertaking develop ment activities of any form there is a feeling that these tribals will never develop and they cannot help it, for the tribal traditions ruin themselves. Thus they leave the development activities to the destiny of the tribals. Some of them are sceptical about the government money spent on them for their development. It is a challenge to the social scientists. But how to meet the challenge? Where is the scope?

The foregoing delineation of facts and the empirical analysis made at some length warrant the relevance of the study of tradition from the development point of view. An academic discourse on tradition and development is held to be beneficial not only for the development agencies deter mined to pursue development activities in the positive way but also for anthropologists (since they are used to the study of tradition) in order to establish the relevance of Anthropology today in National development.

Critical Views on Tradition and Development : The Tribal Perspective

Setbacks in economic development in the less-developed countries have been squarely attributed to the traditional attitudes, values, social structure and institutional ar rangements of these countries. It has been argued, there fore, that unless attitudes and values change and the tradi tional structures and institutions are modified, programmes of economic development cannot make much headway. About such attribution to Indian tradition Professor Dube is not con vinced. Unlike some other Indian social scientists he takes an opposite stand and stresses that Indian tradition in not 'unresponsive to changes in the environment' for in several instances it has demonstrated its remarkable adaptability and innovativeness (Dube, 1981:296), but only "laments that Hindu religious and social thought have more to say on change than development" (Mahapatra, 1981:304). About the change of the attitudes, values and institutions etc. beyond a limit in order to keep pace with the western ideologies of change and development professor Dube is sceptical and ap prehensive of collosal consequences as it may result in 'alienation, anomie and rootlessness'. However, he is hope ful that development could be achieved along traditions of societies and cultures and warns to utilize tradition care fully. To quote Professor Dube, "Bad performance on the development front cannot be blamed on tradition alone. Poor planning and indifferent implementation are often the real causes of failure. All traditions are responsive to changes in the environment and to the imperatives of social harmony and human survival. They are not inflexible but adapt gradually to the changing environment" (Dube, 1981:299). The case study delineated at the outset and the evidences drawn in respect of tradition and development from other parts of tribal Orissa fully corroborate the views of professor Dube on 'tradition and development'. At the same time in these development experiences in the tribal societies of Orissa one finds the answers to the four questions raised by Professor Dube. Is tradition truely unchanging? Answer is, No. Tradition does change. Does it obstruct development? Answer is, it depends how does the development practitioner understand the functioning of traditions in the practical field in its entirety and how he pursues development. How does one go about changing attitudes, values, and social structure or in other words, the tradition itself ? Answer is by assessing peoples' tradition and pursuing development actions in line with their tradition with confidence so that the people do not feel alienated. Assuming that they will be brought about, what will be consequence of these changes ? Answer is, changes brought about in accordance with the process just cited above will have harmonious consequences in the sense that economic development will be in harmony with socio-cultural development.

Further, in order to find answers to the following ques tions raised by professor Mahapatra (1981) in his commentary on Professor Dube's paper (1981):

> To what extent are the traditional Hindu views of change shared among the Mahomedans, Christians and tribal peoples of India at present, even among the rural Hindu-Buddhist-Jain-Sikh masses? Why do the peasents of Punjab and Haryana and in other pockets in South India take to modern ideas, values and techniques for economic development more rapidly than, for example, those in eastern India including Chhatis garh ? Why do the tribal people of North Eastern India, for example, in Nagaland, Meghalaya and Mizoram achieve spec tacular progress in education and economic development in spite of their tradition-bound so-called "primitive" societies?

The following discussion, it is hoped, will highlight bet ter and resolve the dilemma of 'tradition versus development'. Tradition can be comprehended to have three basic components. One is the **historical component** of tradi tion which has been imposed on a group of people from out side in the historical process of accidents and later has been ingrained into the minds and institutions of the people. The second is the **structural/cultural component** of tradition which has been imposed by the people themselves and has been exclusively their own device. These two com ponents manifest at the level of reality. While the histori cal component is more broad-based and it transcends the cul tural boundary of one group and may be shared with the other group in the region, the cultural component of tradition is limited to the people themselves and is local. The third one is the **technical/scientific component** of tradition which manifests at the abstract level and is understood at a com parative level. About such component of the tradition people are conscious since through this they bring about innova tions. For the social scientist the first two components of the tradition may be considered both functional and dysfunc tional while the third component is understood only as func tional, generative, positive and evaluative. Thus a develop ment practitioner or a development scientist need to be aware of these distinctions while operating with the development of any group of people and devising techniques of pursuing development in the field. The answers to the three questions of Professor Mahapatra can be found more in the historical and technical components of the traditions of the people referred to than in their structural/cultural tradition alone. Empirical insight into these of course is warranted. But they can be prognosticated in this way.

While dwelling upon the problem of 'tradition and development' one would be exhorted to ask the question : How far is 'culture and development'? (Madan:1983) Since 'culture' is the domain of the anthropologists, is 'culture and development' to be exclusively discussed by the anthropologists?, and 'tradition and development' to be dis cussed by the social scientists in general ? To resolve this it can be said that both 'tradition and development' and 'culture and development' belong to the similar stretch of phenomena and the ultimate aim of the social scientists is to gain scientific understanding of 'society', 'culture' and also 'tradition'. To quote Professor Dube, "Tradition is to be understood as the total heritage—beliefs, customs, and opinions—transmitted from generation to generation". Under standing of culture is not far away from this. However, since anthropologists have been practically trodding in the field of culture and mostly tribal cultures, the extreme form of tradition-bound cultures or in other words cultures having the very low pace of change and development, the onerous task of development and change be bestowed on the trained development anthropologist which is his legitimate due, so that tradition and development would not be borne in mind as antithetical to each other while pursuing develop ment in the action field.

It may be reiterated that limited employment of Anthropologists in the development plannings and programmes has forced them to suffer from appropriate technical dis abilities which otherwise they could efficiently handle. Given more and more opportunities the anthropologists would not longer remain shy about planned development and change. However, some anthropologists raise the slogan that they are 'students of change' and not 'agents of change'. This is un fortunate. Another misconception among the general public is that the anthropologists are opposed to change and develop ment as they have vested interest in preserving traditional structures of tribal societies. This is wrong. Further the impression goes that the anthropologist is committed to "gradualism" in introducing change. This needs to be dis pelled (Mathur, 1977 : 12). Atleast, all this has been made clear in the case study of the present functioning of the Dongria Kondh development Agency where the development has been rapid.

REFERENCES

Dube, S.C. 1981 Traditional views of Change and Develop ment in Absolute Values and the Search for the Peace of Mankind; Vol. I, Proceedings of the 9th International Con ference on the unity of Sciences, The International Cultural Foundation Press, New York.

Elwin, V. 1950 The Bondo Highlanders; Oxford University Press, Delhi.

Madan T.N. 1983 Culture and Development; Oxford University Press, Delhi.

Mahapatra, L.K. 1981 Commentary on Professor Dube's Paper on Traditional Views of Change and Development in Absolute Values, and the Search for the Peace of Mankind Vol. I.

—— 1981 Barriers and Stimulants to Development in two most backward Gram Panchayats of Orissa; Paper presented in the All India Seminar on Tribal Development held in Bhubaneswar.

Mathur, H.M.(ed) 1977 Anthropology in the Development Process; Vikas Publishing House, New Delhi.

Nayak, P.K. 1982 Forseeable Problems of Displacement: a Study of the Denizons of Indravati Dam Project; Paper being published.

—— 1984 Structure and Function of Clan Feud Among the Dongria Kondh; Unpublished Ph. D. Dissertation.

EIGHT

S. N. Tiwary

Musahars During the National Emergency and the Janata Rule in the Bhojpur District

The Musahar along with other scheduled castes belong to the lowest strata of traditional Hindu caste society. One can well imagine their social position as they were not provided a place in the four-fold division of Hindu popula tion. "Many terms have been used for this category in ear lier literature, such as antyaja, panchama and chandala" (Beteille, 1969:67). They have been facing various kinds of disabilities and exploitation. Popularly they are known as untouchables. Their poor economic condition has been more striking.

No doubt changes have been taking place in the country and also in this section of the society. Changes among them have come along several avenues. Some reform movements have brought changes among some scheduled castes at various periods of time. Through the process of sanskritization at tempts have been made to move up in the hierarchy by adopt ing the style of life traditionally associated with high castes. Some of them inspired by the process of Western ization have tried to adopt Western patterns in dress, man ner and customs.

In independent India concerted efforts have been made for amelioration of the condition of these under-privileged groups. The preamble to the constitution has assured to the economic and political justice, liberty of thought, expres sion, belief, faith and worship, and equality of status and opportunity. It is stated in Article 17 of the constitution that untouchability is abolished and its practice in any from is forbidden. The encorcement of any disability arising out of untouchability would be an offence punishable in ac cordance with law. Article 15(2) prohibits the discrimina tion in the use of public utilities on ground of religion, race, caste etc. There are a number of constitutional provi sions for their welfare and uplift also under the Directive Principles of State Policy. These provisions were later reinforced by legislations like Untouchability Act of 1955, Protection of Civil Right Act of 1976 and others.

Wedded to the goal of rapid socio-economic development through democratic means, the government - the centre and the state - has adopted a package of measures to launch an onslaught on poverty of scheduled castes and other poor. For the sake of convenience, the government policies may be put under two broad categories. In the first place it is that wealth and property accumulated at the upper classes would parcolate to the lower classes and thus general development would be brought out in the country. In other words along with the rich, the weaker and poorer sections would move up as the beneficiaries of trickling down effect of the govern ment measures of development. The second category includes those steps (undertaken mainly under constitutional provisions) which are exclusively meant for amelioration of conditions of scheduled castes and other 'backward classes'. Such measures may be put under the policy of 'reverse discrimination' or 'protective discrimination'.

It was mainly under the first category that modernization of Indian agriculture (where intense use of 'package' of in put was advocated) was started under Five Year Plans. But "Green Revolution experiences in North India have disproved the percolation theory" (Punit, 1982: 172). There, farm as sets, instead of percolating to lower strata over the years, have shown a tendency of being monopolized by rich farmers. It has led to evictions and increased rural unemployment. It has been desired in Five Year Plans that the benefits of economic development must accrue more and more to the rela tively less privileged classes of society. Besides, planning should result in greater equality in income and wealth. Realizing the nonfulfilment of plans' objectives, especially in respect of removing poverty, changes in 'property structure' (Joshi, 1971), and land owernship (Thorner, 1956 'land to the tiller', Dasgupta -

'radical land reform', 1977; Myrdal - 'radical land distribution', 1968), 'structural change' (Hicks - 'non-farm labour' to be in creased, 1971), 'realistic approach' to planning (Tandon, 1978), 'financial descipline' (Minhas, 1974) and others have been suggested.

Having the experiences of prevailing situations in the country, the Congress party under the leadership of Indira Gandhi made it a point to remove poverty (Garibi Hatao) in 1971. The ruling party faced growing unrest in the country which was spearheaded by Jaya Prakash Narayan - towards the end of the five year tenure. Consequently the government declared the National Emergency on June 25, 1975 to check deteriorating law and order situation. Simultaneously the Prime Minister announced the 20 point Economic Programme to tackle economic problems of the nation on a war-footing. Though weaker sections were to be benefitted by the entire programme, the following seven points are directly formu lated for their benefit:

Point 2: Implementation of land ceilings and speeder distribution of surplus land to the landless.
Point 3: Ownership rights of house sites for land less and weaker sections.
Point 4: Freedom from bonded labour.
Point 5: Liquidation of and moratorium on rural in debtedness
Point 6: Raising the wages of agricultural workers
Point 9: Development of handloom sector
Point 10: Improvement in quality and supply of con trolled cloth.

The means for implementation, however, attracted much criticism for being coercive. In the 1977 election, the Janata Party came to power under what was then called 'Janata Wave'. In pursuance with its declared programme of removing poverty and unemployment within 10 years, the Janata Government announced the Rolling plan. The sixth plan was rural oriented, based on wage-Goods Model and not on Heavy Industries Model. Under its Minimum Needs Programme emphasis was put to provide drinking water, house-sites for the homeless, elementary education, rural health care, rural electrification and other needs to the poor. The scheme of total prohibition, for the first time in the country, was implemented. It was expected that the Programme would be the first step towards distributive justice leading to removal of poverty. Emphasis was placed on the development of small- scale and cottage industries which would create more employ ment. The planners expressed the need to implement land reform measures like transfering land to the tillers more vigorously. It was also urged for urgent finalisation of Records of Rights to solve the land ownership problems once for all.

Table 1 : Occupations (main) of Heads of the Households by Caste

Caste	Labour	Cultiva-tion	Caste-Occupa-tion	Service	Business	Total
Brahman	0	29	3	12	0	44
Rajput	0	73	0	12	0	85
Kayastha	0	0	0	2	0	02
Ahir	0	67	0	5	0	72
Kahar	0	21	0	2	0	23
Koeri	0	21	0	0	0	21
Kanu	0	4	13	0	0	17
Kumhar	0	9	4	0	0	13
Teli	0	4	0	2	0	06
Paneri	0	0	0	2	2	04
Hazam	0	4	1	0	0	05
Sonar	0	0	0	0	1	01
Noniya	0	0	0	0	0	01
Barahi	0	0	1	0	0	01
Lohar	0	5	0	0	0	05
Pasi	1	0	0	0	0	01
Chamar	39	13	0	9	0	61
Musahar	121	0	0	0	0	121
Dusadh	31	27	0	10	0	68
Dhobi	0	7	2	4	0	13
Mehtar	0	0	1	0	0	01
Total	192	285	25	60	03	565

Note :- S.N. 1 to 3 - High Caste, 4 to 15 - Backward caste and 16 to 21 Scheduled caste.

Under such development perspectives an attempt is made here to study the condition of the Musahars who "are the poorest and the most backward among the Harijans" (Sachchidananda, 1977: 156) during the period of the Na tional Emergency (June 25, 1975 to March 21, 1977) and the Janata Rule (March 22, 1977 to Jan. 10, 1980) in a village statutory panchayat of the Bhojpur district in Bihar. The panchayat consists of only one village which is a dispersed one. It is located at a distance of 12 K.M. south of Arrah, the headquarters of the district and is under the jurisdic tion of I.A.D.P. (Intensive Agricultural District Programme) Block, Udwantnagar.

Table 2 : Castewise Ownership of land (in acres)

Caste	Land-less	Below-1 acre	1-5	5-10	10-15	15-20	More than 20 acre	Total
Brahman	1	21	11	7	4	0	0	44
Rajput	0	20	19	24	16	4	2	85
Kayastha	0	0	0	0	0	2	0	02
Ahir	4	10	47	11	0	0	0	72
Kahar	9	8	6	0	0	0	0	23
Koeri	0	19	3	0	0	0	0	21
Kanu	7	8	2	0	0	0	0	17
Kumhar	0	11	2	0	0	0	0	13
Teli	2	2	2	0	0	0	0	06
Paneri	2	2	0	0	0	0	0	04
Hazam	0	5	0	0	0	0	0	05
Sonar	1	0	0	0	0	0	0	01
Noniya	0	1	0	0	0	0	0	01
Barahi	1	0	0	0	0	0	0	01
Lohar	0	3	2	0	0	0	0	05
Pasi	0	1	0	0	0	0	0	01
Chamar	44	17	0	0	0	0	0	61
Musahar	120	1	0	0	0	0	0	121
Dusadh	22	46	0	0	0	0	0	68
Dhobi	0	10	3	0	0	0	0	13
Mehatar	0	1	0	0	0	0	0	01
Total	213	185	97	42	20	6	2	565

Numerically the Musahar is one of the most important scheduled casts and forms about 15% of the scheduled caste population in Bihar. Musahars are landless and are mainly agricultural labourers. They lead a precarious existence. They are divided into various branches namely Magahiya, Tir hutiya, Rikhiyasan, Dholbaja, Gidaramara or Kichak, Sak hatora, Rajbanshi, Draboar, Horhowar and Rajaorhi. The first two are regional groups and do not intermarry. The Magahiya Musahars found in Bhojpur and other parts of South Bihar are traditionally regarded as blunt and uncouth. Drinking and gambling are their common recreations. They rear pigs and poultry. Their level of education is extremely poor. They worship a number of gods, goddesses and deities, collec tively about four times in a year and individually also for specific purposes like protection of health of family mem bers, or cure from diseases, marrying a male member of the family and so on. It is generally said by the caste Hindus and also by other scheduled caste people that they are habitual lazy and would not work if they have some grain for next day at home. Among the six scheduled castes namely the Mehatar, the Chamar, the Musahar, the Dusadh, the Dhobi and the Pasi, the position of the Musahar is reported only above the Mehatar in a study on caste hierarchy in the Bhojpur district (Tiwary, 1980).

In the village under study all Musahars live in shanties, some have mudwall thatched. They got legal ownership of house-sites during the emergency. All of them (121 households) depend mainly on agricultural labour and are landless except one who has less than 15 dismals of land.

Except them and other Harijans (excluding Dhobis) none in the village is agricultural labour. Musahars are con centrated at three places, eastern and southern outskirts and extreme north-west side of the village. It is reported that they had about 14 bighas of land in the south of the village still known as Musaharawajot but that had to be auc tioned by the then Zamindar as they could not pay the rent due to famine - about 80 years ago. Except three (two primary and one middle school educated) none is literate while there are some high school and college educated Harijans who belong to other scheduled castes. Differential development is evident if their position with other scheduled caste villages is compared.

Much before the Independence, Jag Jiwan Ram (who belongs to a village near Arrah) toured the district advocating for removal of untouchability and leaving nasty habits like eating dead animal. But Musahars were never approached for their reform. Rather they have been facing disabilities at the hands of other scheduled caste villagers also. They con tinue to eat pork and rat. Before 1967 most of them were not allowed by high caste villagers particularly Rajputs (who own most of the village land and are very dominant) to exer cise their franchise. It was TKS, a wealthy left oriented Rajput who along with a Dusadh caste leader (GR of the village) began to move from door to door among all Harijans including Musahars for votes. He was a candidate for Mukhiya of the village Panchayat in 1967 opposing then sitting Muk hiya, BNS, a Rajput. BNS had been heading the Panchayat from the beginning and has active supports of almost all high castes, many backward castes and some scheduled castes. TKS for his left leaning and acceptance of drinking water even at the hands of Musahars (in Musahar toli itself) was severely criticised in the village. Musahars and other Harijans voted for him and he won. It was the first time that Harijans could vote freely as most of the Ahirs (known for able bodied blunt men in the area) were in his favour. It was the first occasion when landowners particularly Raj puts got jolt. During TKS' headmanship all adult Harijans including Musahars could get teccavi loan of Rs. 50.00 twice by the government in 1971. Blankets and Saris were dis tributed among Musahar and other widowed and old Harijan as relief by the government.They still remember TKS with gratitude. A Musahar recalls;

> "I was a member of the Mukhiya Committee. All of us got Rs. 100.00 in two equal instalments as taccabi loan. The Block Development Officer initially wanted that some land owners should be our guarantors. Mukhiyaji (TKS) alone be came ready to do so and insisted that we would starve if help was not given to us. After some months the Officer with some Block officials came to our village for collection of the loan. Again Mukhiyaji helped us. He was ready to be ar rested. Ultimately they were compelled to return. Now none threatens us for that loan".

Realising the humiliation of 1967, dominant caste vil lagers sponsored YPM, a Brahmin,for Mukhiya against a can didate supported by TKS, GR and some other non-high caste people in 1971. YPM won. Many Musahars were not allowed to vote. They were supporters of TKS' candidate. Till the promulgation of the National Emergency Musahars and other Harijans could receive no help from the government. Under the 20 point Economic Programme several schemes were an nounced for the benefits of rual poor. GR, a Dusadh and ploughman of TKS from 1962 to 1974 had blessings of TKS and has acquantances with some communists of Arrah. He began to organise village Harijans (including Musahars) who were mainly agricultural labourers for more wages as approved by the government by October 1975. Initially he requested Raj put and other land owners for increased wages but was rebuked. One day Harijans announced their strike and stopped the work of their masters. But the Musahars of the extreme north-west side of the village could not do so because of their helplessness. A Musahar recalls;

> "We live at a distance from the village and work mainly in the fields of Ahirs of our tola. If we had stopped their work they would have worked by themselves. They would not have then employed us. Some of them had also threatened us to leave their work at the time of the labour strike".

Besides, four Dusadhs (share croppers, land provided by Rajputs) did not join. TKS had returned from jail after im prisonment of a few months and did not take interest. By March, 1976 many Harijans including Musahars filed cases in the court of the Block Development Officer (BDO), Ud wantnagar, against their land-lords who did not provide min imum agricultural wages as announced by the government. The Block officials including Labour Inspector visited the vil lage several times and tried for a compromise between the two warring groups. Landlords always assured them to pay the new wages but actually did not pay. In the meanwhile landlords began forcible harvesting of Kola lands (provided to attached labourers) by December against the loan due to their attached labour. Then again under the leadership of G.R. many Harijans (including many Musahars) began to file cases in the courts of the Subdivisional Officer (SDO) and the BDO. Banarasi Devi Gupta and an advocate (communist) of Arrah helped them. The SDO known for his articulation to en force the law deputed a police party in the village. In his presence several labourers could harvest paddy crops over their Kola land. He along with the Circle Officer of the Block and some Harijans were named as accused in a case filed by Rajputs. Several cases were also filed by Harijans against Rajputs under Arms Act and Explosive Substance Act. Conflicts continued for more than a year. Both groups were disgusted with the prevailing situation. Ultimately in the beginning of 1977 (before the withdrawal of the Emergency) a compromise took place. Wages and allied facilities were in creased but less than the wages approved by the government. The daily wage was fixed to be 2 seers of rice and one meal and not 1 or 1.5 seers of rice only as was prevalent. While harvesting paddy or wheat a labourer would get one bojha (shĕaf) out of every 23 bojhas instead of 25 bojhas while one bojha out of every 25 bojhas of Khesari instead of 31 bojhas. While threshing paddy or wheat a labourer would get one maund of every 23 maunds of its production instead of every 25 mounds while one maund of every 25 maunds of Khesari production instead of every 31 maunds. Outstanding loan against any attached labourer was liquidated. Loan in kind would be realised from attached labourers in kind without interest and not in cash as then prevalent. All cases filed in courts would be withdrawn by both groups. Ac cordingly these were implemented soon. Some landlords did not like the 'increase', a few of them still put pressure on some Musahars for their loan, contrary to the terms of the compromise. It was revealed that Musahar had never filed a case in any court of law before their strike. During the days of the emergency consciousness among weaker section was so aroused especially among Dusadhs and chamars of the pan chayat that Musahars also found convenient to join the protest.

Then came the rule of Janata Party in March 1977. The Harijan leader and other Harijans including most at the Musahars favoured this party at poll. Other villagers were already against the Congress Party due to emergency ex periences like the labour strike when Harijans raised their heads against them for the first time. Particularly high caste villagers were very enthusiastic over the installation of the Janata Party government and felt some kind of relief (as revealed by some Rajput Young villagers). It is inter esting to note that Rajput leaders and other high caste vil lagers were particular that Harijans should not be benefitted by government. On the other hand they demonstrated their anger by helping these Dusadhs and others who had not joined the strike. A few hand pumps were in stalled near their huts. There were government scheme for repairing small irrigation channels (Karaha) and 'ahars'for storage of water to irrigate lands. Their contracters were Rajputs and F.R. the Sarpanch of the Panchayat, a Dhobi. Some Musahars got the job but it was so manipulated that they could not get wages of several days in the name of non- supply of government fund. The Harijan leader remained busy in preparing ground for his success in the forthcoming Pan chayat election. And none cared for Musahars and other Harijans.

Having some understanding with Ahirs the Harijan leader (GR) stood for Mukhiya and an Ahir (RSY) for Sarpanch in 1978 election. GR was the rival of BNS, a dominant Rajput leader and RS was that of FR, the sitting Sarpanch. For the first time political dominance of Rajputs was challenged by a Harijan. It was reported by many Musahars and others that GR's voters began to reach the polling booth in early hours of the polling day like waves and every one anticipated that he would win. Such anticipation disturbed high caste people. In the meanwhile a high government officer (a relative of a Rajput), some servicemen of the village (called by the high caste candidate for help) and young Rajputs in collusion with polling officials arranged bogus voting. When objected by GR situation became so tense that GR and other Harijans (including many Musahars) had to leave the booth out of fear of beating. GR with some others went to lodge complaint against bogus voting to the District Magistrate, Arrah. Many Musahars could not vote. BNS and RS won. The high caste and many backward caste people were happy. But situation in the village continued to be tense. Consequently the Harijan leader (GR) had to leave the village out of fear and remained in other village for more than a year. This had demoralising effect on Harijans while high caste villagers became more aggressive. Due to their docile nature and weak position Musahars become main target of neglect and harass ment. All of them depend on their labour and remained out of employment for about 5-6 months in a year. So they had no alternative but to become attached labourer of some landlord so that they might have interest free loan during the days of unemployment or lean seasons. But several cases were reported when landlords showed inability to lend more during lean seasons. In such circumstances the landlords 'obliged' the Musahars by requesting some family members to lend in interest and recovery of such loan with interest used to be done by the landlords in very husking ground out of the produce of the Kola lands. It was further reported that after the panchayat election some cruel and cunning landlords began to pressurise attached Musahar labourers for recovery of loan during the days of the Emergency. A Musahar narrates his misery.

> "I have been an attached ploughman of A. Singh. After the labour strike all of us got rid of master's loan. But he always puts pressure for Rs. 500.00. To him this amount I have to pay. He is so strong and dangerous that I fear to leave his work".

Not only that, there are instances where landlords still put pressure for the loan given sometimes (before the strike) to the fathers (who are dead). Dusadhs and Chamars (although many of them depend on agricultural labour) are not harassed in this way. They fear that their crops in fields might be stolen. Musahars are also neglected by 'dealer' (shop owner of control shop) and essential com modities are not provided to many of them in time. They are simple-hearted persons and avoid quarrels with others. Data are available which indicate that whenever they had disputes among themselves, those were settled by the caste elders. No help of non-Musahar was ever sought nor did they approach any panchayat official.

A Musahar views the sufferings in the following way:-

> "We depend wholly on the village Rajputs. We could get employment for 6 to 7 months in a year. So every year we have to borrow grain and cash for meeting the two ends meet. If some one has marriage in his family or some one dies we have no saving to meet the expenditure. Whatever we produce in our Kola lands is taken away by landlords and Mahajans at the hushing ground. It is certain that we would always remain in debt. Landlords provide lands to other scheduled castes but none of the Musahars. They fear that we would not work in their fields if our sufferings are removed. I do not anticipate to be ever out of debt."

Instead of an urge for improvement, exhibition of such apathy and resignation has been shown by many Musahars. This apathy might have been generated by centuries of neglect and exploitation. During the emergency Musahars and other agricultural labourers could have some benefits. Some hope was also aroused but later on - after that situation - it subsided. Rather Musahars (weakest among the Harijans) had to become the target of landlords in more than one ways. Most of them found some hope in a Harijan leader (GR) who himself felt insecure in the village. On the other hand landowning castes particularly the Rajput are not found ready to change their reputation.

Data were collected at the end of 1980 when the Congress party (I) government launched some schemes for rural poor. Again except most of the Musahars, other Harijans could have some benefits like employment in food for work scheme. They continued to be main sufferers. No surplus land was ever reported in this panchayat. Government should take some radical measures for them and they should directly be in volved at the implementation level. Harijans are not homogenous group and so interest of lowly among low must be taken care of. Besides, some efforts should be made to change attitude and behaviour patterns of high caste and other landowning village leaders (help of voluntary or ganisations may be sought for this) and government officials who continue to be apathetic and indifferent. "There is no degradation like indifference....Indifference is the final denial of humanity" (Segel,1968: 125).

REFERENCES

Beteille, Andre 1969 Caste: Old and New; Asia Pub lishing House, New Delhi.

Dasgupta, Biplab 1977 India's Green Revolution; Economic and Political Weekly, Special Number

Hicks, Ursula 1971 Strategy of Development; in Challenge of Poverty in India, (ed.) by Fonseca A.J., Vikas Publishing House, New Delhi.

Joshi, P.C. 1971 Social Dimensions of the Problem of Poverty; in Challenge of Poverty in India op. cit.

Minhas, B.S. 1971 Planning and the Poor; S. Chand, New Delhi

Myrdal, Gunnar 1968 Asian Drama: An Inquiry into the poverty of Nations; Vol. 11, Penguin Press, London.

Sachchidananda 1977 The Harijan Elite; Thomson Press, Faridabad.

Tandon, P.L. 1978 Indian Express; 10th April, Bombay.

Tiwary, S.N. 1980 Caste Hierarchy Among the Scheduled Castes; XV-All India Sociological Conference, Meerut.

NINE

Renu Ranjan

Tradition and Development Among The Scheduled Castes of Bihar

In the Hindu Society several castes whose names vary in different parts of the country have been associated with un clean occupations and suffer from social restrictions, poverty and exploitation by the strong and advanced sections of the Hindus for centuries. Sudras, Panchamas, Antyaja, chandalas and a few other names figure frequently in several documents and village parlance. After independence the Government of India adopted the term "Scheduled Castes" for the said groups. All through the ages, these groups have suffered from social injustice and exploitation leading to their permanent degradation.

In Bihar there are 23 scheduled caste communities. The Bhangi and the Musahar are two such communities. The present paper deals with these two communities. It gives a compara tive analysis of changes taking place in these communities, mainly with reference to their living condition and family pattern.

The word "Musahar" is the combination of two words Musa (rat) and Ahar (food). Thus literally, the Musahar is known as a specific group of Harijans, which is characterised by the peculiar habit of catching and eating rats. They form 15% of the scheduled castes population in Bihar. They are mostly concentrated in the districts of Darbhanga, Saharsa, Purnea and Munger. There is a strong sprinkling of them in Gaya and Patna districts also(Sachchidananda, 1977).

Table 1 : Community Sex, Age and Literacy of the Respon dent

Age(Yrs)	Bhangi			Mushar			Total		
	Male	Female	Total	Male	Female	Total	Male	Female	Total
Up to 30	40	5	45 (30.00)	10	3	13 (8.66)	50	8	58 (19.33)
30 to 40	38	23	61 (40.66)	35	29	64 (42.66)	73	52	125 (41.66)
41 & above	12	32	44 (29.33)	45	28	73 (48.66)	57	51	127 (39.00)
Education									
Literate	67	9	76 (50.66)	2	1	3 (2.00)	69	10	79 (26.33)
Illiterate	23	51	74 (49.33)	88	59	147 (98.00)	111	110	221 (73.66)
N	90	60	150	90	60	150	180	120	300

Most of the Musahars are landless and lead a precarious life. Now a days, they work as agricultural labourers, share croppers and engage in animal grazings. At times, they do brick laying, mining work, packing and loading works, con struction work etc. The level of literacy among the Musahars is extremely low. Child marriage, widow remarriage and divorce are allowed in this community.

Bhangi

The Bhangis or Doms are mainly sweepers and scavengers. They also work in bamboo, straw and cane. At certain places, they supply logs, straw and fire for lighting of funeral pyre. In caste hierarchy among the untouchables, they come at the bottom. Child-marriage, widow remarriage and divorce are prevalent among them. They practice endogamy. They are il literate.

The problems of the scheduled castes in India have received scarce attention of the sociologists. There are only a few sociological studies. In Bihar, Sachchidananda's (1977) "Harijan Elite" and Vidyarthi's & Mishra's (1977) "Harijan Today" are pioneer studies in this field. But no specific study on Bhangis and Musahars has been done so far.

Table 2 : Income and Occupation of the respondents

Income (Monthly)	Bhangi	Musahar	Total
Up to 100	8.7	9.3	9.0
101 - 150	18.0	86.0	52.0
151 - 200	20.0	4.7	12.3
201 - 400	53.3	0.0	26.7
Occupation			
Traditional Occupation	98.0	95.3	96.7
Non-traditional Occupation	2.9	4.7	3.3
N	150	150	300

The present paper is based on the information collected from 300 respondents. A group of 150 each from the Bhangi com munity of Patna Municipal area and from the Musahar Com munity of Nawadah Municipal area was interviewed with the help of a schedule. The details of the respondents are given below.

Agewise distribution reveals that maximum number of respon dents (42%) are in the age group of 31-40 years. Another 39% are of 41 yrs or above. Only 10% of the respondents are thirty years or less.

An overwhelming majority of them are illiterate. Illiteracy is higher among the Mushars (98%) than that among the Bhan gis (49%).

Table 2 shows that most of the respondents are engaged in their traditional occupation and only a few of them have taken up on-traditional callings.

Income of the bulk of the Musahar does not exceed Rs.150/- per month. Relatively the Bhangi is a better lot. Their in come ranges from Rs. 200/- to Rs. 400/- in majority of the cases.

Living Condition

Living condition of the communities will be examined in the context of their housing, facilities available in the houses and nature and kind of food intake.

In traditional Hindu society, dwelling place of a caste is determined in accordance with its position in the heirarchy which is in turn defined in terms of purity and pollution. Ancient Hindu codes advocate separate dwelling for the un touchables like the **Chandals** and **Svapaks** outside the vil lages. Manu (Manu Smriti, Chapter-VIII p. 14) has also described about the housing condition of Sudra, the so- called scheduled castes of today, as they did not have right to property. They were supposed to roam from place to place having no permanent shelter of their own. Thus, social sanc tions forced their segregation-Bougle (1971), Hutton (1963) and Ghurye (1950) have mentioned about some other restric tions regarding their dwellings.

Segregation seemed to be a concomitant of their economic backwardness. Sudra or Untouchables in the past were mostly landless agricultural labourers. They could not have their own land. Thus to have some roof above their head, they were forced to erect thatched huts on plots removed from the main habitation, but nearer to their masters' agricultural land. They were not only outside the villages, but also deprived of any civie amenities. They had to live in clustered hut ments surrounded by filth and dirt, uninhabitable even for animals.

The practice of segregation is still prevalent in village and in small towns. In big towns and cities this is not so strictly maintained.

Housing

Although the Musahars of Nawadah are poorer than the Bhangi of Patna, their housing condition hardly differs. It is deplorable in both the cases.

Table 3 : Ownership of the Houses

	Bhangi	Musahar	Total
Houses owned by them	4.7	4.7	4.7
On rent Land Given by Govt.	0.0	37.4	16.3
Houses or Quarters	23.3	0.0	11.7
Unauthorised Occupation	12.0	60.7	66.3
N	150	150	300

Barring a few respondents none has any holding or land of his own. They mostly live in huts built with their own ex penses on unauthorised land. Some of the respondents live in Quarters provided by their employers. A handful of respon dents have got land from the government and all of them belong to the Musahar. Investigation also reveals that Bhan gis or Musahars have been living in cluster and segregated from caste Hindus. Studies by Khan (1980) and Dubey and Mathur (1972) find the similar situation in other parts of the country.

It is surprising to find out that facilities for water, latrine and electricity are not available even in the quarters provided by the employers. Only two Bhangi respon dents of Patna residing in their own pucca house have these facilities.

Thatched houses are made-up of mud walls with roofs of dry leaves and bamboo sticks. Its flooring is done with mud and cow-dung. It has a window or a small round hole near the roof for the purpose of ventilation. Height of the roof is as low as 5ft. or even less. The doors are made of bamboo sticks and their height is just enough to permit a person to enter.

Pucca houses are made of brick walls with plaster and pucca roofs. These have at least one window with wooden panel and a wooden door. Mixed houses are found to have brick walls but roofs are of tiles. In some cases, walls were plastered, otherwise it was simply white washed. Flooring were usually of mud with cowdung coating. These have windows and wooden doors.

In Patna, Sulabh International has done a commendable work in providing lavatory, drinking water and bathing facilities at public places in or near Bhangi bustees. However, there are some bustees where no such facilities exist. They depend upon roadside public taps for drinking water and bath.

Table 4 : Condition of the Houses

	Bhangi		Musahar		Total	
	Single	Double	Single	Double	Single	Double
No. of room	80.0	20.0	70.0	30.0	75.0	25.0
Separate Kitchen	9.3	10.7	6.7	11.3	8.0	11.0
Ventilation of windows	80.0	20.0	70.0	30.0	75.0	25.0
	150	150	150	150	300	300

It is pathetic to observe that three-fourth of the total respondents have been living with their families in a single room.

This room is used for "bed-room", "store-room", as well as for cooking their meals. At times, it is also used for hous ing their domestic animals. The room is of moderate size. Mishra and Vidyarthi (1977) in their study have also ob served the similar condition. However, only one-fourth of the rspondents have been living in two-roomed huts. A few of them enjoy the facility of verandah. All the houses have holes or windows for ventilation. Thus, over crowding and insanitation are important features of these houses. This phenomenon is not just confined to the untouchables of Bihar, it is a common sight all over India (Currie and Means 1945; Bose and Malhotra 1965; Agan and Suiger 1965, Khan 1980).

No arrangement for sanitation or drainage in these huts in available. During the rainy days, the whole area becomes al most inaccessible. It becomes a hell, full of mud, filth and heaps of garbage. About three decades ago, Sharma (1958-59) reported that the houses of the lower castes could be iden tified even from a distance. This is true even today.

Living condition of the respondents can also be assessed on the basis of the household materials they posses. In the possession of household materials, economic condition and exposure to urbanism play certain role. The Bhangi of Patna have shown a tendency to acquire modern household materials. A large number of them have bicycles, transistors, watches etc. Some of them have kerosene Oil stove as well. The Bhan gis have cots in general and few have also chairs and tables. Among the Musahars of Nawadah, these materials are rarely found.

In case of household utensils, brass and aluminium utensils are commonly found among the Bhangis, in addition to earthen wares. Some of them have steel utensils as well. In the case of Musahars, such utensils are almost absent.

Acquisition of improved variety of household materials by even the Bhangis of low income families indicates a change in their standard of living.

In the matter of preparing and taking meals, the Bhangis are found to be a better lot than the Musahar. However, a large number of them cook and take meal once a day. This shows their pitiable condition.

It is a matter of great satisfaction that both the com munities show aspiration for betterment. All of them aspire to have own house with all necessary amenities like drinking water, latrine and electricity. The Musahars want to possess agricultural land.

Family Pattern

This includes the types of family, decision making process in a family, age at marriage, age-difference at the time of marriage among the spouses, attitude towards divorce and widow-remarriage and prevalence of dowry as well as bride price.

In Hindu society, the joint family is said to be the dominant form, though at the turn of the century, this is gradually being replaced by nuclear type. However, there is doubt whether joint family was ever the dominant form among the lower castes. Such doubt arises from the fact that joint family centers around land and that the lower castes had traditionally been deprived of landed property. Studies by Kolenda (1968), Shah (1974), Sachchidananda (1977) and Mali (1979) indicate that nuclear type of family is popular among the scheduled castes. The present study of the two com munities corroborates. Nuclear than joint family is more prevalent among these communities, irrespective of the fact that the Bhangi is exposed to urban influence and the Mushahar lives in rural milieu.

In a joint family, decision making is found to be centralised or individualised, whereas in nuclear family it is democratic or decentralised. In the case of the two com munities, decision making is found to be neither in dividualised nor totally family based. It is in between the two.

Although males enjoy an upper hand in this matter, females are not altogether ignored. They have almost equal say in the affair. However, a female hardly decides anything inde pendently. She seeks comment of her husband or adult children. But a male does not depend as much on his wife or children as on his parents, if alive.

The study reveals that with age a male becomes gradually self-dependent in regard to decision making. Another impor tant fact is that the Bhangi males decide a matter in con sultation with their children. Thus a tendency of family based decision is found in these communities.

Economic independence and decision making are closely re lated. When both husband and wife earn, they do not depend absolutely on each other for decision on every issue. In certain cases wife dominates her husband. As soon as the children start earning, their status is raised. They take decision independently on personal issues and take active part in familial issues.

Age at Marriage

In order to stop the practice of child or early marriage legislation has been enforced in the country, according to which marriage before the age of 18 years for girls and of 21 years for boys is a punishable offence. Therefore, it will be interesting to see if the attitude of the people un der study has changed. This will be assessed in terms of the actual age at marriage and the age preferred for marriage.

It is evident from the table that actual age at marriage has increased with the passage of time. The male Bhangi whose current age exceeds 40 years were married at the age of 14.6 years whereas those who are 30 years or less, got married at 17 years. Similarly, actual age at marriage for the Bhangi females has increased from 11.8 years to 14 years within a decade or so.

Table 5 : Mean-age of the respondents at the time of their marriage

Age group (Yrs.)	Bhangi		Musahar	
	M	F	M	F
Up to 30 years	17.0	14.0	15.0	12.5
31 to 40	16.0	13.5	14.2	12.0
41 & above	14.6	11.8	14.0	11.0

In the case of Musahar also, there is a tendency towards an increase in the actual marriage age. But compared with that of the Bhangi, it is substantially less. While the in crease for the Bhangi males and females is 2.4 years respec tively, this is merely 1 years and 1.5 years respectively for the Musahar males and females. This difference seems to be accountable to the urban-rural differences.

Preferred Age at Marriage

It is likely that younger persons would prefer higher age at marriage for their sons and daughter than the middle age and old aged persons.

It is evident from the table that only the Bhangis of younger age group are in favour of higher age for marriage of their sons between the age of 21-25 years. None of the Musahar respondent agreed to marry his sons so late. This difference of opinion may be due to urban influence. The Bhangis are not ready to marry their sons till they are settled or have completed their education.

However, it is apparent that the respondents of younger age group, irrespective of relative difference between the communities prefer higher age at marriage for their sons.

Table 6 : Preferred age at marriage for children

Prefered age (Yrs.)	Bhangi		Musahar	
	B	G	B	G
11 - 12	0.0	0.0	0.0	31.3
13 - 14	0.0	42.7	0.0	67.3
15 - 16	6.0	56.0	14.7	5.3
17 - 18	27.3	1.3	44.7	0.0
19 - 20	46.7	0.0	40.7	0.0
21 - 25	20.0	0.0	0.0	0.0

* B - Boy: G - Girl

In so far as the age of marriage for girls is concerned, notable difference is found between the communities. None of the Bhangis prefers marrying their daughter before the age of 13 while about one-fourth of the Musahars want to do so. On the whole, both the communities emphasise that girls should be married between 13 and 16 years of age.

Preference for age at marriage reflects that early or child marriage is still prevalent among the communities. Legal sanction against early marriage is yet to be opera tive.

Age Difference Between the Spouses

According to legal provision a boy or a girl cannot marry before the age of 21 years or 18 years. This means that age difference between the couple should be of at least three years. In practice it is hardly followed. Usually 5 or 6 years difference is maintained.

The table indicates that the bulk of the respondents prefers 6-10 years' age difference between husband and wife. Only one-fourth of the Bhangi like to have the difference of five years. There are equal number of persons in both the communities who prefer the difference to ten years or more.

Table 7 : Preferred age difference between the Spouses

Age group	Bhangi			Musahar		
	5 Yrs.	6-10 Yrs.	11 & above	5 Yrs.	6-10 Yrs.	11 & above
Up to 30	51.1	44.4	4.4	0.0	92.3	7.7
31 - 40	22.9	65.6	11.5	0.0	85.9	14.1
41 and above	0.0	68.2	31.8	0.0	82.2	17.8
N	24.7	60.0	15.3	0.0	84.7	15.3

Although an indication of value change is found in certain section of the Bhangi, traditional value dominates and guides the bulk of the persons in these communities.

Dowry

Traditionally the custom of dowry was confined to the up per caste Hindus only. But now-a-days the practice of dowry has made inroads into the social life of the scheduled castes also.

In the lower starta of Indian Society, women are engaged in gainful occupation, and therefore, they are considered an economic asset to the family, whereas in the higher strata they are regarded as an economic liability as most of them remain engaged in household work. Thus, in lower section, when a girl is married, it means the loss of an earning mem ber to the parents of the girl. This loss is compensated by "bride-price". It may be regarded as the customary amount paid for the bride to her parents at the time of marriage (Srinivas, 1942).

Since scheduled castes women cling to gainful occupation, the custom of bride-price is expected to find a place among the communities under-study. Our study reveals the opposite response. Due to the impact of higher castes and urban in fluence, the rece' of dowry is considered a symbol of prestige in these commur'

For those who have some education, it is a necessity. In the case of the Musahar, dowry is paid only in kinds such as wrist-watch, bicycle or transistors etc. But among the Bhangi both cash and kinds are paid. The practice of bride price is still prevalent but it is given to the girl in the form of silver ornaments and clothes but not to her parents.

Attitude toward Widow-remarriage

Remarriage of widows was not approved in ancient India. Manu and Yagyavalka said that the widows must not mention the name of any other man after husband's death. Vatsyayan placed the sex - relations with widow in the same category as with a prostitute (Malik : 1979).

But in the past, among the scheduled castes, widow- remarriage was widely practised. At present also widow remarriage among scheduled castes is permissible. But it seems that they are gradually going against this. The table reveals that a sizeable section of the respondent disfavours widow remarriage.

This is more prominent among the Bhangi than the Musahar. It is interesting to note that more females than males are against this practice.

Table 8 : Attitude towards widow-remarriage

	Bhangi			Musahar		
	Male	Female	Total	Male	Female	Total
Favour	55.55	33.33	46.66	73.33	50.00	64.00
Against	44.44	66.66	53.33	26.66	50.00	36.00
N=	90	60	150	90	60	150

Those who favour this practice say that when one becomes a widow at an early age she should remarry, for her maintenance. Without remarriage there will be corruption in society.

Those respondents who oppose it say that after remarriage her children would be neglected and deprived of parental love.

Divorce System

The phenomenon of separation and divorce is an old as well as a common feature among the scheduled castes. Either of the couple has the right to divorce. But now-a-days it seems to be an uncommon affair. The study shows that the majority of the respondents dislike the practice of divorce. Only one-fourth of the respondents s still favour this practice.

Studies conducted by Vidyarthi and Mishra (1977) and Sachchinanda (1977) indicate the similar attitude. Sachchidananda reports that with the that with the influence of the diverse forces of change, the majority of the respondents are against the prevalence of this practice; there are some who are strongly in favour of it.

Table 9: Attitute towards Divorce

	Bhangi			Musahar		
	Male	Female	Total	Male	Female	Total
Favour	21.11	28.33	24.50	22.22	28.33	24.66
Against	76.66	71.66	74.66	77.77	71.66	75.33
Undecided	2.22		1.33	-	-	-

Those who are in favour this practice pleads that if any one of them is unfaithful adjustment is hardly possible. If the conjugal life is not happy, there should be divorce.

Those who oppose it say that due to the practice of divorce, children often suffer. The couple should have faith on each other and try to adjust even in the worst situation. In order to support their argument, they cite the examples from high caste persons, who have been making compromise and trying to adjust by all means. This shows that the scheduled castes have been emulating the practices prevalent among the upper castes.

Conclusion

It is clear from the above analysis that income is not the only factor to determine one's living condition. People of some income brackets differ in material possisson. While the Bhangis show a tendency of acquiring modern amenities of life, the Musahars seem to be indifferences towards it.

The Bhangis and the Musahars aspire for a house of their own with basic amentities like drinking water, latrine and electricity. The Musahars also aspire for possessing some agricultural land. Thus the common view that the lower castes have low level of aspiration and do not think of their future does not dominant among the caste Hindus but it has hardly ever been prodominant among lower castes. Due to economic hardship, they live in nuclear families.

Decision making in lower caste families is hardly centralised or individualised. Like the male members, females are entitled to take decision. Decision making is found to be decentralised where all adult members par ticipate in the process.

The Musahars prefer early marriage as compared to the Bhangi. But in both communities marriage is solemnised at an age earlier than what is required under the law. Since the younger people prefer higher age than the older persons, it may be expected that after some time, people would reach the legal age for marriage.

In all communities, certain age difference between the spouses is considered desirable. However, there is no uniform view in regard to ideal age difference. The majority of the Bhangi and of the Musahar prefer 6-10 years of dif ference.

But younger Bhangis speaks for lesser age difference. It is five years of less. None of the Musahars likes this dif ference. All of them opt for higher age gap. It may be that the Bhangis are in urban milieu and the influence of edu cated urban people have changed their view.

Dowry is becoming more popular among the Bhangi than the Musahar. Among the Musahars, both dowry and bride-price are found. Thus the social practices of caste Hindus are making inroads into the life of the scheduled castes.

The practice of widow remarriage is on the decline in the communities. Strong disfavour for it has been shown by the Bhangis. The Musahars are yet to develop a strong view against it. Divorce is highly disapproved by the people of both the communities.

The cultural life of the scheduled castes is said to be different from that of the caste Hindus. They have certain norms and practices which can be considered "modern" at the present time. But surprisingly, they have been leaving these norms and values and adopting those of caste Hindus. This means that they have been getting out of one tradition and entering into another. This process may be termed sanskritization but it is surely detrimental to development.

There is a common notion that once a group or community moves away from its traditionally prescribed way of life it adopts modern norms of life and moves towards development. In the case of the scheduled castes or lower castes, this does not seem to be applicable.

REFERENCES

Agan, Tesaie & Suiger, Elaivehuch Ka, 1965 The House; Kansas state University, New York.

Agarwala, S.N. 1964 Some Recent Trends in Age at Marriage in India; Paper presented at the Asian Population conference in December, New Delhi.

Bougle, C. 1971 Essays on the Caste System;Combridge Univer sity Press, London.

Dubey, S.N. & Mathur, Usha 1972 Welfare programme for scheduled Castes; Economic and Political Weekly, Jan. 22, Vol. VII, No. 4

Fuchs, Stephen 1949 The children of Hari: A study of the Nimar Balahis in Madhya Pradesh, India; New Order Book Co., Ahmedabad.

Goode, W. 1965 The Family, Prentice Hall of India, New Delhi.

Ghurye, G.S. 1957 Caste and Class in India; Popular Book Depot, Bombay.

Hutton, J.H. 1963 Castes in India; (4th ed) Oxford Univer sity Press, London.

Kapadia, K.M. 1958 Marriage and Family in India; Oxford University Press, Bombay

Kapadia, K.M. 1959 Family in Transition; Sociological Bul letin,Vol. VIII, No.2, Sept. 59.

Kolenda,P.M. 1968 Religion, Caste, and Family structures A Comparative Study of the Indian Joint Family; in Miltion Singer and Bernard Cohn (ed) Structure and change in Indian Society, Aldine Publishing Company, Chicago.

Khan, M.A. 1980 Scheduled Castes and their Status; Uppal Publishing House, New Delhi.

Malik, S. 1979 Social Integration of Scheduled Castes; Ab hinav Publications, New Delhi.

Mishra, N. & Vidyarthi L.P.1977 Harijan Today; Classical Publication, Delhi.

Parsons, T. 1953 Revised analytical approach to the theory of social stratification; in Bendix & S.M. Lipset (ed) Class, Status & Power-Reader in social stratification; Free Press, Glencoe.

Ross, A.D. 1961 Hindu Family in its Urban Setting; Univer sity of Toronto Press, Toronto.

Sachchidananda 1977 The Harijan Elite; Thomson Press (India) Ltd. Haryana

Shah, A.M. 1974 The household dimension of the family in In dia - A field study of Gujrat village and review of other studies; University of California Press, Berkley.

Srinivas, M.N. 1967 Caste in modern India and other Essays; Asia Publishing House, Bombay.

Srinivas, M.N. 1942 Marriage & Family in Mysore; New Book Co.Bombay

TEN

Anirudh Prasad

Changing Lifeways and Thoughtways of Musahars in Bodh Gaya

Several studies have been made on the problems of the Scheduled Castes in the states. There are also some com munity specific studies highlighting socio-economic and cul tural aspects of the Chamar, Bhangi, Dusadh and Dhobi (Michael 1972, Sachchidananda 1977, Vidyarthi 1977, Mukerji 1980, Shyamlal 1984).

This paper attempts to examine socio-economic condition as well as the lifeways and thought-ways of the Musahar living in Bodh Gaya region of Bihar. The Bodh Gaya region has five Blocks viz. Fatehpur, Mohanpur, Barachatti, Sherghati and Bodh Gaya Block itself. The concentration of the Musahar in these Blocks is high. Some Voluntary organisations have been making substantial efforts for the development of Musahars in the region. In order to have an assessment of the percep tion of the Musahars and their attitude towards changing lifeways and thoughtways, Musahar and Harijan leaders of the region were interviewed. Musahar who were in close touch with the Samanwaya Ashram and the Chhatra Yuva Sangharsh Vahini and other agencies involved in their upliftment were also interviewed. In addition some studies of the Musahars in the region were conducted with a view to knowing the changes in their lifeways and thoughtways.

The Musahar which is the most backward and the poorest of the Scheduled Castes, constitutes about 3% of the total population and 23% of the Harijans in the State. In respect of their population, they come to third position among the Scheduled Castes, being next to the Chamar and the Dusadh. Although Musahars are found in all parts of the State, their concentration is mainly found in the districts of Derbhanga, Saharsa, Purnia and Munger. In the district of Bhojpur, Patna, Gaya, Nawadah and Nalanda, they are also in good num bers. The Musahars are known by different names. In South Bihar, They are known as Bhuiyan or Rajwar. In the plateau region, they are called Manjhi.

The Musahar as a community is divided into two sub-Castes. The Magahiya Musahar is found in Bhojpur and some districts of South Bihar. They are traditionally regarded as blunt and uncouth. Another sub-caste known as Tirhutia is found mainly in Darbhanga and some districts of North Bihar. They are said to be calm and courteous.

Table 1

Occupation	Total work Force (Persons)	% of the Total work force
1. Cultivators	41,897	4.98
2. Agricultural Labourers	777,151	93.40
3. Livestock, Forestry Fishing etc.	6,978	0.83
4. Mining and quarrying	3,989	0.48
A : Primary Sector	830,015	98.60
5. Household Industries	1,373	0.16
6. Manufacture other than household	2,605	0.31
7. Construction	1,468	0.17
B : Secondary Sector	5,446	0.65
8. Trade and Commerce	762	0.09
9. Transport & Storage	1,444	0.17
10. Other Services	3,466	0.41
C : Tertiary Sector	5,672	0.67
Total workers A + B + C	841,133	100.00
Total Non-workers	959,196	

Source : Census of India, 1971: It includes Rajwar & Bhuiya too.

The Musahar belongs to the bottom in the caste hierarchy of the Harijans. They are the real **antyaja** who are at the level of abject poverty. They have been subjected to ex ploitation and oppression for centuries. Their women have also been subjected to sexual exploitation by the Zamindars, Mahanthas and rich persons. Consequently they have lost their selfconfidence and self-respect.

Musahars depend on labour particularly on agricultural labour for their livelihood. Many of them are bonded labourers. In fact, they are under customary obligation to work on the farms of landowners. The landlords generally give them meagre wages in kind. The main reasons of their bondage are indebtedness and customary or social obliga tions. Almost every Musahar is in debt. They hardly have any surplus to repay loans.

The following table shows the participation of the total work force of the Musahars in the different occupational categories.

It is evident from the table that of the total work force, agricultural labourers constitute more than 93%. They have very little opportunity to be engaged in the secondary and tertiary sectors of the economy.

Literacy rate among Musahars is extremely low. Their dis tribution according to level of education in 1971 is presented in Table 2.

It is apparent from the table that about 1.8% of the total population of the Musahar is literate in Bihar. Thus, Musahar children are deprived of education in schools from the very beginning. Their parents do not realise the value of school education as they send their children to tend cattle rather than go to school.

In the Blocks under Study, Musahars account for 45% of the total Scheduled Castes population in the district according to 1971 census. Earlier, Musahars of this region were primarily engaged as agricultural labourers in Bodh Gaya Mahanth's (Shankar Math) land. Now some of them have started working in temple construction (Under the temple renovation Schemes of Bodh Gaya), road construction and repairs works etc. A large number of them are also engaged in rickshaw pulling at Bodh Gaya town. Due to lack of required skills, they do not get employment in other sectors of the

Table 2 : Literacy rate among Musahars in Bihar in 1971

Level of Education	Urban		Rural		Total		Total	% to total
	Male	Female	Male	Female	Male	Female	Person	person
1. Illiterate	23,673	21,870	859,803	862,604	883,476	884,474	1,767,950	98.0
2. Literate	1,062	119	16,768	922	17,834	1,041	18,871	1.0
3. Primary or Junior	857	47	10,902	333	11,759	380	12,139	0.8
4. Matriculate	144	2	1,124	8	1,268	10	1,278	
5. Technical degree	1	-	-	-	1	-	1	0.2
6. Graduate	71	-	-	-	71	-	71	
7. University degree or post-graduate	-	-	-	-	-	-		
Total :	25,824	22,038	888,597	863,867	914,405	885,905	1,800,310	100.0

Source : Census in India, 1971

economy. However, agriculture is still the main stay of their livelihood. It may de noted here that some families were given land ranging from 0.5 acre to 3 acres under the Bhoodan and Gramdan Scheme.

II

A number of voluntary organisations, social workers and activists have been working in the area to mitigate the miseries of the deprived and down-trodden sections of the people. Two important voluntary agencies working here are Samanwaya Ashram and Chhatra Yuva Sangharsh Vahini. These organisations have been implementing their socio-economic and motivational programmes among the Musahars. These agencies not only supplement government work but are free to try out innovative experiments to ameliorate their condi tion.

The Samanwaya Ashram,[1] a Sarvodaya Organisation, based on Gandhian Values was established by Acharya Vinoba Bhave in 1954. Since its inception, the Ashram has been engaged in multifarious activities for the betterment of Musahars under the able leadership of Shri Dwarko Sundarani, a devoted fol lower of Vinobaji.

The main activities of the Samanwaya Ashram are education, agriculture, dairy farming, mechanical workshop, medical services, Village reconstruction, land development, cultural activities, placement programme, feeding and health care centre for pre-school and non-school going children, programme for social change like compaigns against dowry, untouchability, debt redemption, abolition of bonded labour, discouragement of child marriage etc. and other relief serv ices to the Musahar community of the study area.

In the field of education, the Ashram has made con siderable progress by establishing seven Balwaris and two residential Schools for Musahar boys in its operational area. About 700 children are getting education in these educational institutions. Apart from teaching regular cur riculam, they are taught the rudiments of agriculture, dairy etc. About 2500 acres of Bhoodan lands have been

1. Samanawaya Ashram essentially aimed at evolving a syn thesis of the teachings of all religious and an integra tion of the life of the Musahars through Bhoodan and Gramdan.

distributed among the landless Musahars. The Ashram has provided them some facility for irrigation, improved seeds and agricul tural implements. Cattle raising is done by the students of the Ashram themselves. There are 70 milch animals in the Ashram. This has attracted the attention of local villagers. During our study we found that nearly 15 students were taking training in repairing diesel pump and in electric motor binding. The local farmers often came to the Ashram for repair of motor and pump. In the field of health serv ices, the Ashram has a medical unit which provides services to the poor Harijan families. Village reconstruction is one of the important activities of the Ashram.

The Ashram helped the Musahars in restoring to them their lands which were appropriated by the previous donors. The Ashram with the help of Bhoodan Yojna Committee provided them both the ownership and possession of land as well as homestead deed. Children's festivals (Bal Mela) are held every year in the Ashram. The Musahar children organise the cultural programme. The plays are mostly based on social life. The Ashram has given employment to 21 such students who have completed Ashram's education. Most of them are teachers. A few are employed as motor mechanics, tractor and jeep drivers. The nutrition programme covering about 463 children is being run at different centres of the Ashram. The Ashram has been able to provide milk to over 1600 Musahar children in the operational area.

These activities of Samanwaya Ashram are spread in Fateh pur, Mohanpur, Barachatti and Bodh Gaya Blocks of Gaya dis trict. It may be noted that these activities are not merely a programme for social and economic change of Musahar com munity of the area. They are not merely concerned with relief and charity work as the Community Development Blocks do. These activities intend to bring new values of life for Musahars by integrating educational, spiritual and develop mental programmes as mentioned above. They also train com mitted social workers from among the Musahar children for dedicated work in the villages (Prasad, 1986).

The Chhatra Yuva Sangharsh Vahini which was born out of J.P. Movement in 1974, was very active in Bodh Gaya region since 1978. The Vahini emerged to fight the exploitation and oppression perpetrated by the Shankar Math of Bodh Gaya. It was deeply involved in the struggle of the landless poor Harijans, particularly,

Musahars of the region for re- distribution of some of the vast tract of **Benami** land con trolled by the Math. It became a well known and well- documented struggle for social justice by non-violent means.

The Vahini organises the Musahars of the area to work together. It has been playing important role in creating so cial awareness and motivating the poor Musahars of the region. It also looks after the interest of Musahars when they face difficulty with the Block officials and landlords of the region in getting benefits of government schemes and minimum wages. Besides, it provides legal aid to the Musahar Victims by instituting cases in the Harijan Police Station and intimating the P U C L (People's Union for Civil Liberty). There are several such instances which are records of Vahini's programmes for the welfare of Musahars of the region. As a matter of fact its work is quite different from the Samanwaya Ashram. Its work is mostly motivational, promotional and educational rather than relief and economic oriented (Prasad, 1985).

The Community Development Blocks in the region run a num ber of welfare programmes for the Harijans as a whole. But it has been observed that the Musahar Community derives little benefit from these programmes. This is partly due to lack of initiative among the Musahars for getting the benefits of the programmes. For these reasons till recently hardly they received benefit from Harijan Housing Scheme, Old Age Pension scheme and the Harijan residential schools run by the Block officials in the region. During the course of our study it was found that only three Musahar students were getting education in the Harijan residential school at Matihani, Bodh Gaya. As many as 10 disabled and old men from the Musahar community were getting Rs.30/- each per month under the old age pension scheme. However, the Musahar is yet to benefit from the programmes like the Integrated Rural Development, Special Component programme etc.

Besides the voluntary organisations and the government in stitutions, a number of activist groups like Kisan Sabha, Indian people's Front, Gram Sabhas of the Musahar community and P U C L etc. are engaged in improving the conditions of the Musahars in the region. While the Kisan Sabha and the Indian People's Front look after the welfare of the Musahar alongwith the other castes of the Harijans and on their be half mediate with the landlords and the Block officials for minimum wages and other benefits. They also provide legal aid to the Musahar. As many as 17 Musahars of the region un der study have got justice under the scheme of legal aid so far. The Gram Sabhas of the Musahars have recorded a noteworthy achievement in mobilizing both the physical labour i.e. **Shramdan** and financial resources i.e. **Gram Kosh**. Although the amount in the Gram Kosh (Village Fund) is neg ligible, a sense of saving is being developed among the Musahars of the region.

Thus, the role of Voluntary effort as well as the govern ment agency appears very important in changing the life style of Musahars of the region through providing them economic and promotional programmes.

III

Now we discuss the changes taking place in the life-ways and thought-ways of Musahar Community in Bodh Gaya region of Bihar. The criteria for determination the changes taking place in the field of material ways and liberation of mind ways (thought ways) of the Musahars of the region being con sidered are.

1. Fear,
2. Lack of initiative,
3. Social belief, and
4. Culture of silence (Passivity).

There is now a great deal of awakening among the Musahars of the region. Earlier they were so afraid of the musclemen of the Mahanth that they could not stand freely before them. Now they are no longer afraid of the red turban musclemen and other officials and can talk to them with boldness. Now the Musahar women take active part in the processions launched by the Chhatra Yuva Sangharsh Vahini from time to time. Not only that, the Musahars do not allow themselves to be cheated or exploited by moneylenders, government offi cials, contractors and even Mohanth of Shankar Math. They resist atrocities committed on them in their daily life. They can now be seen taking tea in the tea stall installed near the Math premises. They sometimes take active part in election campaign organised by the Municipal Corporation and others.

Earlier self-initiative was totally absent among the Musahars of the region. Such initiative was also lacking even among the leaders of the community. Now the situation has gradually changed. Self-initiative to performing the community welfare or individual development among the Musahars of the region has been developing gradually.We may cite here one example of Baleshwar a very poor Musahar Youth. He was brought in the Samanways Ashram for education at the age of five. He was keenly interested in social work and has been engaged in such activities since the age of 15 when he was a student. Apart from Musahars, other scheduled castes of the region have great respect for him. In view of his potentialities, Ashram appointed him a teacher. He was married with Joyti, an Ashram girl. No dowry was paid in their marriage. They were both employed as teachers and posted at the Balwari in the village of Bapugram. They built their own house and settled in that village. Both the couples started earning about Rs.600/- p.m. from their teaching job. In fact, he wanted to become an independent leader of his own caste. After some time, he gave up his job in the Ashram and continued to do voluntary social service and motivational work for the Musahar along with several other young Musahar workers who had at different times left the Ashram. He succeeded in setting up an institution named 'Musahar Seva, financially supported by OXFAM (OXFORD FOR FAMINE RELIEF). Presently, he is doing some social work among the Musahars of the region. Thus, Baleshwar is not only able to organise the Musahars, he is also able to mobilise some resources for the development of his community of the region. His future plan of work is to train social workers from among the Musahars of the region for dedicated work for his own community.

Fatalism in the Musahar community is being eroded. Until the early seventies, Musahars of the region clinged to their traditional customs and rituals. There was no marital relationship between the Magadhi Musahar and Tirhutia Musahar. Child marriage was very common in the community. There was no commensal relationship with members of the Chamar, Mehtar and other untouchables. Now the situation has changed. Attitude towards social customs like dowry, funeral feast and habit of drinking liquor among the Musahars of the region are undergoing considerable change. Incidence of child marriage has decreased to a large extent . A sense of cleanliness and sanitation and use of clean water have developed among them. Now they are trying to get rid of so cial evils, superstition and dirty social habits. Musahar youths are gradually organising themselves and discussing the issues of dowry, atrocity, rape, arson, drinking water problem, corruption, and other social disabilities. In fact,they have been trying to raise consciousness regarding the problem of superstition, social beliefs and other dis abilities. Thus, the Musahar of the region is gradually shaking off old norms and values and adopting a new culture of hope.

Earlier Musahars were at the level of abject poverty. Their economic conditions were very deplorable. Their daily wage was so meagre that they could not think even for their children. Some of the Musahars of the region were eating palm fruits instead of cereals. Now poverty of Musahars has been mitigated to some extent. A little smile has come on their depressed faces. The Musahars who could not even think of a day ahead have now started thinking in terms of better life. Now they have tendency to save seeds and other agricultural inputs for the following season. We may cite here a few examples of Musahars dwelling in the region and their economic development. There are 32 Musahar families in Vinobapuri village situated in Bodh Gaya Block. They are settled on a barren Bhoodan land of about 20 acres. They were, by and large, bonded labourers of the upper caste families earlier. The Samanwaya Ashram started taking steps for improving their miserable condition. The Ashram succeeded in freeing them from the clutches of landlords and Mahanth in 1978. The Ashram provided them all the facilities for their settlement. Apart from homestead land, Ashram provided them some Bhoodan land for cultivation. Their land was reclaimed with the Ashram's assistance. House and drink ing water wells were constructed. Agricultural implements were given to them for cultivation. Now they grow crops on the land. Before their settlement on Bhoodan land at Vinobapuri, they were **Kamiya** (bonded labour). Now they are capable of taking lands on lease from the upper castes for cultivation. They produce their basic requirements of cereals and pulses. Musahars of the village decided on self- help instead of asking others to help them. The Musahar tolas have been able to mobilize the entire village labour force for constructing wells and community hall. It has also been able to raise a good amount at Gram Kosh for the vil lage development. Now they are able to increase their surplus earning from self-cultivated agricultural and or chard produce.

We may cite another example of Ramchandra Musahar. He was brought in the Ashram at the age of eight as an orphan. He used to work in the workshop and learnt repair of machines during his stay in the Ashram. After a few years, arrange ment was made by the Ashram to send him to Jamshedpur for getting training in the workshop. There he took training in motor driving. After his training, he took driving job. At present, he is well placed and associated with a local Harijan M.L.A. He is getting Rs. 600/- p.m. He his happy with his family. During agricultural season, he also cul tivates his land which he got in Bhoodan. There are several such examples with indicate that the Musahar in the region have moved from tradition to self-reliance and development.

Culture of silence was found in the Musahar community. They never resisted injustice. They were not supposed to fight for their rights. Perhaps they did not know their rights. Even if the Musahars were aware of the rights, they were not prepared to assert them. In fact, the Musahars, by and large, had been living in the culture of silence. This may be partly due to centuries of economic deprivation and partly due to repressive system of bonded labour.

If we look at the Musahar of Bodh Gaya region, we find that some changes are taking place in the culture of si lence. Women folk among the Musahar community of the region is more active and articulated. They have their own or ganisation named 'Mahila Sabha' were some basic problems like minimum wage and exploitation are discussed. They par ticipate and take active part in Satyagrah under the leader ship of Chhatra Yuva Sanghrash Vahini. The Musahars, par ticularly the knowledgeable among them, know about the government programmes and schemes and they seek their share of the benefits mentioned in it from the respective Block officials of the region. It has been reported that several marches have been organised by the Musahars before B.D.O.to mitigate their grievances.

Much awareness exists among the Musahars of the region regarding the need of education for their children. They are not merely interested in education but sometimes they seek white collar job. We find that about twenty Musahars of the region are employed as teachers in the Samanwaya Ashram and its sister agencies. Besides, some Musahars have been placed in sub-centres as motor mechanic-cum-tractor driver and as agricultural teacher-cum-extensive workers. We may put here an example of Dharmnath, a social worker of Mohanpur Block. He was an orphan boy. He was associated with a rich and up per caste family of Bharatpur village at the age of 8. He was not happy in that condition. He came to know of the Samanwaya Vidyapith at Bagha where Musahar boys were taught. Once he fled away from the richman and reached the Vidyapith for education. He used to live and study in the Ashram. He narrated his story that the rich man paid Rs. 6/- only for the coffin of mother and he became bonded labour of the rich man. After completing the Ashram education, be left Vidyapith and settled down in his own village. He started cultivation on Bhoodan land. Later on, he was married at the age of 18 in a nearby village. Presently, two of his children, a daughter and a son,are in the Vidyapith. Not only that 10 more Musahar boys from this village being in spired by Dharmnath are taking education in Samanwaya Vidyapith. Earlier they were engaged in grazing their pigs like other Musahar children of the village. This shows that the Musahars of the region are gradually realising the value of education. This also shows that enlightened Musahars of the region are trying to change their life and thinking.

IV

Musahars of the region have recorded considerable change in view of their life style in their material culture and thoughtways through the liberation of mind. This changing attitude of Musahars is apparent in the field of fear, leadership, poverty, education and their social beliefs. However, the change is more apparent in the sector of al leviation of poverty, education and leadership. It has been taking place due to the active participation of Chhatra Yuva Sanghrash Vahini and Samanwaya Ashram. Both the organisa tions are engaged for the development of the Musahar Com munity for a long time. Some social scientists who had the opportunity to see the living conditions of Musahars, are of the opinion that Musahars have by and large changed in dress,styles of living, self thinking and also some of their habits. However, perception of the change that has been taking place in the habits and old values of Musahars may differ from one section of people to another depending upon their level of understanding and feeling. The change that has taken place in the life style of Musahars may not appear much to outsiders but those who have seen Musahars of the region before this change may consider it miraculous.

REFERENCES

Beteille, Andre 1969 Caste: Old and New; Asia Publishing House, New Delhi.

Mahar, J. Michael 1972 Untouchables in Contemporary India; University of Arizona Press, Tucson.

Mukerji, A.B. 1980 Chamars of Uttar Pradesh, a Study in so cial Geography; Inter India Publication, New Delhi.

Prasad, Anirudh 1985 People's Perception of the Atrocities Committed on Harijans in Bihar; Journal of Social and Economic Studies, Vol.2 Number 1.

Prasad, Anirudh 1985 Voluntary Effort in the Development of Musahar Community in Bihar; (mimeograph); A.N. Sinha In stitute of Social Studies, Patna.

Prasad, Anirudh 1986 Samanwaya Ashram in the Service of Harijans; Janki Prakashan, New Delhi.

Sachchidananda 1977 The Harijan Elite; Thomson Press, Faridabad.

Vidyarthi L.P.1977 Harijan to-day: Sociological, Economic, Political, Religious and cultural analysis; clasical, New Delhi.

Shyamlal 1984 Bhangis in Transition, Inter India Publication; New Delhi.

ELEVEN

Ramesh P. Sinha

Restriction on Participation and Role in Decision Making : Women in Rural Bhojpur

Any attempt to assess the social position of women in a society should ideally start from the social framework. So cial structure, cultural norms and value systems are impor tant determinants of women's roles and their position in society. They influence social expectations regarding be haviour of the two sexes, both as individuals and in rela tion to each other. Social traditions influence in shaping attitude as well as behaviour pattern of human groups: emerging trends can not be viewed in isolation from them.

The response of the structural forces of change is not easy to predict. Social structure can stimulate certain trends of development and change but, at the same time, it can also thwart the development. Changes in the normative structure and in the organizational forms of society do not take place in unison: the difference in their pace often creates hiatus. Thus we find that reforms in law and educa tional policy do not always make the desired impact because of the normative and structural unpreparedness of the society to accept their goals and means.[1] Religion, family and kinship, roles and cultural norms delimiting the spheres of women's activities obstruct their full and equal par ticipation in the life of the society and in the achievement of their

1. For details, see **Women's Right : Myth and Reality**, Sac hchidananda and Ramesh P. Sinha, Roopa,Jaipur, 1984.

full potential. Thus for the development of the society, particularly in the Indian context, the social position of women will have to be related to the living realities of the social and cultural contexts of their present position. One may venture to assume that if a society provides adequate opportunities for women, they would tend to make significant contribution towards social development. Any restriction imposed on women on their par ticipation in social activities as well as in family deci sion making would delimit the process of development of that society.

II

Historically, the social position of women in the Indian society has been resilient. In the Vedic age, women enjoyed relatively high position[2] in the Indian society. They en joyed freedom for spiritual progress and intellectual development. Vedic texts are replete with references to rituals recommended for ensuring the birth of a learned daughter (Asthana, 1974,1). Women had absolute equality with men in the eyes of religion; they could perform ritual sacrifices independently and were not regarded as an impedi ment to religious persuits. Marriage was a religious neces sity to both the man and the woman, since neither could reach heaven without being accompanied by the duly married consort. The position of wife was an honoured one in the family; widow remarriage, within the family, was permitted. However women could neither hold nor inherit property (Dube,1963,184).

The changes that took place during in the age of the Brahmans(1500 to 500 B.C.) in the position of women were slow but gradual. **Upanayana** of girls was still in vogue and they were allowed to pursue educational attainment. However, as Altekar (1938,410-11) states, in this period the system of sending out girls to teachers or centres of education was discouraged. Therefore religious and educational training became possible only in the case of the girls of rich and cultured families. A tendency was now apparent which stipu lated curtailment in the religious rites and privileges of the average woman, many functions of religious rites now came to be assigned to men. However ideals of marriage and the mutual relations of the

---

2. The famous saying **Yatra Nari Pujyante Ramante Tatra Devata**(God lives there where a woman is worshipped) sig nifies the high position accorded to women.

husband and wife continued to be the same as they were in the earlier age. Divorce was per mitted to the wife though the permission was not extensively utilized. Widow-remarriage was still permitted, but women had ceased to attend public meetings.

The position of women during the age of Sutras and Epics (500 B.C. to 500 A.D.) changed considerably. The introduc tion of the non Aryan wife into the Aryan household was largely responsible for this change (Dube, 1963,185). When the Aryans and non Aryans proceeded to live together peace fully, intermarriages became inevitable. However, the non- Aryan wife, with her ignorance of the Sanskrit language and Hindu religion, could not enjoy the same religious privileges as the Aryan consort. Thus there began deteriora tion of women's status, which was caused due to the com plexity of the rituals connected with the Vedic sacrifices. Instances where the husband attempted to associate the non- Aryan wife with his religious sacrifices led to the priests declare that the non-Aryan wife was unfit for such religious rituals. When this rule was defied, women were declared un fit for Vedic studies and religious duties. Consequences of this change were stupendous.

The age of marriage for girls was lowered,their education was discontinued and their status in the family was lowered. Since **Upnayana** was usually performed at an early age the marriage of girls was also regarded ideal at an early age. Widow remarriage was opposed and was finally interdicted by about A.D. 500 (Dube, 1963,186). But it gave rise to the provision of property rights. Since widow remarriage was shunned, class of childless widows arose, and society had to devise an honourable means of enabling them to maintain themselves. Although no definite rules were envisaged, in course of time different regional customs were evolved al lowing varying degrees of proprietary rights to women.

The theory of the perpetual tutelage of women, propounded by Manu[3], was clearly formulated and expressed during this age. It was ordained that the father should protect her in the childhood, the husband when she was married and the son when her husband was no more: at no stage was she to be left unprotected. Gruadually it

3. There are exhortations by Manu that Women should be kept under control...in childhood,to her father : in youth to her husband, and when her lord is dead,to her sons...A woman must never be independent.

was assumed that a woman desired no independence; she ought not to do anything on her own responsibility in childhood, or youth, or even in old age.

During the post-Smriti period also the position of women continued to change. From the theological point of view women came to be regarded as of the same status as the Sudras.[4] Although, widow remarriage had generally become taboo, child-widows were allowed to marry upto A.D. 500. However this practice was shunned. Although permissive legislation was adopted in 1856, the prejudice against widow remarriage was so deeply entrenched that legislation could not leave any appreciable and perceptible impact.

Although the practice of **Purdah** was opposed around 12th Century A.D., it was revived with the onset of Moghal em pire. **Pardah** thus became a way of life for women. Customs like **Stridhana** was introduced and extended by including in it property acquired even by inheritance and partition (Asthana, 1974).

During the British rule in India Legislation was used to bring about significant modifications in the structure of society. Reference has been made to the abolition of **Sati**, and Purdah. Subsequent legislation recognised inter-caste marriage, as also widow remarriage. The age of marriage was raised, the divorce was permitted under certain conditions. Special facilities were provided for women to acquire modern education. They were also provided with increasing employ ment opportunities in certain selected spheres.

After independence, marriage and divorce laws have been modified, ensuring a greater measure of equality to women. Women now have a legal share in property. Educational and employment opportunities have now been amplified. They have an equal right to Vote.

III

Inadequate as the above survey of women through the ages is, it nevertheless gives us an idea of the resilient posi tion of women in

4. It is said that Tulsidas grouped women with drums, morons, Shudras and cattle as objects fit to be beaten.

the different historical periods of the evolution of Indian society. Although women are now legally emancipated, several restrictions have been imposed on them which reflect latent as well as manifest dimensions of the position of women in the Indian society. These restrictions are socially sacrosanct and inexorable. These have been shaped by the authority of classical texts and teaching of religion. Participation of women in social and economic ac tivities outside home is stigmatic. Although numerous women now go to work, the fact remains that women as a rule seek work out of economic need rather than to get even with men (Nanda, 1976,XV).

This leads one to surmise that women, as a social rule, suffer from several limitations and that rural women would be in more precarious condition. The present exercise makes an attempt towards unravelling the social position of women. Limited in scope, this paper tries to examine restrictions imposed on women in their social and economic activities. It also tends to delineate the extent to which women are con sulted (thus indicating their position within the family) in important decisions made in the family. As indicated ear lier, the intention of this paper is not to provide holistic picture of the position of women in rural Bihar but to give an indication as to what their social position is in contem porary time. To put it succintly, the objectives of this paper are,

(a) to examine restrictions imposed on rural women in respect of their participation in socio-economic activities, and
(b) their role (i.e.how far they are consulted) in family decisions. These two objectives have been examined with reference to some background variables like caste, age, ex posure to mass-media and the type of family (nuclear-joint) of the respondents.

The present paper is based on data from the project 'Awareness of Legal Rights among Women' sponsored by the Ministry of Education and Social Welfare, Government of In dia. In this paper a total of 120 women, all married and falling within the age range of 18-49 years were selected on the basis of probability samples. These women hailed from three villages of Bhojpur. Villages were selected by drawing two concentric circles on the map of Bhojpur, keeping urban areas in the centre of these circles. Care was taken to en sure that the listed villages were not only twenty kilometers away from the centre but also from the vicinity of any other urban centre. The population figures of these villages were

Table 1: Social Background of Respondents

For-ward VILLAGES	CASTE			LITERACY		FAMILY		MEDIA EX-		AGE			
	For-ward	Back-ward	Sche-duled	Illi-trate	Lite-rate	Nucl-ear	Joint	Un Ex-posed	Expo-sed	19 Yrs. to below	20-29 Yrs.	30-39 Yrs.	40 Yrs. and above
Posawa (N-40)	15.0	50.0	35.0	75.0	25.0	47.5	52.5	72.5	27.5	0.0	52.5	27.5	20.0
Sandesh(N-40)	17.0	62.5	22.5	95.0	5.0	32.5	67.5	92.5	7.5	7.5	37.5	37.5	17.5
Purhara(N-40)	70.0	15.0	12.5	97.5	2.5	52.5	47.5	70.0	30.0	2.5	32.5	27.5	37.5
Total (N-120)	34.2	42.5	23.3	89.2	10.8	44.2	55.8	78.3	21.7	3.3	40.8	30.8	25.0

drawn and three villages were selected by using the table of random numbers. Respondents were selected with the help of random technique and data were collected with the help of interview schedule.

Besides questions on age, caste, family restriction, deci sion making, there were questions on respondents' exposure to mass-media. Media exposure was operationalised in terms of frequency of utilization of radio, newspaper and cinema. Respondents were asked to determine in case of radio- listening and newpaper - reading, whether they were exposed once a week, twice-thrice a week, four times a week or everyday in a week. In case of cinema, they were asked to report the frequency of exposure occurring during the last six months (i.e. how many visits) from the date of inter view. After assigning scores to frequency of exposure, the total scores on all these channels were calculated to ascer tain specific position of respondents in respect of exposure to mass-media.

Background Characteristics of the Respondents

Women from rural Bhojpur were all married and the bulk of them belonged to the age group 20-29 years (40.8%). However Inter-village comparison revealed that women from Posawan were Younger (52.5% belonging to age group 20-29 years) than those from Sandesh (37.5% forming the age group 30-39 years) and Purhara (37% were above 40 years of age). The overwhelm ing majority of women was illiterate(89.2%) and illiteracy was pronounced more in Sandesh (95%) and Purhara (97.5%) than among women from Posawa (75%). The Backward (42.5%) and upper caste women (34.2%) were in majority. Living in joint family was still a norm (see table 1) but it appeared to be weaning its significane. Thus 55.8% respondents came from joint family against 44.2% nuclear family-dwellers. The bulk of women was not exposed to mass-media except 21.7% women who were exposed to media communication.

The above description reflects different characteristics of social background of the sampled women. Although women were different in respect of these characteristics across the three villages, village-wise differentiation has not been attempted as it does not constitute an objective of this study.

Table 2 : Restriction on Women's Activities across background Variables

Sl. No.	ACTIVITIES	RESTRICTION PERCENTAGE	CASTE			MEDIA EXPOSURE		FAMILY		AGE				
			For-word	Back-word	Scheduled	Un Exposed	Exposed	Nuclear	Joint	10 Yrs & below	20-29 Yrs	30-39 Yrs	40 Yrs. above	Total
1	2	3	4	5	6	7	8	9	10	11	12	13	14	15
1.	Going out to work	46.7	66.1	30.3	3.6	62.5	37.5	64.3	35.7	5.4	48.2	21.4	25.0	100.0
2.	Leaving house alone	30.8	67.6	27.0	5.4	56.8	43.2	62.6	32.4	10.8	43.2	18.9	27.0	100.0
3.	Talking to males other than relatives	36.7	50.0	40.9	9.1	63.6	36.4	61.4	38.6	9.1	56.8	18.2	15.9	100.0
4.	Talking to husband in presence of elders in the family	40.8	55.1	36.7	8.2	61.2	38.8	59.2	40.8	8.2	46.9	28.6	16.3	100.0
5.	Having male friends	95.8	34.8	49.5	21.7	78.3	21.7	43.5	56.5	3.5	40.9	29.6	26.1	100.0
6.	Having female friends whom husband dislikes	95.0	35.0	42.1	22.9	78.1	21.9	42.1	57.9	3.5	42.1	29.8	24.6	100.0
7.	Participation in public life	90.8	37.6	42.2	20.2	76.1	23.9	43.1	56.9	3.7	41.3	29.4	25.7	100.0
8.	Going to melas with friends	77.5	40.8	43.1	16.1	78.5	21.5	48.4	51.6	4.3	37.6	29.0	29.0	100.0
9.	Visiting relatives at own will	67.5	44.4	37.0	18.5	71.6	28.4	45.7	54.3	4.9	46.9	27.2	21.0	100.0

10. Using Family Planning methods	92.5	34.2	42.3	23.4	83.8	16.2	37.8	62.2	3.9	42.6	28.7	24.7	100.0
11. On being face to face with father in the presence of husband	5.8	71.4	28.6	0.0	57.1	42.9	57.1	42.9	0.0	28.6	28.6	42.8	100.0
12. On being face to face with father-in-law/husband' selder brother	30.8	59.5	32.1	8.1	70.3	29.7	59.5	40.5	5.4	51.3	24.3	18.9	100.0

IV

Restriction on Participation

Twelve questions were put to each respondent to known the types of activities which were prohibited to wives. The questions were 'do you encounter restrictions on the follow ing activities : (1) going out to work, (2) leaving house alone (3) talking to males other than relatives, (4) talking to husband in presence of elders in the family, (5) having male friends (6) having female friends whom husband dis likes, (7) participating in public life/social work (8) going to melas'with friends (9) visiting relatives at will, (10) using family planning methods (11)on being face to face with father in the presence of husband (12) on being face to face with father-inlaw/husband's elder brother.

The respondents were asked to report in yes-no answers. Responses are summarised in Table 1. For each item which the respondent answered in affirmative, one point was scored. The total score thus reflected the total number of restric tions imposed on married women (for details, see B.N. Muk herjee, (1974,1975).[5]

Analysis of restriction data (see table-2) reveals that in rural Bhojpur, married women were not allowed to have male friends (95.8% women reporting this restriction), par ticipate in public life (90.8% reporting restriction) and use family planning methods (92.5% reporting restriction). More than 70 percent of the respondents did not have freedom to go to village fairs while more than 60 percent encoun tered restriction in visiting their relatives at own will. All the sampled women thus experienced restriction in varied proportion. The minimum restriction reported was two (by one woman only) and only three women reported to have encoun tered all the twelve restrictions. Restrictions indicating social and familial control seemed to be more critical items[6] wheras items

---

5. Restrictions on women's activities have also been ex amined by B.N. Mukherjee with similar items. (See B.N.Mukherjee, 1974, 1975).

6. The extent of familial control is significant. About 31% women are not allowed to face their fathers-in-law/husbands' elder brothers. Marriage seems to restrict father-daughter relationship. 5% of the married women encountered restric tion on being face to face even with their father, in the presence of husbands.

indicatiang economic freedom (i.e. goin out on job) were less critical.

Analysis of restriction data across background variables (ref. to Table2) revealed that restriction imposed on married women was pronounced more among upper caste women and women of lower age group (i.e. below 20 years). The married women from upper castes and nuclear family were restricted more in respect of economic than social ac tivities. Laxity of restrictions on economic activities is a matter of necessity, women from the scheduled castes, ir respective of their marital status do go out on jobs, they are earning members and therefore their talking to males other than relatives and family members is not stigmatic. Restriction on women from nuclear families in respect of going out on jobs is perhaps due to lack of people who may substitute for them in their absence.

It thus appears that upper castes in rural Bhojpur limited the activities of women to the home only, whereas women of the Scheduled castes participated in economic activities, outsided the home.

Drawing women into labour and job depends on tradition, Gadgil says, "Ability to keep away manual work has been an important distinguishing sign of socio-economic status. Therefore non-participation of upper caste women in work outdoors is everywhere considered as a value" (Gadgil, 1955- 7). Gadgil's observations are buttressed by Yurlova. She says "in many cases women's work outside home is regarded as a social taboo particularly among upper caste. As for the poor section the bulk of whom belong to lower castes, the social taboo is not so widespread" (Yurlova 1981, 180-192).

Role in Decision - making

In order to examine married women's role (i.e.their say) in decision-making[7] in family matters, the following ques tions were asked : Are you consulted in important family decisions like (1) marriage **gauna, donga** and the like, (2) education of your children, (3) adoption of family planning methods (4) your consent on

---

7. Items were taken from B.N. Mukherjee's study (1974).

Table 3 Women's Say in Decision Making across background Varables

CONSULTED IN FAMILY AFFAIRS	Family		Media Exposure			
Sl. FAMILY MATTERS	Yes	No	Nuclear	Joint	Unexposed	Exposed
1, 2	3	4	5	6	7	8
1. Marriage/Gauna etc.	*46.3	51.7	36.2	63.0	81.0	18.9
2. Education of Children	45.8	54.2	38.2	61.8	80.0	20.0
3. Adoption of F.P.	5.8	94.2	57.1	42.9	28.6	71.4
4. Consent on Adoption	5.8	94.2	57.1	42.9	28.6	71.4
5. Buying/selling domestic assets	15.0	85.0	44.4	55.6	83.3	16.7
6. Keeping money for domestic Expenditure	70.8	29.2	44.7	55.3	76.5	23.5
7. Has property in name*	0.8	99.2	0.0	0.0	0.0	0.0

Sl. FAMILY MATTERS	CASTE			AGE				
	Forward	Backward	Scheduled	Up to 19 Years	20-29 Years	30-39 Years	40 Years	Total
	9	10	11	12	13	14	15	16
1. Marriage/Gauna etc.	29.0	43.6	29.3	-	39.6	24.1	36.2	100.0
2. Education of Children	29.1	43.6	27.3	-	40.0	25.5	34.5	100.0
3. Adoption of F.P.	85.1	14.3	-	-	42.8	42.8	14.4	100.0
4. Consent on Adoption	85.7	14.3	-	-	28.6	57.1	14.3	100.0
5. Buying/selling domestic assets	66.7	27.8	5.5	-	33.3	22.2	44.5	100.0
6. Keeping money for domestic Expenditure	37.6	38.8	23.5	3.5	34.1	35.3	27.1	100.0
7. Has property in name*	-	-	-	-	100.0	-	-	100.0

* Only one women had property in her name and she hailed from joint family and was not exposed to media communication. She was an upper caste woman.

adoption of the same, (5) buying/selling of land and other important domestic items - and(6) do you keep money for day to day expenses (7) do you have any property in your name.

Although women in rural Bhojpur found their major respon sibilities in the preparation of food, care of children and home, they did not have the necessary power and authority in all spheres of family life. More than 50 percent of the to tal married women (See table-3) did not enjoy confidence of their husbands and other family members: They were not con sulted in important family affairs. The numerical distribu tion reveals that 20% women were not at all consulted, 21.7% were consulted on one issue, 22.5% on two-three issues while 26.7% were consulted on five-six issues. Interestingly, none of the married women was consulted on all the seven issues of family affairs. Thus the majority of rural women enjoyed subordinate position in important family matters and were not consulted even on matters like adoption of family plan ning measures.

When the data on decision-making were tabulated (ref. Table 3) across respondents' age, media exposure, caste and the type of family, it was found that the married women belonging to joint family, those who were not exposed to mass-media, enjoyed more 'say' in decisions made in impor tant family issues. Thus more than 50 percent of women from joint family and those from 'unexposed' category were con sulted in matters of marriage and the like, education of children, and buying and selling of domestic goods and as sets. However in matters of adoption of family planning methods, women, exposed to media as well as those who lived in neculear families, were consulted more than their other counterparts.

Reasons for variation in response in the above context have not been explored, which requires further investigation in this area.

V

The data incorporated and analysed earlier tend to yield interesting results. Women in rural Bhojpur are subservient to men (i.e. husbands), they encounter restrictions on so cial and economic activities.. Restriction on economic ac tivities is pronounced more among upper caste women. The married women have lesser say in the decisions made in the family.

If in a family in which the husband is the decision-maker in domestic matters in which wife perceives a low position (i.e.lesser say, having little effect on decisions) in deci sion making vis-a-vis husband and other members of the family and in which her activities are predicted, then such society may be said to be tradition-ridden.[8] This is so be cause under a subservient position, the wife hardly gets an opportunity to use her potentialities. Because of her low position (lesser say) in family matters (thus having low position in the family) and restriction on her activities, she has very limited scope to participate in roles outside the home.

The opposition to increasing opportunities for women's participation in socio-economic activities springs from con servative view regarding women's proper role in society, where proper imposes clearly, and often rigidly, defined limits to the activities that women may or may not parform. Traditional values impose restrictions not only on women's activities outside the home but also within home. tradition provides ideological and moral bases for the accorded status and institutionalised role of a woman in a rural society. Thc social restrictions on women and also people's notion about their proper role in the domestic and extra-domestic spheres are largely derived from the traditional conceptions of women's basic characteristics, her assumed virtues and vices and the stereotypes regarding her nature and capacities. It thus seems that the contradictory attitudes expressed about women in classical texts persist even today. On the one hand they are regarded as the highest embodiment of purity and power, on the other they are viewed essen tially as weak and dependent creatures requiring constant guarding and protection. While the former view seldom gets overt expression, the latter is determined by covert norms which define her actual position.

Men are superior to women is the theme and it has many latent and manifest dimensions. Women is regarded as more susceptible to pollution. She may be easily defiled and her purification is difficult. In a 'pollution-purity' conscious society, as Dube states (Dube, 1963,

---

8. Tradition here refers to behaviours characterised by "Sacred sanctions, roles defined by rituals ..." (See Bellah 1965); "as the psychic attitude-set for the habitual workday and to the belief in everyday routine as an inviolable norm of conduct" (See, Weber, 1947) or "explicit reference is made to the past"...(See Shils, 1961).

191), the significance of this view is crucial. It gives rise to dual morality. The one governing the males and the other governing the females. The underlying assumption of the dual morality syndrome is 'Man is strong and capable of looking after himself' and 'Women is weak and dependent on man for security'. It tends to establish male dominance and female dependence. It also restricts female activities and outdoor activities and most of the major decision-making roles are thus the domain of man. In the traditionally-oriented society,the stereotype suggesting the desirability of the life-long protection to a woman from childhood (by father) to old age (by son) is still in vogue.

Pursuantly, intertwined with this belief, women tacitly assumes her complimentary role in which the superiority and dominance of male is not only taken for granted but is also jealously guarded. Her going out to work is uncommon and so cially unacceptable. Andre Beteille and T.N. Madan (1975, 161-162), while portraying the position of women, make a very apt and vivid revelation" ....no woman is allowed to walk out in the street unaccompanied by a man....If a hus band has friends visiting him,his wife stays in another room....The form and degree of strict observance of these rules varies depending upon caste, locality, etc." While ex amining the causes, Gore (1968,159) opines that restrictions on women arise from "fear of being uncoventional".

To sum, concerted efforts made toward legal emancipation of women notwithstanding, old customs and ideas continue to exert great restricting influence on women. These old cus toms have tremendous ability to resist changes that affect women in family and social life even today.

REFERENCES

Altekar, A.S.1956 The Position of Women in Hindu Civi lization, Motital Banarasi Das, Banaras.

Asthana, P. 1974 Women's Movement in India, Vikas Publishing House, Delhi.

Bellah, R.N.(ed.) 1965 Religion and Progress in Modern Asia, Free Press, New York

Beteille, A.and T.N. Madan 1975 Encounter and Experience, Vikas Publishing House, Delhi.

Dube, S.C. 1963 "Men's and Women's Roles in India : A Sociological Review" in B.E. Ward (ed.) Women in New Asia,UNESCO, Paris.

Gadgil, D.R. 1965 Women in Working Force in India, Govt. of India Publication,

Delhi.

Gore,M.S. 1968 Urbanization and Family Change, Popular Prakashan,Bombay.

Mukherjee, B.N. 1974 "The Status of Married Women in Haryana, Tamil Nadu and Meghalaya" Social Change, March.

Mukherjee, B.N. 1974 "Restrictions on Married Women's Activities", Indian Anthropologist, Vol. 4, No.2.

Mukherjee, B.N. 1975 "Awereness of Legal Rights among Married Women" Indian Anthropologist, Vol. 5,No.2.

Nanda,B.R. 1976 Indian Women : From Purdah to Modernity, Vikas Publishing, Delhi.

Sachchidananda and Ramesh P. Sinha 1984 Women's Rights : Myth and Reality, Printwell Publisher,Jaipur.

Shills, E. 1961 Tradition, Faber and Faber, London.

Weber, M. 1947 The Theory of Social and Economic Organiza tion, Oxford University Press, London.

Yurlova, E. 1981 "Some Aspects of Women Employment", in India's Problems of Development, USSR Academy of Science, USSR.

TWELVE

B. B. Mandal

Norms and Practices in Chield Development: The Case of Rural Bihar

The constitution of India has made several provisions for care, protection and prevention of exploitation of children. A number of legislations have also been promulgated in the country to uphold these rights. But it was only when the United Nations came out with the 'Declaration of the rights of the child' in 1959 that India started taking steps through action oriented programme to guarantee these rights. The Declaration affirms the rights of the child to enjoy special protection and facilities to develop in a healthy and normal manner, to have special security, adequate nutri tion and medical services, to grow up in an atmosphere of affection and love and to receive education and protection from exploitation[1] As a sequel to this Declaration, the Government of India initiated for the first time a programme for child development under the Social Welfare sector in the Third Five Year Plan.

In August, 1974 the government of India formulated the Na tional Policy Resolution for children. According to the resolution, the state is to provide adequate service to children both before and after birth and through the period of growth to ensure their full physical, mental, emotional and social development. The state shall progressively in crease the scope of services so that within a reasonable time, all children in the country enjoy optimum conditions for their balanced growth. The measures suggested for achieving the objective are: a comprehensive health programme, i.e. nutritional services for removing protein and calorie deficiencies in the diet of children, expectant and nursing mothers, nutrition education of mothers, free and compulsory education for all children upto the age of 14 years including non-formal education for pre-school children, promotion of physical education and recreational activities, prevention of exploitation of children, and spe cial facilities for children with different types of dis abilities. Special provisions have also been made for children of weaker sections like the scheduled castes and the scheduled tribes (Rajendran, 1980).

An important development that can be attributed to the Na tional policy is the initiation of the scheme of integrated child Development services which aims at providing a package of services to children below 6 years, and expectant and nursing mothers. The package of services consists of sup plementary nutrition, immunization, health check-up, referal services for children and mothers, pre-school education, recreation, health and nutrition, education of mothers and provision of safe drinking water (Department of Welfare, 1974).

The different programmes evolved and launched in the country for the child have two basic aims. They intend to deliver benefit to the children of weaker section in their physical and mental growth on the one hand and on the other tend to create certain values which in turn will reflect a set of new norms defining child care and child development. The new norms will replace those old norms which are out dated and proved to be devoid of reason in the present con text.

Every culture contains a large number of guidelines which direct conduct in particular situations. Such guidelines are known as norms. A norm is a specific guide to action which defines acceptable and appropriate behaviour in particular situations. Norms are enforced by positive and negative sanctions, that is, rewards and punishment. Sanctions may be informal such as an approving or a disapproving glance, or formal such as a fine or a reward given by an official body (Johnson, 1960).

Norms may be divided into two broad classes. Some norms specify positive obligations in terms of roles and sub groups. For example, the positive obligations of a family are not the same as those of a business concern. Again posi tive obligations of a father (a social role) are not the same as those of the son or a daughter (a social role). This class of norms is obligatory and may also be called rela tional because of the fact that they specify the positive content of relations between role-occupants and between sub- groups. The second class of the norms is permissive rather than obligatory. They may be called regulative, since they do not differentiate between roles or sub-groups. They regu late the behaviour of the people regardless of their roles.

Norms, whether they are relational or regulative, remain ineffective in influencing the behaviour of persons so long as they are not institutionalized. A norm is said to be in stitutionalized when the following four conditions are met. Firstly, a large number of members of the society or of a group (if the frame of reference is a narrow one) should be aware of the norm. Secondly, those who are aware of the norm should accept it in principle. Thirdly, many of those who accept the norm take it seriously and have internalised it. Lastly, the norm should be sanctioned, that is, a large num ber of the members have accepted to abide by the norm in ap propriate circumstances.

It is already mentioned above that the government, through its different developmental programmes for the children, in tends to create a set of norms regarding child care and child-development which must be internalised by the majority of the Indians and must guide human action in appropriate circumstances. In doing so, the government attempts to re place those norms which are traditional and seem to be ap propriate for proper child care and development from the context of the advancement in human knowledge.

II

In this paper we attempt to identify those norms which need to be internalised and substituted for the older ones as well as to delineate how far traditionally sanctioned norms are compatible to the new norms. For the sake of con venience of analysis, traditionally sanctioned norms will be called social practices and the guidelines to be in stitutionalised will be referred to as norms.

Antenatal Period

A number of norms guide the behaviour during antenatal period. They are as follows: (1) the pregnant women must get antenatal check up at least thrice prior to delivery; (2) she must be immunised against tetanus; (3) she must receive balanced diet or 2400 calories per day. Applicability of the first two norms depends upon two conditions. First, there must be adequate medical facilities available within easy reach of the concerned population. Secondly, the people must be aware of the facilities and of the measures required during gestation period.

According to the latest available information, there are 19 hospitals, 665 primary health centres and 7,699 primary health sub-centres to serve the rural population in Bihar. In addition, there are 986 dispensaries. Every primary health centre is expected to have three doctors. Thus the number of doctors posted in the primary health centres comes to 1995. In addition to their job requirement in primary health centres, they are required to visit health sub- centres a least once a week.

The statistical information given above reveals an inter esting account of the situation prevailing in rural Bihar. There is one primary health centre or a hospital for a rural population of 89,467 persons spreading over an area of2 49.5 sq. kilometres. The primary health centre is located at the Block Headquarters. If it is centrally located in the block, people living on the boundary of the area have to travel at least 8.9 kilometres.[1] In reality it is hardly so. Thus a person intending to attend a primary health centre has to trek down more than this distance. Similarly, a health sub- centre covers a population of 7,948 persons and an area of 22.2 sq. kilometres. Average distance between the people living at the boundary of its respective area and the sub centre comes to 2.6 kilometres. This distance may not seem to be far for a pregnant woman. But since sub-centres are looked after mainly by the Auxilliary Nurse Midwives, a pregnant woman who wants to have routine medical check up as well as treatment for anaemic diseases may not like to come to a sub-centre. Doctors posted at primary health centres are expected to visit sub-centres at least once a weak. But in reality this does not happen (Mandal, 1979, 1984 and 1985).

---

1. Formula used for calculating the distance between a primary health centre and the people living at the boundary of the area of it is as follows: A where A=Area of the PHC which is assumed to be circular in shape; =3.1416 approximately.

Doctors posted in primary health centres cannot be blamed for this. In addition to their routine duty in the centres, they are required to attend family welfare clinics and or ganise family planning camps from time to time. At present there are 1,995 doctors in rural Bihar who serve in 665 primary health centres and 7,699 sub centres. Every doctor serves nearly four sub-centres which spread over an area of 85.5 sq. kilometres. In other words, he has to travel a dis tance of nearly five kilometre one way to attend a sub-centre. Every primary health centre has only one jeep which often remains out of order for one reason or another. When it is in order, it is used mainly by the medical officer. The other doctors require to arrange their own conveyance. Most of the sub-centres are not linked with roads and during rainy seasons they often remain cut-off from the primary health centres.

Under the prevailing circumstances, it can hardly be ex pected that the pregnant women will be given routine antena tal check-up. Studies reveal that a few pregnant women, mostly from the well-off families, consult doctors in case of serious complications. In the first instance, they are taken to village quacks and on their failure, to doctors at primary health centre or nearby town. Under the anaemia con trol programme, folic acid and iron tablets, worth of thousands of rupees, are distributed among the poor pregnant women. But the number of actual beneficiaries may be counted on fingers. Most of the rural folk are unaware of such free medicines.

According to the norm, an expectant mother is required to have tetanus vaccine in three doses in the case of the first pregnancy and in two doses in subsequent pregnancies. It is administered from four to nine months of pregnancy and time gap between the doses may vary from 30 to 45 days. It is found that awareness of it among the villagers is almost ab sent. Only a few villagers, particularly those living in the vicinity of primary health centres, have some vague idea about it. Only some of them approach a doctor and get it done on payment.

During the gestation period, a woman is required to have balanced diet for her own health as well as for that of the child. Requirement of such diet seemed to have been known to the people of ancient India. In recognition of its impor tance, it was given religious sanctity in the form of "Ghod Bharai". In course of time, however, it lost its sig nificance and now it retains only its ritualistic overtone. In the present time availability of antenatal nourishment is related to several factors. Firstly, it is related to the economic condition of the family. In poor families, proper nourishment is unexpected for obvious reasons. But in well- to-do families also this is seldom provided. Secondly, it is conditioned by social status of women in families and in society at large. Females are considered socially inferior to men. This is reflected throughout a women's life and so cial practices manifest ample evidence of this inferiority. Birth of a female child is considered inauspicious and a so cial curse. In so far as the requirement of nourishment of pregnant women is concerned, it is mainly determined by those women who have crossed the age of reproduction. Their decision is often regulated by the traditionally approved practices than by notions of nutrition. Thirdly, practices regarding 'food distribution' system in the family provide lesser opportunity for nourishment of females. Food is dis tributed more in accordance with the status and position of an individual than for nutritional requirement. The head of the family and other adult male earners are served first, while women and female children receive what is left over. Male members hardly bother what and how much is left over. In the distribution of food, delicious items go in larger quantity to adult men. Similar distinction is maintained be tween male and female children. Thus pregnant women starve nutritionally and their starvation increases due to timing pattern of food intake. The usual time of taking breakfast by a women, irrespective of whether or not she is pregnant, is around 11 a.m. The lunch time varies from 2 p.m. to 3p.m. The dinner is over by 8 p.m. The time gap between dinner and breakfast is to the tune of fifteen hours or so. If digest ion needs a four-hour time, a woman remains in empty stomach for eleven hours. In the case of a pregnant women, it causes irreparable harm. If she seeks to take food in between or early, it brings ridicule. Moreover, she is afraid of mother-in-law's mandate.

Intranatal period

One of the important determinants of maternal and neonatal mortality is related to obstetric care. Medical science prescribes that the pregnant woman must be placed under the care of medical staff in primary health centre or sub-centre at the time of delivery. As this facility may not be avail able for all, it alternatively prescribes for a nurse or a trained Dai to attend on her. The fulfilment of the norma tive condition rests on three conditions. Firstly health centre or sub-centre must be within approachable distance. According to the available statistics, a health centre or a sub-centre lies within a radius of 2.6 kms. which can easily be approached in dry season. During the rainy season, however, it gets delinked with its surrounding human habitat. Secondly, a health centre or subcentre must be equipped with necessary facility. A health sub-centre is staffed by an Auxilliary Nurse Midwife. At time, she is as sisted by a health worker. Their presence at the sub-centre is uncertain as they are also charged with family planning responsibility. Bed-population ratio in rural areas is ex tremely inadequate. There is one bed for a population of 11,000 persons. Thirdly, enforcement of the norms is condi tioned by the availability of trained Dais in villages. In order to fulfil this condition, a programme of training the conventional Dais has been launched. Till March 1984, a to tal of 56,029 conventional Dais had been oriented with the current scientific knowledge of obstetric care. But these trained Dais are not uniformly dispersed all over rural areas. In certain areas, either they do not exist or their number is negligible. Moreover, in the absence of follow-up action, they have lapsed into conventional ways of obstetric care. Even if these pre-conditions are met adequately, norms may remain ineffective. Customarily every village has a num ber of conventional Dais and each has a fixed clintele. The break in the relationship is considered undesirable and may also pose problem in future. Moreover, child birth is ex clusively a private affair. Obstetric care at health centre or sub-centre is derogatory from the view of traditional norm.

Postnatal period

Infant and child morbidity and mortality are precipitated by the interaction of malnutrition and infection. To counter this situation, medical science and science of nurtition provide a number of guidelines to child care and health. These guidelines are as follows: (1) Infant must be breast- fed within three or four hours after birth; (2) first milk of the mother must not be wasted; (3) Infants must receive adequate supplement to breast milk from fourth month of in fancy and sufficient food in the early years of childhood; and (4) infant must receive immunization against common preventable diseases.

In rural areas of Bihar breast feeding is the most common phenomenon. Rural mothers are more concerned about their children than about their own physique. The physique con sciousness as prevails among a section of urban women, has not percolated down to rural areas. However, mother's milk is not fed to the infant immediately after birth. First, he is given a few drops of honey and this is followed by water mixed with sugar candy for a day or so.

Breast feeding starts after a day and in certain cases after two days. In case the infant has a low birth weight, he is breast fed by some other lactating mother and not by his own mother. First milk of the mother which is commonly called 'Fenus' or 'Finsa' is not fed to the infant as it is considered unwholesome and it may cause diarrhoea. Some people think that by taking out a few drops of breast milk, effect of evil spirit is warded off.

Conventionally, an infant is not given any supplement to breast milk till the age of one year or dentition (Mandal 1979,1984, and 1985; Verma, 1985), Solid food is given only from early childhood. With the increase in age, quantity of food increases. Rarely any attention is paid to its quality. Thus rural children receive poor supplement to breast milk in the later part of infancy and insufficient food in the childhood.

The major causes of infant and child mortality are common preventable diseases and gastro-intestinal infections. Many of these causes of death are amenable to immunization. The best period for immunization against polio, tetanus, diph theria, whooping cough and measles is the infancy, that is, between 3 to 9 months. The vaccines are said to be made available in primary health centres and sub-centres. But these remain mostly unutilised or under utilised. There is little effort by the health staff to immunise the child and the villagers are also ignorant of it. A recent survey of certain development Blocks reveals that about one percent of the children in these areas received vaccination but most of them did not receive the required number of doses of it (Mandal 1984, and 1985).

III

The facts stated above reveal that little effort has been extended to encourage use of government health care facilities. Few people are aware of promotive services being offered, even of immunization or antenatal services. There are frequent reports of charging for medical services by primary health staff which are supposed to be free. The Auxilliary Nurse Midwives are charged with responsibility for preventive and promotive services including antenatal care. In recent years their family planning responsibilities have allegedly taken over their entire effort; consequently the wider task of health care has become difficult. Neither the primary health centre staff nor the Auxiliary Nurse Mid wives effectively cover the required target population. Achievements in preventive and in maternal and child serv ices are far below requirement.

Acceptability of health care and child care is also hampered by the conflict between traditional norms and those advocated by extra-familial institutions. Resolution of this conflict is a long term issue. It is directly linked with educational level of the people and with their individual economic status. But health awareness among the people need to be created. Increased health education is needed par ticularly of the parents who should know the different dis eases against which infants can be immunised, the number of doses for each vaccine and the age at which the vaccines are to be given. The parents should know the nutritional requirements of mothers and children, the quality and quan tity of food to be given and the age at which supplement to breast milk to be given. The efforts in this direction have to be stepped up through radio broadcast, printed materials and interpersonal communication.

The recent recommendation by the study group consisting of social scientists, AIR and ICDS functionaries to use the media Radio for broadcasting messages on mother and child care is a sound move (Verma, 1985). It is hoped this will facilitate or accelerate resolution of conflict between traditional norms and those advocated by the extra-familial norms.

It, however, does not mean that tradition and development are always in incompatible relations. In fact, they are at times in agreement with each other. Traditional norm of breast feeding, for example, has been re-emphasised by the science of nutrition. It attempts to re-educate those edu cated urban-based mothers, who refuse breast feeding, regarding its necessity for proper physical and mental development of the child and of the mother.

Some of the traditional norms have been continuing mainly because the people are unaware of any better alternatives. For example, the child is given supplement to breast feeding only after dentition or when he is one year old or so. By food the people mean only that which is eaten by chewing. Naturally an infant is given supplementary food in the early year of childhood. Awareness about supplementary food which does not require chewing, can reverse the present tradi tional practices. The people are also not aware of any bet ter obstetric care than what is available at present in the villages. Inavailability of modern obstetric care is the major reason for the continuance of the services by tradi tional dais.

Ignorance delays acceptance of developmental norms. The people, for example, are not aware of immunization. The availability of necessary vaccines is also inadequate. Necessary knowledge about immunization will facilitate its internalisation.

Developmental norms may be in conflict with traditional norms when the internalisation of former norms necessitate change in structural relations. Women in our society are considered inferior to men. This notion governs the relationships between the sexes. If the pregnant woman is given preference in respect of food intake, traditional norms regarding food distribution in the family are upset. Similarly, acceptance of modern norm for small size family assumes absence of hankering for male children. It follows that there would be no distinction between male and female children. This is in contradiction to societal norm. Tradi tional norms may therefore hinder institutionalisation of developmental norms when they encourage structural change.

It may be concluded that norms regarding child development can be institutionalised with lesser 'difficulty if they do not pose challenge to the continuance of traditional norms. The conflict between traditional and developmental norms can be resolved only with the passage of time and with the grow ing awareness about the inadequacy of traditional norms in achieving the concept of development.

REFERENCES

Johson, H.M. 1960 Sociology: A Systematic Introduction, Allied Publishers Pvt. Lt. Bombay.

Mandal, B.B. and Sinha, K.K. 1979 Rural Children (Mimeographed), ANSISS, Patna.

Mandal, B.B. 1984 Social Inputs in Area Development : Khagaria; (Mimeographed), ANSISS, Patna.

Mandal B.B. 1985 Social Inputs in Area Development : Bagaha of West Champaran; (Mimeographed) ANSISS, Patna.

Ministry of Health & Family Planning, 1984 Health Statistics of India; Govt. of India.

Department of Social Welfare, 1974 Programme of Integrated Child Care Services; Govt. of India.

Rajendran, M.M. 1980 National Policy for Children; in "Profile of the Child in India-Policies and Programme", Min istry of Social Welfare, Govt. of India.

UNICEF 1981 An Analysis of the Situation of Children in In dia.

Verma, K.K. 1985 Integrated Report on the Studies on Profile of Children for Media Support to ICDS Programme; (In Hindi), (Mimeographed), ANSISS, Patna.

THIRTEEN

Hetukar Jha

Colonial Legacy and Higher Education in Bihar

Development in education is closely linked with social progress. Therefore, the system of education of any society has to be analysed for understanding the way it works - it may contribute to social change in one context from one point of view while in another context of time and space its working may cause dissatisfaction in the society concerned. As far as the situation of Bihar is concerned, the observa tions and conclusions of several seminars, inquiry com mittees and journalistic reports narrate in vivid terms the threat arising out of the free play of sectarian forces and government control to the field of education here.[1] In the present paper, an attempt has been made to explain these two trends in terms of colonial legacy by drawing references from the records of the history of British rule in India.

Inditially, the East India Company Government followed the policy of neutrality towards education in India. However, some voluntary associations such as Calcutta Free School society, Calcutta Benevolent Institution, the Society For Promoting the Education of the poor, the Bombay Native School Book and school society etc. and a few individuals like Warren Hastings and Jonathan Duncan

1. Jha, Hetukar, Colonial Context of Higher Education in India (Patna University from 1917 to 1951: A Sociological Appraisal); Usha Publishing New Delhi, 1985, p. 11.

took a steps for the cause of education on their own.[2] Simultaneously, ef forts were also made for the incorporation of education as one of responsibilities of the East India Company which succeeded in a way as a clause of education was included in the East India Company Act of 1813.[3] This clause set out two broad objectives of education in India, first[4] "the revival and improvement of literature and the encouragement of the learned natives of India" and second, "the introduction and promotion of a knowledge of the sciences among the in habitants of the British territories in India". The Act however, remained silent about on the way these objectives had to be pursued and consequently, the period from 1813 to 1835 witnessed a constant conflict of ideas which were ad vanced on this issue.

There were protagonists of elitist education who did not reconcile to the views of those of mass education. The former group was also divided into two camps, the acciden talists and the Orientalists. The court of directors to the Governor-General in Council of Bengal favoured the ideas of promoting oriental education of Persian/Arabic and Sanskrit in 1814.[5] Subsequently, the General Committee of Public In struction was constituted in 1823 which also followed the policy of supporting Oriental education justifying the adop tion of filtration theory of education as a matter of policy.[6] The filtration theory implies that [7] "knowledge in troduced from abroad should descend from the higher classes and gradually spread through their example". However, voices were raised against the filtration theory of education in 1823 and the need for educating the children of the then peasantry was emphasized.[8] Though the General Committee of Public Instruction remained firm on its above mentioned policy, the issue of mass education did not subside.

2. Ibid, pp. 20-21
3. Ibid, p. 23
4. Sharp, H. (ed.) Selections From Educational Records; Part-1, Government Printing, Calcutta, 1920, p.22
5. Ibid, pp. 22-23
6. Ibid, p. 23
7. Host Mackenzie's note on the policy of the General Com mittee of Public Instruction Dated the 17th of July 1823, see Sharp H, op.cit, pp.57-60.
8. Jha, Hetukar, op.cit, p.26

William Adam, a strong advocate of Vernacular or mass education, was appointed by Bentinck in 1835 to inquire into the working of this education which had a large network in Bihar and Bengal at that time.

Table 1

	UPPER CASTES	NO.			
1.	Brahman	256	22.	Barhi	35
2.	Magadha	468	23.	Suvarnabanik	31
3.	Kayastha	220	24.	Aguri	21
4.	Rajput	150	25.	Luniar	20
			26.	Kansyabanik	20
	Total	1094	27.	Chhatri	1
			28.	Barayi	1
		(37.5%)	29.	Churihara	1
			30.	Kayali	1
	NON UPPER CASTES		31.	Kahar	102
			32.	Napit	39
1.	Gandhabanik	540	33.	Mali	16
2.	Teli	271	34.	Banawar	14
3.	Koiri	200	35.	Beldar	8
4.	Halwakar	66	36.	Khatki	2
5.	Sunri	56	37.	Tanti	1
6.	Kurmi	55	38.	Mahla	1
7.	Swarnakar	51	39.	Kalwar	18
8.	Mahuri	41	40.	Baiti	1
9.	Goala	38	41.		
10.	Tamil	16			
11.	Bhatta	15		Total :	1777
12.	Sanyasi	14			
13.	Lohar	13			(61 %)
14.	Lahari	13			
15.	Kumar	10		SCHEDULED CASTES	
16.	Kandu	9			
17.	Yugi	8	1.	Dosad	23
18.	Bundela	4	2.	Pashi	22
19.	Patowar	4	3.	Dhobi	1
20.	Vaishnava	2	4.	Musahar	1
				TOTAL :	47
					(1.61%)

Adam's report is quite revealing in the sense that it provides the most elaborate account of Vernacular education which prevailed at least during the early nineteenth cen tury. There were more than a lakh of Vernacular schools in the villages of Bihar and Bengal.[9] In

---

9. Basu, A.N. (ed.) Reports on the state of Education in Bengal (1835-1838) By William Adam; University of Calcutta, 1941 p.480

Bihar, he personally conducted the survey of such schools in the villages of Tir hut (North Bihar) and South Bihar (Patna - Gaya). In the districts of south Bihar, there were two hundred and eighty five schools with teachers drawn from both upper and non- upper castes.[10]

Table 2

TIRHUT

UPPER CASTE

		NO.
1.	Rajput	62
2.	Kayastha	51
3.	Brahman	25
4.	Magadha	18
	Total :	156 (31.07%)

NON UPPER CASTES

1.	Rajput	62
2.	Kayastha	51
3.	Brahman	25
4.	Teli	29
5.	Mayra	28
6.	Swarnkar	25
7.	Kandu	18
8.	Aguri	17
9.	Kurmi	11
10.	Luniar	9
11.	Goala	8
12.	Kahatriya	7
13.	Koiri	5
14.	Tamil	4
15.	Kumar	4
16.	Kansari	4
17.	Kaivarta	2
18.	Chhaipikar	2
19.	Parsua	2
20.	Lahari	2
21.	Sutar	2
22.	Kahtti	1
23.	Mahla	6
24.	Dhanuk	5
25.	Napit	4
26.	Kahar	2
	Total	341 (67.92%)

SCHEDULED CASTES

1.	Pashi	5
		(0.99%)

A list of the students of these schools was prepared by Adam who also mentioned the names of the castes from which those

10. Ibid, p.243

students were drawn.[11] This list has been presented in table I under the categories of upper castes, scheduled castes (lower castes) and other castes (consisting of the rest). Besides the Hindu students, there were one hundred and seventy two Muslim students whose sects have not been mentioned.[12] Table I shows that the majority of stu dents were drawn from non-upper castes. Even schedule caste members has an access to this education at that time. Almost similar was the situation in Tirhut (see Table-2) when Adam had visited the Vernacular schools (eighty in number) there.[13] Teaching profession at this level was not the mo nopoly of the upper castes.[14]

The syllabus was more or less uniform in both the parts of Bihar and covered courses on commercial accounts, agricul tural accounts and some works of Hindi.[15] This uniformity in the contents of instruction over a large tract of land indi cates that this system of education was fairly institu tionalized and was closely related to the needs of the people at large.

Adam wanted this network of education to be supported and improved, as according to him, this was the real national education and this alone could help in national regenera tion.[16] But the attitude of the Government was already decided in favour of the elitist education. In the twenties of the last century, the conflict centred around the issue of Oriental education versus English education both of which were meant for elites only. The case of English education however gradually gained in strength at it was supported by David Hare, Raja Ram Mohan Roy, christian missionaries and[17] "the middle classes ... to whom a knowledge of English was a sure passport to service and who, therefore, clamoured for the introduction of English". Anglo-Indians and Junior civil servants also joined hands with the above.[18] Later, Macaulay gave a final blow to

11. Ibid, pp.244-245
12. Ibid
13. Ibid, pp.245-247
14. Ibid
15. Ibid
16. See Introduction by A.N. Basu, op. cit, p.XXVI
17. Ibid, P. XV
18. Jha, Hetukar, op.cit, p.31

the orientalists by forwarding a long minute[19] for the cause of English education in India in 1835 to William Bentinck who gave his [20] "entire concurrence to the sentiments expressed in this Minute". Macaulay asserted that mass education was not practicable, Oriental education was a waste of talent and resources and English education was the only hope for the future of India.[21] He recommended in clear terms that [22] in one point I fully agree with the gentlemen to whose general views I am opposed...it is impos sible to attempt to educate the body of the people ...We must at present do our best to form a class who may be in terpreters... a class of persons Indian in blood and colour, but English in tastes, in opinions, in morals and in intel lect. To that class we may leave it to refine the Vernacular dialects of the country, ...and to render them by degrees fit vehicles for conveying knowledge to the great mass of the population". The 'gentlemen' who Macaulay opposed were the orientalists and the one point on which he agreed with them was the policy of filtration theory of education against that of mass education enunciated above. Education in India began to take a shape in accordance with the sug gestions of Macaulay. Mass education was ignored. Oriental education was discouraged and English education was favoured to grow among the upper and the upper middle class people so that the latter might work as "interpreters" between the rulers and the ruled. The objective of English education was defined in a way that only the upper sector of Indian society could have an access to it and above all its primary function was limited to serve the rulers' interests. Educa tion in India thus became sectarian in scope and subordinate to political sphere.

Some Scholars of the history of education in India such as H. Sharp[23] and B.B. Misra[24] contend that the education in troduced under the colonial rule was a middle class educa tion based on the freedom of opportunity. But, the essence of the filtration theory of

---

19. See Minute of Hon'ble T.B. Macaulay, dated the 2nd February, 1835, Sharp, H., op.cit, p.107-117
20. Ibid
21. Ibid
22. Ibid, p. 116
23. Sharp, H. op.cit, Introduction p.III
24. Misra, B.B. The Indian Middle Classes, Oxford Univer sity Press, 1961, p.149

education (discussed before) which was adopted as a matter of policy to be pursued in In dia by the authorities of the East India Company Government, is not compatible with the above interpretation of English education as a middle class education. Freedom of oppor tunity in this context was meant only for the upper sector of society. The net work of Vernacular education centres in villages could not flourish as the Government refused to support it. At the sametime, the British also adopted a policy of resumption of revenue-free grant of lands on which these institutions depended for their maintenance.[25] These two policy decisions eventually led to the collapse of the system of Vernacular education which existed at the grassroot level. Freedom of opportunity in the context of education for the people in general could have been meaning ful at this level alone. But, that was denied; the British policy, rather, paved the way for the elite sector's monopo lization of education in India which was a departure from the situation that existed before.

There were two kinds of education in Bihar in those days, viz. classical education and Vernacular education. Classical education included Persian/Arabic and Sanskrit. In the early nineteenth century, there were five hundred and twentynine Persian/Arabic schools in Tirhut and Patna - Gaya taken together.[26] The total number of students was 2084 (101 Arabic and 1983 Persian).[27] Among the Persian students, the representation of Hindus was approximately two times more than that of Muslims.[28] The Hindu students were drawn from various castes, both high and low, such as Kayastha, Brah man, Rajput, Bhumihar Brahman, Teli, Kamar, Napit, Kurmi, Koery, Kalal, Swarnakar etc.[29] It is, thus, clear that this education was open to all irrespective of caste and communal consideration in the same way as was the system of Ver nacular education discussed before. In this respect, Sanskrit education alone

25. Stevenson-Moore, C.J. Final Report on the Survey and Settlement Operation in the Muzaffarpur District 1899; Government Printing Press, Patna, p.85

26. Basu, A.N. op.cit, pp.287-290

27. Ibid

28. Ibid

29. Ibid

was an exception as it was confined to only Brahmans.[30] Elsewhere, it has been discussed by the author of this paper that this education had already fallen in a state of decadence.[31] Persian had replaced it as a lan guage of state administration much earlier and therefore, its relevance in this context had been lost. The eighteenth century was a long period of political turmoil and transi tion and this might have effected the loss of the Zamindars' and Rajas' patronage on which Sanskrit education depended to some extent. The cumulative effect of these factors was that its significance could not be appreciated beyond the sphere of religious rituals. The situation was perhaps different in pre-Mughal days when philosophical importance of Sanskrit was acknowledged widely.[32] However, it is difficult to admit what scholars such as R.V. Parulekar, Pandit Sunder Lal, J.P. Naik and others believe that the educational sector as a whole was not accessible to non-upper castes before the introduction of English education.[33] Education included all the three types **viz.** Sanskrit, Arbic/Persian and Vernacular. The data available in this context, discussed before, present a picture contrary to the view held by the above scholars. At least in Persian/Arabic and Vernacular educa tion which attracted the largest number of students, caste and communal factor were not at all considered. There were eight hundred and ninety four schools of Vernacular and Persian/Arabic education in Tirhut and Patna-Gaya whereas the number of Sanskrit schools in these two regions taken together was only eighty five when Adam had conducted his survey.[34] This shows that the combined sector of Persian/Arabic and Vernacular education virtually had an overwhelming appeal in comparison with that of Sanskrit education among the consumers of education who represented both high and low layers of society. Therefore, the view that educational consumption depended on sectarian con sideration before the introduction of English education can not be held valid.

It was the colonical power which imposed this rationale and that too for facilitating their own rule. State superor dination or

30. Ibid
31. Jha, Hetukar, op.cit, pp. 40-41
32. Roerich, George, The Blue Annals; Motilal Banarasidass p.390
33. Pal, Dharam, Our Village School Master; The Times of India. Sunday Review, August 21, 1983 p.8
34. Basu, A.N. (ed.) op.cit, pp.287-290

control of education was also a new experience in India as never before in history could one find an evidence of this kind in any field of philosophy, litera ture, grammer etc., though a tradition of employing scholars in courts continued till recent days.

The tradition of English education was, thus formally in augurated in 1835 for the then elite sector to serve the colonial interests. These two considerations formed the core of British policy in this respect.

For a few decades following 1835, English education was practically ignored by Bihari elites. [35] The situation changed in the last quarter of the nineteenth century when they realized the importance of this education for con solidating their status.[36] Then, they took keen interest in expanding the higher education in Bihar. After the estab lishment of Patna College (in 1863), five colleges were set up in Bihar by the end of the last century. Four of which (Viz. T.N.J. College, now T.N.B. College of Bhagalpur, B.N. College, Patna; Diamond Jubilee College, Now R.D. and D.J. College, Monghyr; and Greer Bhumihar Brahman College, now L.S. College, Muzaffarpur) owed their existence to the ef forts of upper caste influentials[37] (Zamindars and English educated men). Only one, St. Colomba's College was started by the Dublin University Mission at Hazaribagh.[38]

The last quarter of the nineteenth century was also a period of the rise of sectarian tendencies in Bihar. The up per caste elites started organizing their respective caste associations for securing benefits to their caste men.
[39] Later, non-upper caste men also followed them in this ven tures.[40] The British authorities following its policy of divide and rule instigated such activities.[41] Job in ad ministration became a central

35. Jha, Hetukar, op.cit, pp.47-48

36. Ibid

37. Ibid

38. Ibid

39. Ibid, p.48

40. Ibid

41. Ibid, p.117

issue behind Bihari-Bengali feeling which eventually caused the speration of Bihar and orissa from Bengal in 1912.[42] The early decades of the precent century in Bihar were so dominated by the sectarian forces that even the creation of Patna University in 1916-17 could not escape their thrust.[43]

At the time when Patna University bill was introduced, M.M. Malaviya, Tej Bahadur Sapru and C.H. Setalvad objected vehemently to the provision of state control over the university.[44] Important journals such as *The Times of India, The Modern Review, Hindu, Indian Social Reform, Punjabi* etc. also expressed dissatisfaction in this context.[45] But, the Bihari elites (represented by Krishna Sahaya and Mazharul Haque) welcomed the Patna University bill which provided for government control in the matters of the appointment of the Vice-chancellor and the composition of Senate and Syndicate. [46] The Bihari elites were under the spell of anti-Bengali agitation and wanted to get rid of "the continuance of ...dependence on the Calcutta University for educational requirements".[47] This helped the Government in in stitutionalizing its control over the university in accord ance with its education policy of 1835 discussed before.

The university started functioning under the vigorous con trol of the state government though voices were raised against it at times by individuals such as Sachchidanand Sinha and a few local Journals.[48] An analysis of the avail able registers of admission forms of Patna University shows that until 1942, approximately 92% of the total number of students came from the upper castes.[49] Since upper caste men dominated the elite sector before independence, one may as sume that this centre of higher education worked exclusively for

42. Ibid, p.54
43. Ibid, pp.55-57
44. Ibid, p.59
45. Ibid, pp.60-61
46. Ibid, pp.59-60
47. See "Speech of Krishna Sahaya" Bihar Provincial Tracts I, Published by Rajendra Prasad, Bankipore.
48. Jha, Hetukar, op.cit, p. 120
49. Ibid, p.80

the promotion of elites' interests. The spirit of the resolution of 1835 which emphasized the sectarian bent in education (discussed before) was, thus, manifested without any alteration in Bihar.

The elites who were granted the privilege of English education in the beginning gradually realized that this could help in reinforcing their status. Consequently, since the second half of the last century, influentials of each constituent caste of the elite sector started making efforts for securing more and more of this privilege for their respective caste men, as this opened the gate for securing other privileges also. Sectarianism, thus, came to dominate social and political life in Bihar and began to effect the university education also. It became so rampant on the cam pus that in 1946 Sir C.P.N. Sinha, the then Vice-chancellor, expressed his annoyance at this phenomenon.[50] In 1950, again, Sarangdhar Sinha who was the Vice-chancellor then, made his dissatisfaction with this trend clear to the mem bers of the Patna University Senate.[51]

Until 1951-52, Bihar had only one university viz. Patna University. This university is, therefore, considered to be the pace-setter for other universities which have been es tablished after independence. The sectarianism and govern ment control which came in force in this university at the instance of the colonial power, gradually became so much in stitutionalized in the educational sphere here during the period before independence that even the present day campus life not only of the Patna University but of all the other universities of this state succumbs to their grip. Under the circumstances, it is necessary for the policy-makers as well as the educationists to evolve a suitable strategy for coun tering these colonial legacies in order to promote the quality of education.

---

50. Ibid, p.122
51. Ibid.

FOURTEEN

C.S.P. Sinha

Tradition and Development : The Context of Education

When the two terms 'Tradition' and Development' are jux taposed with each other, they could mean either of the three:

a) Tradition as a motive/source for Development,

b) Tradition as an obstacle to development,

c) The two terms being desparate in nature have a mere sym biotic relationship. By and large, however, when people talk of them as such they take it mostly in the second sense which may not always be correct.

In the context of a country like India called "Mahamanver Samudra" by Tagore - with history going back to millenia and a cockpit of races and people coming together fighting, mixing and then living together, it is very difficult to define the term tradition very accurately. Then we have the twofold division adopted by many sociologists and his torians, the **Great tradition** and the **Little Tradition** (Srinivas: 1972 p. 26) with accompanying features like those of Brahmanization or sanskritization (Ibid p. 1-46) on the one hand and Tribalization (Ibid. p. 19) on the other. There is hardly any custom prevailing among the Hindus and Muslims - the two major communities that is not an admixture of the two. Historically speaking we have the queer phenomena of simultaneity of ancient, medieval and modern traditions flourishing side by side not only in case of communities but at times discernible as a backdrop of an individual's dif ferent roles and his behaviour pattern.

From bullock cart (with investment as big as railways) to sattlelite all jostling together is really a wonder. Development, too, is one word with many facets. It could be used in case of an individual from a psychological point of view when it is referred to his growing maturity over the years - may through his whole life. In the context of Society it could mean more of social cohesion, Society's capacity to be stable and changing simultaneously, a ra tional, secular scientific outlook on life of its members (which means predominance of the rational over the irra tional forces buried deep in society's psyche). In the field of politics we associate it with national identity, good government ensuring equality of opportunity for all, more of popular participation in day today governance of the country. In the economic field, where, incidentally, the term is used most frequently, it stands for a high level of production both at primary and secondary levels, a system of equitable distribution and a high level per capita consump tion of amenities of life, e.g. (1) Good and nutrition; (2) Clothing; (3) Housing including sanitation; (4) Health facilities; (5) Educational facilities; (6) Information Media; (7) Energy consumption; (8) Transportation (Myrdal, G: 1968, Vol. I; 538). We usually associate it with higher life expectancy with a low rate of population growth. The developed economy is visualised as one which is by an large self-reliant and has crossed the threshold of 'take-off,[1] stage, where internal savings, generate income sufficient to upkeep the nation as a whole as also individual's constitut ing it prosperous. One could think of many more fields both from the view point of individuals and society where the concept of development could be applied with justification.

As things stand today economic considerations have become all too important and therefore when we talk of education in the context of development, we have to stress more on the economic life, of the community or the nation.

Education incidentially has traditions of its own. When ever a gathering of teachers is addressed by politicians in variably there is a reference to the glorious tradition which they partake-tradition not only going back to Nalanda or Vikramshila but to the Upnishadic

1. The term was first used by W.W. Rostow in his 'stages of Economic growth (Cambridge 1960) and has since then became fashionable to use it in the context of economic growth of the 3rd world countries. Rostow proposes a non-Marxian model of economic/social development in the said book.

period as well. Teachers of today who are mere jobbers are reminded of their being descendents of Vashistha, Vishwamitra and Yajnvalkya. Even the Holy Qoran is quoted to the effect that 'seek learning from four quarters of the world'. "It is no use preaching homilies on the nobility of the teaching profes sion. Hunger and want deprive one of all idealism" (Jha; A.N. 1954, p. 103). Again unfortunately, there is another tradition as well of the late Moghul and early British period reflected in sayings like -

"Man Malin Tanse Ati Chhin Tin Kanh Rai Mudarris Keen".[2]
"Parehn Pharsi Bechen Tel Dekho Yeh Kudarat Ka Khel".[3]
"Aab Aab Kari Beta Marige Kabhi na Manga Pani

Aisi farsi beta parhen - apne pran sirani"[4] & so on. **Aruni**, **Eklabya**, **Uttank** and **Satyakama**[5] can not play the role of super go for our student community of today. An appeal to Brahmanic, Buddhist or Islamic Traditions of learning is equally irrelevant today for the simple reason that 'Sarva Dharma Rajdharme Prevista'.[6] As is the ruler so is the Dharma[7] not in the narrow sectarian sense but in the larger sense of Rta [8] holding the Universe together by sheer moral force.

Unfortunately the second, if not the first generation, of learners of modern schools and colleges became its greatest critics. Regarded as a foreign edifice planted on the native soil with no roots,[9] being imparted in an alien tongue which inspite of 150 years or more has not reached the 2nd man in a hundred. With an eye on job rather

2. An adege popular in Bhojpuri speaking areas of U.P. and Bihar, depiciting the poor quality and status of the teach ing profession.

3. Another common saying widely prevailing in Bihar till the time when persian used to be the language of culture in Bihar and speaks of the uselessness of classical education.

4. Reinforces '3'.

5. All are referred to in early Upnishads.

6. A saying attributed to Bhishma in the Mahabharat (Shantiparva).

7. Raja Kalasya Karanam'. Mbh: SP 69-71.

8. A Vedic term standing for cosmic law; providing the basis for 'Satya' Truth which is its effect.

9. The idea was first elaborated by Arther Mayhew in his 'Education in Modern India'.

then character, con cerned more with degree and examination than with knowledge, producing a hybrid **'Babu'**, Bhadra Lok'[10] not at ease either at home or office it was all useless, nay harmful. As Ravindranath put it poetically, it was just like a light flickering in a fast moving train with darkness all around.[11]

As ill luck would have it all our efforts whether taken at the initiative of great man like Tagore and Gandhi or pursued by various reformist associations like Arya Samaj and Ramkrishna Mission or as a result of measures taken by the Government at the advice of individuals, committees and commissions have failed to produce the desired results. There may be found some jetsam and floatsam left around in a few institutions here and there of all these suggested measures but on the whole we have a system of education that has failed to serve the cause of development, economic, so cial or political, leave aside its own.

We therefore have to answer two related questions: one what is to be done to set the house of education in order and second, what do we expect from education to do for development ?

As for the first question, the answer has been, debated for more than a century by officials - non-officials, teachers, non-teachers all alike. Everyone feels that our education suffers from wrong priorities. We should have had more schools and fewer colleges for general education - more in stitutions for technical training at the lower level than prestigious Engineering and Medical Colleges and All-India Institutions, more emphasis on adult/social education im parted through voluntary agencies than formal schools which we have failed to provide with bare necessities for their sheer existence. (Myrdal, G., 1968, III p. 1651-96). Teachers at each level are working more on trade union lines than as path finders for social change. In the hopeless run for quantity - quality has been sacrificed. Even the ig norant masses have a feeling that middle school graduate of a generation earlier was better equipped than a matriculate of today. With the whole gamut of selective telective tests on All-India basis for merit scholarship, with all our search for

10. A theme popularised by Cambridge School of historians of India's freedom struggle (Treating in rather federal character notably by Anil Seal in 'Soundings in S.E. Asian History'and 'Emergence of Indian Nationalism'.

11. Rabindranath Tagore in 'Letters on Russia' (Ruser Chithi).

'national talent' - our education continues to be urban oriented, elitist in nature and cut off from the na tive soil. Not that these ills have not been diagnosed - what is lacking is the will in us to give it a different direction. It reminds one of Schopenhaur's dictum that 'you could do as you please but you could not please as you would please'. Even political parties claiming to be mouthpiece of the downtrodden have little or no policy on education. When the Kerala Government in 1957 attempted to nationalise mis sion schools, the Government itself had to go; when West Bengal tried to replace a primer in Bengali which smacked of feudal culture, it was forced to retrace its steps by the intellectual gainst of Bengal like Suniti Chatterji and Nihar Ranjan Ray. Both cases show how thin is the veneer of democracy in India. For mere survival we have not been able to get rid of English either. There is a craze for English medium schools which have spread like wildfire all over the country. Curriculum has been enriched, better text books are available, teachers are toleravly better paid than their counter-parts of the days of yore. Examination papers have been remodelled on new lines but it has not been well managed with results all too well known. One has a feeling that this is all due to the weakness of a 'soft state', (Myrdal, G. op. cit I, p.66), in an old society but a new nation'. We have tried to plan but at every stage we have fumbled, the number of educated unemployed goes on increas ing, the erosion of talent through brain drain persists.

As for development in different fields we find confusion worse confounded. Caste which was losing its grip became all too important because of politics of elections at different levels. Caste did serve a very useful purpose both in North and South India for the spread of education. Many a school and college was set up by different castes primarily for educating their children but none of them exclusive in character. Now that all the institutions from Primary to University (which enjoys a notional academic freedom as the purse strings are held by state government or the U.G.C.) are under the thumb of Government. The queer phenomenon of teacher absentieesm has made its impact felt at all levels of education. The two revolutionary ideas mooted by Indian Education Commission (1964-66) which called its Report "Education For National Development", those of common school and neighbourhood school' were rejected by the Parliamentary committee set up to examine it. Nor could the two national policies enunciated in 1968 and 1979 by congress and Janata Governments respectively dare talk about it.

Even the N.E.P. keeps almost mum... The three language formula was cold storaged mostly by Hindi States (which brought in Sanskrit through the backdoor) and militant Tamil and Bengali sub-nationalism. The same fate overtook work experience and so cially useful productive work which had killed Bapu's craft in the nascent stage of Basic Education.

The same scenerio is repeating itself in the field of economic development. Gross National Product and per capita income have gone up but number of people below poverty line as defined by Government itself has gone up in equal measure. Land Reforms have helped only the upper crust of large tenants and all schemes launched by government for rural uplift and uplift of the poor have made the rich richer and the poor poorer.

However, there is no reason to despair. We could still delineate some of the broad features of development, economic, political and social, where education could play a crucial role provided, of course, if its own house is set in order.

All-round development of a society demands a growing knowledge (of which the quantum is supposed to be doubling every 7 years) now in different fields to be widely diffused either through formal/non-formal schooling, (in the context of India, 'Deschooling (ILLICH, 1, 1973) is ruled out at the moment though the 'school may be dead' (Reimer, E. 1971) in the West and may be providing only 'compulsory miseducation;). Mass media fortunately has cast its net wide.

It further requires both trained personnel at different levels of work with a further provision for their updating their knowledge and skills.

Above all it demands a forward looking scientific outlook on life on the part of society in general and teachers in particular.

This means that we have to have a corpus of job analyses which would help us in planning the training programmes at different levels. It further requires that education to serve the purpose must be deemed a life long process.[12] Education has been conceived as a preparetion for the unknown - this means we have to keep our doors and windows open all the time. But as Gandhiji put it - "he would like fresh wind blowing into his house from all directions - but not so strongly as to throw him off his feet".[13] This clearly means that education though oriented to the future need not be cut off from the past. History it to the people what memory is to the individual. It helps them realise and maintain their identity.

We had a very rich tradition of oral education in our country.[14] Katha and Kirtan, Lilas and dramas - all kept our people - though illiterate in the technical sense - alive to what was best in our tradition which was highlighted by Anand Cooumar Cooumar Swami in his 'Bughear of literacy' published as early as 1949. Now the most revolutionary educationist of today Paulo Friere is saying precisely the same thing.[15] J.P. talked about **participatory democracy**. Friere tells us about participatory education - where there is mutual give and take between the teacher and the learner and which aims at avoiding the 'banking' method wherein pupils are on the receiving end only.

Thus a happy blending of tradition with modernity[16] in education alone could help education play the crucial role it is supposed to do.

Education at best is a sub-system of the social system and left to itself, it is bound to be stagnant and moribund, positively harmful for social growth.

---

12. UNESCO 1973 'Learning to be': A summary of the Report has been published by NCERT. The companion volume 'Education on the Move' (Delhi 1973) provides the background papers on this them. IIEP (Paris) has published an annotated bibliog raphy, with the same title (listing English & french titles only).

13. Mahatma Gandhi in his 'Basic Education' - a collection of his writings on Education published by Navjivan Trust.

14. For details, K.M. Sen's Hinduism (Penguin) and V.S. Agarawal's ~Prachin Bhartiya Lokdharma' may be found help ful.

15. Paulo Friere, Pedagogy of the Oppressed (Penguin 1973) argues his case rather convincingly.

16. The theme is fully discussed in 'Old Societies & New States' (Ed) clifford Geertz (Amerind): Indian Edition, New Delhi, 1971.

Development - especially economic development - has a dynamics of its own. It creates new needs, new relationships and releases new social forces. What education could do is to make them a little polished by making people acquire so cial sensitivity, social knowledge and social skills. Even the most illiterate farmer has taken to new agriculture most avidly. Industrialisation has weakened the forces of parochialism, casteism, untouchability and all such social evils. Films have broken the language barrier. So what education could do for development was simply this. The haphzard change working in the wake of industrial changes could be made more meaningful to serve the purpose of society as a whole. This is not to say that education be made all too subservient to the demand of developing economy- after all education can not be conceived as totally cut off from tradition. As Dr. Zakir Hussain put it, 'education is subjective revivification of the objective goods of culture'.[17] After all, it is tradition that keeps us bound together. Tradition itself as such is not a bondage; it is rather a source of inspiration provided we do not become what Alberuni told about his contemporary Indians - dogmatic and inward looking and having a feeling of self-righteousness which was uncalled for'.[18]

It has been established by economists of education on em pirical evidence that if per capita income is to go up say from $ 200 to $ 300 per annum, literacy must reach 40%. Literacy beyond 70% ceases to be operative from the view point of economic growth.[19] But even this limited target is far off.

Next we have to create genuine leadership at the inter mediate level by imparting them knowledge of what has been called

---

17. The phrase is from Dr. Zakir Hussain's 2nd Patel Memorial lectures : Education Reconstruction in India.

18. The famous passage from Al-Berui from his Indika is an oft quoted one and is taken here from Jaichand Vidyalankar's 'Bhartiya Itihas Ka Unmeelan' (Hindi Bhawan, Jullandhar).

19. The theme has been eleborated in Russell, G. et:el:ed 'Planning Education for development' Vol. I : Models and Methods at System Planning of Education. Cambridge Mas sacheusetts 1980. The relationship between Economic growth & that of education is rather dubious, only with advances in Technology in late 19th & early 20th century - the relation ship, has emerged in form of educational Economics - see also Blaug ; Readings in Economic of education.

intermediate or appropriate technology[20] in different trades and vocations. We are spending too little on R & D with the result that functional research is being neglected. Above all, only through education, we could arouse people's dormant powers - a will to achieve and perserverence in the face of most heavy odds. In brief what we need today for all round development of the nation is the 'education for character' as Buber would have liked to call it.[21]

REFERENCES

Government of India 1966 Report on the Indian Education Commission; Publication Division, Delhi.

Illich, Ivan. 1973 Deschooling; Penguin Books, Middlesex.

Jha, A.N. 1954 Symposium on 'Future of Education; Publica tion Division Government of India, Delhi.

Myrdal, G. 1968 Asian Drama, 3 Vols, Penguin Books, Mid dlesex.

Reimers, E. 1971 The School is Dead; Penguin Books, Mid dlesex.

Srinivas, M.N. 1972 Social change in Modern India; Allied Publishers, Bombay.

---

20. Schumacher, E.F. in 'Small as Beautiful' Calls it 'Intermediate Technology' (Indian Reprint 1977 - Delhi). See also 'Appropriate Technologies for third world Development, Ed. Robinson A Macmillan, London, 1979.

21. Buber, M. Between Man and Man - in the essay on 'Kerscheinstciner's educational ideas - Education as character'.

FIFTEEN

K. Gopal Iyer and Manjit Singh

The Subaltern in Bihar Through Tradition and Development

The ideology of the elite is the dominant ideology of a particular period. Throughout the colonial period the subal tern classes (Guha, R., 1982) had their own distinct politics, culture, and ideology. This was reflected from time to time in the violent mobilization of the subaltern which sharply distinguished it with elite ideology. This persistence of structural dichotomy is a unique feature in the understanding of the reality in the context of tradition and development. In the historical process the ideology of the subaltern though made its presence felt, was not power ful enough to overthrow the elite ideology. The elite ideol ogy reflected the interests of the dominant classes during the colonial period like capitalists, landlords, moneylenders, bureaucrats and their ilk. The subaltern classes consisted of the industrial labour, the rural poor consisting of poor peasants and agricultural labourers in cluding the underprivileged tenants.

In Bihar the landlords were the most powerful class who represented the dominant elite ideology. However, they were a culturally heterogeneous group. Their unit of operation was limited to their own hegemonic cultural areas. The three such distinct elite cultural entities were represented by Bhojpuri, Mithila, and Magahi culture. The Rajput-Bhumihar combine in Bhojpur and Magahi culture and the Brahmins in Mithila culture represented the hegemonic group. The parts of Chotanagpur and Santal Parganas had their district tribal cultural roots which was dominated by the upper castes con sisting of Rajputs and Bhumihars in particular. The subal tern classes in Bihar during the colonial rule were drawn overwhelmingly from the tribals, Scheduled castes and lower sections of the backward castes. They were either proto- working class, marginal and small peasants, the inferior tenants, agricultural labourers, and bonded labourers. They were encapsulated within the framework of hegemonic cultural region like the Bhojpuri, Mithila, Magahi and the bastard upper caste cultural domination in Chotanagpur and Santal Pargana areas. The subaltern were under the subjection of severe feudal oppression of the dominant culture. They bled them white. One of the striking feature of the subaltern was the relative strength and weakeness of their cultural in stitutions and cultural identity. The tribals as a subaltern class have sharply distinctive cultural features which separate them from other subaltern brethren consisting of Scheduled Castes and emasculated sections of backward castes. The tribals had a distinct language, religion, cul ture, and social organization. Their specific historical ex perience also marks them into a distinct group among the subaltern. The exposure to the exploitation at the hands of upper castes trinity - consisting of landlords, traders, and moneylenders also supported by bureaucrats during the colonial period was marked by absolute levels of exploita tion leading to land-alienation, pauperisation, proletarianization, and bondage. They were a class-for- others and not a class-for-itself. Their Scheduled Caste and emasculated backward caste brethren in the other hegemonic cultural regions of Bihar were subjected to exploitation through rack-renting, usury, and bondage. Yet the tribals as a subaltern class could revoke their cultural strength to confront the elite culture from time to time and sent shivers through their spine. In the absence of a cultural strength rooted in the past, the scheduled castes and emas culated backward castes exhibited passivity and resignation. When the levels of extraction and exploitation reached its zenith the tribals exhibited their hostility towards all those parasitic groups which seized the tribal lands. They militantly fought against them so long as they were still capable of defending themselves. The superior strength of the dominant culture did push them back ultimately but the state of resistance-resisgnation-resistance has been a striking feature of the subaltern tribal culture as con strasted to their Scheduled Castes and emasculated backward caste brethren. Specific mention may be made of such tribal cultural ingenuity as the internalization of concept of 'Diku' in their phenomenology, the strength of their tradi tional social organization, and their informal communication system like the circulation of twig and the beating of war drum. The strength of such cultural institutions not only gave to the tribals the enjoyment of 'limited freedom' within the framework of the hegemonic culture; it also helped them in collective mobilization and yielding extraor dinary pressure on the invincible British domination who were forced to bring suitable legislations to preserve whatever property was left with them and also to recognize the legitimacy of their cultural institutions. Notwithstand ing the instrument of 'culture of revolt' utilized by the tribals, the exploitation by the hegemonic culture continues to be a part of their phenomenology. The pattern of response by the tribals even today continues to be embedded deeply in past cultural roots. The Scheduled Caste brethren, on the other hand, acted as instrumentum mutum throughout the colonial period. The history of culture of repression has experienced a remarkable continuity for them despite the development of the hegemonic culture. The partial departure for them is the contemporary history where the radical pos ture adopted by a section of the peasant organizations have inculcated in them a 'culture of liberation and confront- development of underdevelopment for them both during the colonial period and in the contemporary period.

A level of caste-class convergence has been one of the characteristic feature of the Bhojpuri, Maithili and Magahi cultural region. While the landlord class was invariably drawn from the upper castes, the substantial tenants were drawn from the intermediate castes consisting of Yadavas, Kurmis and Koeris, and the subaltern classes were drawn from the Scheduled Castes, and emasculated backward castes. The period from the thirties of this century has marked a cru cial phase for the intermediate castes who revolted against the landlord class. They could enjoy the fruits of their struggle during the Post-Independence period when substan tial chunk of them emerged as peasant proprietors. The green revolution further boosted their material conditions lifting them to the status of dominant peasant castes in Bihar today. Their rise on its turn accentuated the oppressive and exploitative conditions of the subaltern classes consisting of scheduled castes and emasculated backward castes. The whole weight of the hegemonic culture ol upper caste - in termediate caste combine has fallen heavily on those subal tern classes. The emancipation of the subaltern in these dominant cultural regions of Bihar have become a colossal problem which has to match the 'culture of violence' of the elite with their own. The conscientization and confrontation posed by the subaltern to the elites in the contemporary history of Bihar is one of the silver-lining. The heightened exploitation of the natural resources in tribal areas have increased the prosperity and development of the dominant classes and further accentuated the development of under development of the tribals. The liberation of the tribals is not only a class question but also a cultural question. The framework of 'Jharkhand' and the concept of 'Jharkhandi' is the crucial reference point for their mobilization and liberation.

While the response of the subaltern in the different dominant cultural regions of Bihar has not only been a con tinuity of resignation and apathy, but also characterized by 'flight' or 'migration'. It is to this aspect that attention will be focused in remaining part of the paper.

Scenario of the migration of the rural poor in the past and today

The trends in the migration in the recent past would help us to understand the contemporary migration in proper perspec tive. The accounts of early migration in the country par ticularly during the second half of the nineteenth and the beginning of the twentieth century, have been adequately described by Sen (1977), Mukherjee (1951), Royal Commission on Labour in India (1981), and Omvedt (1980). These studies highlight the nature and causes of migration of indentured labour to other countries and internal migration to tea plantation and other industries. The identured labourers were sent to Mauritius, British Guiana, Trinidad and other places where sugarcane plantations had grown on a large- scale. The deportation of identured labour took place be tween 1930-1870. The number exported rose to half a million within these forty years which consisted of men, women and children. Intermediaries were the key persons to recruit them from various parts of the country who kept them half fed in the course of the journey and some even died on the way. The recruitment to the tea gardens, particularly in As sam, started in the latter half of the nineteenth century and continued until the beginning of the Second World War. Bulk of these workers were from Bihar, U.P. and Orissa. In 1921 nearly 5 lakh tribals from Chotanagpur districts went to Assam tea gardens and another 7.25 lakhs went to Bengal from the six districts of North Bihar. Though the migrant labourers did not consitute a very significant proportion to the total population of the country but they constituted quite a sizable proportion to the total population (ranging from 11 to 26 percent) of the districts from which they migrated. The extent of migration was so high from parts of U.P. that there was not a single family which did not sent at least one family member either to Assam tea garden or Bengal and Bombay (cf. Cansus of Banaras, 1911). The migrants were mainly drawn from the reserve army of landless labourers followed by the small cultivators with uneconomic holdings. Economic factors like drought, famine conditions and other natural calamities acted as strong push factor to throw the rural poor out of the village. These high migrant districts were characterised by feudal exploitations. 'Slaves with generational bondage were rampant in these dis tricts and the debts were contracted mainly for marriage and other social ceremonies. The worst form of serfdom was found among the tribals in Chotanagpur and Santal Parganas'. The large proportion of migrants from the districts of North Bihar like Muzaffarpur, Darbhanga, Bhagalpur and Monghyer were drawn from scheduled castes such as Dusadh, Chamar, Musahar etc. Certain social fectors like caste disabilities and associated stigma also contributed to push the wretched of the earth from their villages. The recruitment of the tribals from Chotanagpur and Santal Parganas were mainly un dertaken through intermediaries who were known as 'sirdars'. They constituted the real scum of the earth as bulk of the money advanced to them by the planters were siphoned off by them and very little went to the workers. At the work site the hirelings and musclemen were employed to prevent the workers from leaving the work sites. Those recruited to the coal mines and industries were in no better situation. The wage rates in industries were appallingly low as the wage rates in rural areas primarily governed the wage rates in industries as well. The workers from the districts of North Bihar, however, were not recruited through intermediaries but mostly went on their own. The remittances were very meager. In 1921 the average annual remittances by the migrants from North Bihar was Rs.30 per year and from Chotanagpur only Rs.13 per year. These remittances were mostly used to clear the debt and could hardly be utilised for meeting the subsistence needs of the members of their family. The benefits were thus siphoned off by the surplus sector. On the other hand, the remittances from the migrants of higher economic and upper caste strata were utilized to increase their land holdings and their control over labour.The result was that the migration accentuated the al ready existing inequalities in the districts with very high migration rates. Migration thus became central to the life and economy of the migrant workers. The migration was male dominated. Greater part of the migration was seasonal and circular in nature. Such seasonal migration was found suitable even to Assam tea gardens as it provided a greater labour supply.

The tentative generalisation of the migration pattern in the past can be summed up so as to provide a direction to under stand the subsequent migration. The migrants were mostly drawn from the lowest social and economic strata. The long distance migration was much higher than the short distances one. The type of migration was rural to urban. The recruit ment of the tribals was more through intermediaries and hence under less free conditions as compared with their counterparts in North Bihar and U.P. Omvedt (1980) who analyses the pattern of migration in the past suggests that the agrarian regions which contributed to colonial work migration had primarily feudal relations and the place to which they were recruited (mines, plantations and factories) were capitalists in the sense that workers sold their labour power to capital. The feudal agrarian relations were so dominant that it affected the forms of exploitation in in dustry as well. The study of Sen (1977), Mukherjee (1951), and Royal Commission (1931) observe that the districts with high migration rates were characterised by worst form of feudal exploitation.

It will now be appropriate to refer to the study of Standing (1981) who tries to examine the link between mode of produc tions and migration. His thesis is that feudalism impedes migration. while semi-feudal and capitalist modes of produc tion provide greater propensity to migrate. This is at tributed to strong ties and dependence of the rural poor on their masters in feudal modes of production. On the other hand, such ties get weakened in the semi-feudal and capitalist modes of production. Further he states that the mobility of labouring population was an essential condition to the growth of capitalism. Peasant migration has sometimes tended to preserve feudal modes of exploitation in capitalism. His observation seems generally to be applicable to the colonial work migration in India. There has been very little labour mobility in the feudal modes of production which characterised the Indian economy during the Mughal period. The emergence of proto-capitalism (plantations, in dustry and mines) created adequate conditions for labour migration and that too under state patronage. Further, the development of capitalism was associated with feudal forms of exploitation. This also substantiates the proposition ad vanced by Standing (1981).

The foregoing description makes it evident that the migra tion among he rural poor before Independence was mainly in the direction of rural to urban. The contemporary migration of the rural poor is showing a new trend i.e. rural to rural migration. This is also clear from the contemporary census data though one tends to be skeptical on the authenticity of these census data to capture the flow of seasonal migrant labourers. Nevertheless, one could discern the trend based on census date. Ashish Bose (1973) has analysed the migra tion stream based on 1961 census. According to him the predominant form of migration in India is rural to rural. In the case of males he finds that this type of migration ac counts for the largest number of migrants in regard to short and medium distance migration and only in the case of long distance, rural to urban type of migration becomes predominant. However, for females regardless of the dis tance, the main type of migration is rural to rural. Gosal and Krishna (1975), Bardhan (1977), and Premi (1980) also emphasise on the predominance of rural to rural migration based on the 1981 census data. Similar phenomenon of growth in migration to rural areas of Punjab, has been reported by Laxminarayan (1981).

The micro-studies also throw light on the trends of migra tion. There are plethora of studies on rural to urban migra tion but there is great paucity of work on rural to rural type of migration. The studies of Connell **et al.** (1976). Breman (1978) and Jayaraman (1979) provides insight on rural to rural migration.

The study of Connell **et al** (1976) covers a comprehensive ground on the major micro-studies on rural to rural migra tion. One of the major findings is that migration is the child and the father of inequality. He suggests that it is from the village where land is most unequally distributed that migration rates are the highest. For the poorest migrants, the phenomenon of migration is increasingly a wandering search for work and even if the search succeeds it is unlikely to do more for his family than prevent a decline into even deeper poverty. Intra-village inequality espe cially of landholding comes out as the most important single variable underlying both pull and push. The forty Indian village studies indicated that the strata of agricultural labourers contributed to migration on a large-scale. The other major findings is that increasing distance is in general associated with declining propensity to migrate. The pattern of migration initially is circular which is succeeded by direct migration. The migrants are younger in age, male-selective, and uneducated. While poverty comes as a major cause to migrate, but certain social considerations like conflict within the nuclear family, caste stigma etc. also act as an important motive force to migrate. Ravenstein's (1985) low that distance deters migration has been strongly substantiated by the authors to account for the contemporary process of migration. Relating to seasonal migration the authors find that the villages with single cropping act as stimulus to migrate. They have observed that the success of green revolution also has increased the flow of rural to rural migration. Among the impact on the village of origin they observe that the absence of young men leads to paucity of innovators and leaders; the remittances seldom lower the inequality in the village, usually it can accen tuates it; the remittances are invariably utilised to meet the subsistence needs and debt repayment and rarely for agricultural production.

The study of Connell *et al* (1976) tries to place the finger at the roots of the problem. The focus on agrarian relations factor acting as the major stimulant for the rural poor to migrate has received inadequate attention so far. This study gives a positive push to think seriously in that direction. Though the study does not reflect on the historicity of the problem, yet the studies of Mukherjee (1951), Sen (1977) and Royal Commission Report (1931), tend to collaborate the agrarian relations factor outlined by Connell *et al* (1976). However, Connell *et al* (1976) fails to probe into the his toric roots of the problem which led them to follow the path of Ravenstein. They also hold that there is an inverse relationship between the distance and the rural poor to migrate. The studies of Mukherjee, Sen and Royal Commission demonstrate it adequately that poverty has not been a bar rier to long distance migration. The difficulty with the census data as earlier pointed out hardly capture the seasonal flow of migration. The long distance rural to rural migration of the poorest stratum has hardly attracted the attention of the researchers. Such constraints lead the scholars to fall into the Ravenstenian trap.

The study of Jayaraman (1979) relates to the migrant tribal labourers from the agriculturally backward region to the agriculturally developed region of Kaira district in Gujarat. The villages of origin is the one-cropped area whereas the Kaira district which is the destination work place affords them enough work for a few months. The lean season in the villages of origin coincides with the busy season at the destination. The migrants are mostly poor peasants possessing handkerchief plots of land and that too characterized by low yield. The economic factor inducing migration is so strong that over 86% of the households in the district of origin send at least one member to the des tination district. The per worker earning of Rs. 153 for three months is utilised for meeting the subsistence needs. Thus this study lends support to Connell's (1976) findings that migrants are drawn from the lowest stratum and their earnings are utilised for subsistence and not for productive purposes.

Bremen's study (1978) is significant to demonstrate the relationship between capitalist development in agriculture and the exploitation of migrant labourers. The study relates to the migration of seasonal labour from the agriculturally backward regions of Maharashtra (i.e. Khandesh) to the developed region of Gujarat i.e. Bardoli district, where cooperative capitalism in agriculture is firmly rooted. The cane-crushing industry and the cultivation or sugarcane is highly intertwined. The membership to the cooperative sugar cane industry was restricted to the middle and rich peasants who had to buy share from the cooperative sugarcane to the factory. The caste-class covergence was very high as the kulaks who were the members of the cooperative sugarcane factories also belonged to the dominant Kunbi Pattidar caste. They also wielded powerful political influence. They were successful in accummulating enough wealth with the in troduction of sugarcane crop and the novel way of the or ganisation of disposing of the produce. The large influex of the migrant labourers had made the local labourers jobless. The district of origin was one-cropped area with poor ir rigation facilities. They would migrate during the lean season to the destination where the sugarcane cutting opera tion required labourers on a large scale. The migrant labourers were drawn from the landless labourers and poor peasant categories who also belonged to very low castes. The migrants were recruited through well-knit intermediary sys tem. They were advanced loans at the village of origin and were brought to the destination through the intermediaries known as *mukadams*. These intermediaries also controlled their movements at the work place. On the completion of their work they were deported to their villages through the intermediaries.

They were working under bondage as they were not only tied through debt but were also kept under physical surveillance. There was close collusion between the railway authorities and intermediaries. The migrant labourers were paid very low wages. On an average the labourer received only Rs.1.20 for the whole day's work. They would be also required to work at night when the sugarcane was to be loaded. The net income was abysmally low which substantiated the fact that they worked for survival i.e. could only reproduce themselves and could and reproduce the family members. The employers preferred the cheap migrant labour to the local ones. The landlords were effectively organised and exercised a strong- hold in bureaucracy and local politics. Bremen (1978) ob serves that the present production relations results in the rise of systematic exploitation of rural poor. The study highlights the feudal modes of exploitation co-existing with capitalist modes of production.

The phenomenon of migration of the rural poor in the past and to-day reveals certain common and some differential fea tures. The propensity to migration in the past was facilitated due to the impact of British policy e.g., the disintegration of handicraft industries, the proletarianisa tion process, population pressure, transition in agriculture from feudalism to semi-feudalism, the introduction of protocapitalism in the form of tea plantations, industries etc. The economic factors were mainly responsible for mas sive labour migration. The colonial labour migration was both voluntary and involuntary in nature. Wherever feudal holds were strong accompanied with acute bondage and in debtedness, the migration was more involuntary in character (e.g.Chotanagpur) and where agriculture was in transition to semi-feudalism, the migration was free or voluntary in character (e.g. North Bihar). This also had a differential consequence on the recruitment pattern in the two places. Intermediary form of recruitment dominated the Chotanagpur districts. The labourers from North Bihar migrated on their own. It also affected the pattern of exploitation at work place. The tribals in Assam tea gardens worked under condi tions of bondage whereas the North Bihar and Eastern U.P. workers employed in the industries in Calcutta and Bombay worked under relatively free conditions. This substantiates the contention that capitalist modes of production can co- exist with feudal forms of exploitation. The contemporary phenomenon of labour migration which is gradually becoming rural to rural migration also indicates similar trend. For example, the study by Bremen (1978) amply substantiates the fact that the capitalist modes of production in agriculture is positively associated with the feudal forms of exploita tion. The districts and regions with high migration rates are the ones characterised by semi-feudal modes of produc tion or backward agriculture. This has been the trend both in the past and today. The contemporary migration is more from the less developed regions in agriculture to more developed regions. i.e. from the semi-feudal modes to the capitalist modes of production. One could hypothesise on this basis that regions characterised by semi-feudal modes of production accompanied with large reserve army of agricultural labourers also do not uphold the Ravensteinian thesis that the poor migrate only to short distances. The early migration of the rural poor in the country was charac terised more by long distance migrations. Both the past and contemporary processes of migrations strongly justify, the fact that the migrant workers overwhelmingly represent the rock-bottom in the economic and caste hierarchy in the vil lage. The finding of Connell **et al** (1976) that migration is the child and father of inequality is strongly supported both by the migration process in the past and today. The studies emphasize that the remittances are not sufficient even to meet the subsistence needs. The patterns of migra tion are seasonal and cyclical in nature. The migration is male dominated and includes high proportion of young adults.

Focus of the study

The present paper intends to explore the phenomenon of migration of workers from Bihar to Punjab Agriculture. It focuses on the differential conditions of the migrant labourers from North and South Bihar to Punjab Agriculture with respect to the harassment faced during the travel from Bihar to Punjab their socio-economic characteristics, wage rates and conditions of employment etc. In order to have an indepth understanding, the samples of migrant labourers were selected from two villages of Ludhiana district (one of the most developed district in agriculture in Punjab, and four villages of Hoshiarpur district (one of the agriculturally backward districts). The data was collected during the agricultural season of 1980-81.

Harassment to the seasonal migrant labourers on travel

Here the attempt is made to discuss the difficulties faced by the seasonal migrant labourers on their travel from North Bihar to

Punjab and the treatment meted out to them on their arrival at the railway station in Punjab. The migration takes place on a large-scale during the peak agricultural seasons in Punjab. These are wheat harvesting, paddy transplantation and paddy harvesting. The wheat harvesting, and threshing are spread over a period of one month starting from the second week of April to second week of May. The paddy transplantation starts from third week of June and continues till and of July. Paddy harvesting-cum-threshing operation is spread throughout the month of October. The major flow of migrant labourers also coincides with this. It may also be mentioned that the peak season in Punjab also coincides with the lean season in North Bihar.

The labourers from North Bihar come to Punjab via two routes. Some of them board the train at Muzaffarpur to Delhi and take a train to Punjab. However, bulk of them travel from North Bihar to Lucknow and board the trains to Punjab (The Tribune, June 8, 1981). In order to have an idea of the difficulties faced by them during the course of the travel investigator spent few night at Ludhiana railway station and also made short visits to other stations like Rajpura and Khanna. The major time was spent in Ludhiana station which was undertaken for two days in the third week of March 1980 and one week spread to the first fortnight in April 1980. This was followed by short visits to Ludhiana, Rajpura, and Khanna in October 1980. It was not possible to observe the conditions of the workers during the course of the travel from Bihar to Punjab. Hence the difficulties faced by them during the course of the travel is based only on the inter views of the labourers at the stations in Punjab and in the field situation. However, the treatment meted out to them at the railway stations by the ticket collectors, policemen, and the employers are based on observations, interviews, and snaps of photographs. Of all the railway stations in Punjab, most of the migrants get down at Ludhiana station and only a small section of migrants get down at other points (The Tribune, June 8, 1981).

As the labourers travel in large number during the peak season one can notice that the trains carrying them are not only completely packed from inside but a large number of them travel on the roof of the train (The Tribune, June 8, 1980). They not only face the rough weather but also have to face more risky situation. The over-bridges through which the trains pass, the hanging metal wires, and other objects which could hit the heads and cause injuries to those perched on the roof top are some of the dangers to which the migrants are exposed. The interviews revealed few cases of accidents met by those travelling on the roof top who met with serve and fatal injuries.

The difficulties faced by them during the course of the journey is the beginning of the travail. Their are other difficulties which await them at the railway stations in Punjab. The investigator had occasion to personally observe those difficulties particularly at Ludhiana station. As soon as the trains are due to enter the Ludhiana station, the ticket collectors and the railway policemen become quite alert and active and take their respective positions. As soon as the migrants get down at the stations, the ticket collectors and policemen check the tickets. They are hardly treated as human objects. The migrants have to cross over- bridge to reach the exit gate. Some of the migrants have to surrender the tickets even before they cross the over- bridge. As a result some of them are detected as travelling without ticket at the exist gate. The exit gate also present an interesting scene. The labourers are usually in small groups with an informal leader. In the process of moving out of the exit gate some of them are held back either on genuine or flimsy grounds. They are then taken to the ticket collectors room which prominently displays the board, "May I help you". What actually goes on inside the room is the reverse of this. In that room one can find beside the ticket collectors and the detected migrant labourers also the rail way policemen. It is also surrounded by the employers. Such migrant labourers who are able to give the demanded money are immediately released. Others who show recalcitrance are even undressed to check if they have some money twisted in their clothes. The unfortunate victims are those who do not have money. The employers mainly look for such cases. They pay the amount to the ticket collectors and policemen and whisk such labourers. They are not only able to have control over such labourers but also extract work from them at low wages.

This is not the end of their travail. Large number of employers are found waiting outside the station to get hold of the labourers. Some of the employers even spend two to three nights at Ludhiana station in search of labourers. As the flow of migrant labourers to Punjab is not a very recent affair, most of the migrants, who have been visiting for past few years, not only know the village where they have to go but also have prefixed their employers. The major victims are the recent migrants. As soon as they get out of the sta tion, they are surrounded by employers who drag them to their side. One could also notice that some employers bar gain with some migrant labourers, particularly with those who have visited Punjab more than once. The flow of migrats was very high during April 1980 but it was very less during the paddy harvesting season in October 1980 (The Tribune Oct., 2,1980; Punjabi Tribune Oct. 23, 1980). During this season one could observe the forcible capture of labourers at the railway station and being whisked away in tractors (The Tribune Oct. 2, 1980; Punjab Tribune Oct. 23, 1980.

The number of labourers getting down each night from the various trains during April, 1980 varied from 1000-3000. The Tribune of August 18,1980 (Punjabi Edition) estimated that about 3 lakh migrants visited Punjab during April, 1980. The study on migrant labourers by Grewal and Sidhu (1979) es timate that normally 2.1 lakh migrant labourers visit Punjab every year during the peak period. However, the number was much less during October, 1980. While the migrants in March- April 1980 started arriving to Punjab in large numbers season of 1981, the migrants arrived very close to the peak period. This also had its impact on the wage fluctuation in the 1981 harvest period. Those labourers who visit Punjab in the month of April start returning to Bihar from the end of May which extends to the end of July. Those who return by the end of May, they work only in the peak season of wheat harvesting and thashing season. Those who return by the end of July also participate in the peak season of paddy transplantation. Some of them also stay back for paddy har vesting and thrashing operation though there is also a fresh flow of migrant labourers during paddy harvesting season. The return of the migrants is also fraught with dif ficulties. One can find thousands of labourers forming long queue at the ticket window. As soon as the trains are in the platform the labourers hurry-up to move inside the train and also occupying their seats on the roof of the train with their little belongings. As the train moves from the plat form the labourers from the roof top almost lie down to prevent getting hurt from objects above their heads.

Socio-Economic Characteristics of the migrants

The interview of the migrants in the two villages of Lud hiana district i.e., Bassian and Udhowal was conducted in two periods so as to cover all the peak agricultural season in 1980. The first phase was extended from April to July, 1980 and the second phase from

September to October, 1980. During the first phase 41 groups and in the second phase 38 groups were interviewed. The migrants always come in groups which range from 4 to 20 and the average size of the group was eight. Of the total group nearly 7.5 per cent were from three districts of Eastern U.P. and the rest were from various districts of North Bihar. The district of Monghyr, Saharsa, Darbhanga, Muzaffarpur, and Samastipur contributed to the major share of the migrants. Other districts which sent lesser number of migrants were Sitamarhi, Motihari, Madhubani, Begusarai, and Bhagalpur. The migrants had started visiting Punjab from 1972 but the majority among them visited only since 1979. The caste representation was heterogenous with predominance of backward castes. While scheduled castes were 14 per cent, upper castes 2 per cent and the rest 84 per cent belonged to various backward castes. The studies of Grewal and Sidhu (1979) and Singh (1981) have also come to similar findings. Among the back ward castes Yadav and Malahs were the most numerous. One of the interesting feature was that the groups were either from a single village or from two adjoining villages. In Punjab a considerable portion worked in a single village and the rest worked in two or more villages. Literacy rate among the migrants was rather low. Of the total labourers 78 per cent were illiterate and the rest had read below sixth standards. The family size for 40 per cent was upto five, for 34 per cent 6 to 8 and the rest had more than eight members in the family. Each group also had close relatives. Of the total number of groups nearly 26 per cent were constituted of a single caste, 33 per cent of two castes, and the rest of more than two castes. Agricultural labourers and poor peasants constituted quite a sizeable proportion of the migrants. Only 37.5 per cent among them had some amount of land, i.e. 24.5 per cent had less than one acre, 8.9 per cent had up to two acres and 4.2 per cent had up to five acres. Most of the labourers were married who constituted 78 per cent of the total labourers. Bulk of them were very young, i.e. around 66 per cent were below 25 years, and the rest above 25 years. Those below 15 years constituted one per cent. Singh (1981) found in his study that 81 per cent were in the age range of 18 to 35 years. The study of Grewal and Sidhu (1979) revealed that 71 per cent were in the age- group of 20 to 40 years. The predominance of the young among the migrants is substantiated in all these studies. It was exclusively male migration.

Indebtedness was quite rampant among the migrants. Around 73 per cent among them were indebted. It was a characteris tic feature that most of them had borrowed money to cover their travel cost for Bihar to Punjab. Institutional lending hardly figured. Among the various sources of indebtedness 65 per cent were indebted to the village money-lenders, 25 per cent to the village agriculturists, and the rest to rela tives and friends. The amount taken as debt varied. Around 63 per cent had borrowed less than Rs.750/-, 35 per cent had borrowed between Rs.750 to 2000 and the rest more than Rs. 2000. The period of indebtedness incase of 84 percent of the labourers was less than two years and for the remaining more than two years. The purpose of borrowing was mainly to meet expenditure on social ceremonies, subsistence needs, and to cover rail fare. Only 15 per cent had borrowed for investing in agriculture. The rate of interest for the majority ranged from 36 to 72 per cent. Their asset structure was quite meagre. Nearly 56 per cent had no livestock.

Wage rates and conditions of Employment of Migrant Labourers

The wages in the villages of origin ranged from Rs.4 to Rs.5. The workers come with skeleton clothes. They somehow pull on with it when they come during summer months of wheat harvesting. It, however, makes a good deal of difference when they are here in the cold weather particularly during paddy harvesting. In the absence of blankets and other warm clothes, they pass their nights in difficult conditions. They do not usually have proper place to stay. The wage rates for most of the peak operations is undertaken on con tract which is fixed per acre. The wage rates in the two villages of Bassian and Udhowal of Ludhiana district for various operations during the 1980-81 agricultural seasons are given in Table-1.

The wage rates over the years have been on the decline ex cept for paddy harvesting cum-thrashing. The reason for the higher rate for paddy harvesting is because it needs more mandays per acre. Another reason was that during paddy har vesting in 1980, the flow of migrant labourers was much less (The Tribune Oct. 2,1980, Punjabi Tribune, Oct. 23, 1980). The mandays required to accomplish the per acre work for each operation varies. The number of mandays required per acre for wheat harvesting, paddy transplantation, and paddy harvesting cum thrashing are respectively 8,10 and 22. Wheat thrashing operation is paid in terms of daily wages. The per acre contract wages, however, do not give an idea of the wages accruing to individual labourers. When calculated the wages rate per migrant worker, the picture which emerges can be discerned from the figures in the Table 2.

The average number of days work available and per head saving (after meeting the cost of food) for different agricultural operations can be discoured from Table 3. The net earning to the workers varied according to the number of days stayed and worked in Punjab. Three distinct paterns of migration have been observed. The first stream of migrant workers come during wheat harvesting and stay until paddy transplantation i.e. for an average of 100 days. The second stream consist of those who come during wheat harvesting continue to stay until paddy harvesting, i.e. for an average of 200 days. The third stream is represented by those who come during paddy transplantation and stay until paddy har vesting, i.e. for an average of 120 days. There are others, particularly the fresh migrants, who stay for only one operation as they find it hard to adjust in an entirely new situation and that too, as they are more gullible and easy prey to exploitation. The shorter they stay the less is the saving. However, long duration stay is also not a paying proposition in absolute terms. This is because during the intermittent duration of the two peak periods, work is not regularly available and so the workers are prepared to work even on low wages. They remain unemployed for several days during the lean periods. In such places where cotton and maize are grown, some work is available during the lean period also. The average number of days that the migrants remained unemployed during the three migratory streams are as follows:

1.	Between wheat harvesting and ransplantation	30 days
2.	Wheat harvesting to paddy arvesting	75 days
3.	Paddy transplatation to paddyarvesting	45 days

The period of forced hybernation depresses their earnings and savings considerably. The average earnings (less the food costs) for each of the three streams of migrants is as follows:

1.	Wheat harvesting to paddyransplantation	Rs.680
2.	Wheat harvesting to paddy arvesting	Rs.860
3.	Paddy transplantation to paddyarvesting	Rs.760

When the travel cost, up and down, is taken into account, the average savings associated with the three patterns of migration are respectively Rs.543, 720 and 620. If their en tire duration of stay for the three patterns of migration is taken into consideration average daily earnings range from Rs. 4 to 5. Inspite of the period of intermittent unemploy ment their migration to Punjab does appear to be an economic proposition. This is ensured if the workers are paid genuinely by the employers. The interviews have revealed that in certain cases the employers pay only part of the wages and the poor labourers cannot protest. In other cases they are also cheated as they do not have proper concep tualisation of the acreage. This approximates the prevalent average wage rates at their village of origin. One could argue that if the migrant workers get work throughout the year in the village origin, their massive migration to Pun jab agriculture can be arrested. Of the three streams of migration, the largest influx is accounted for by the first stream, followed by the second and third. The labourers remit part of their savings to their village home. There were instances of money being withheld in the post offices of the village of origin which is utilized for money-lending by the postal employees. The interviews could capture few such cases (For such irregularities also see Indian Express, Chandigarh Edition, August 31, 1981, p.9).

Recruitment pattern of tribals

While the seasonal labourers to Ludhiana migrate volun tarily, the recruitment pattern of tribals in Hoshiarpur district and adjoining area is regulated through inter mediaries. The demand for permanent labourers arises from the pemliar agrarian conditions of the district. It is also facilitated from the fact that some people from Hoshiarpur district have been engaged in the district of Ranchi in various occupations like the moulding workshops, transport business, etc. The farmers and the recruiting agents could establish contacts with their acquaintance at Ranchi and secure help in recruiting the tribal labourers. Initially three farmers from Tanda area brought tribal labourers to work on their own farms. Their availability on cheap rates and also their hard work attracted attention of some in dividuals who wanted to mint money by recruiting them for a song and selling them at profitable rate. Initially in early 70's three persons were involved in this trade. They later withdrew from this business in as much as it stigmatised their reputation.

The vacuum thus created was immediately filled in by new contractors not with a strong laid base put with a wide and intimate contact with political and bureaucratic elites. One such person discovered during the course of the field visit turned out to be a school teacher who felt no qualm of con science in this operation as a slave trader. A gross widow of a military personnel from Tanda outbidded him. She had several of her agents prowling about the railway station forcibly transporting migrants to her dungeon to exact work and sell them to the needy farmers. To ensure that they did not escape the migrants would be locked in dungeon. The poor tribals would not be allowed to go out to answer even the call of nature. Since it would entail an extra coust of vigil, a tin container was placed in the room to enable them to urinate. Every means was considered fair in recruiting the tribals. She could take the law in her hands not only with the connivance of the minions of law but also with their active participation in perpetration of such crimes. These new contractors streamlined the whole process of trade in human beings to match with the demand for labourers. These contractors in Hoshiarpur have their agents at Ranchi who operate through sub-agents at the village level. The agents collect the potential migrants to a common place in Ranchi who would then be transported to Hoshiarpur. On ar rival here they are sold to the farmers in the district of Hoshiarpur of adjoining area for a sum ranging from Rs.200 to Rs.400. Many of these contractors do not own holdings large enough to employ these labourers. Distress sale would again reduce their profit. To circumvent this difficulty these labourers would be sent in groups to farms nearby during the day times. They would work in lieu of two square meals a day and keep coming to the concentration camp main tained by the contractor until the final buyers could be found out. The final buyers, i.e. the farmers, would be asked to deduct the commission charges from the wages of those who migrated from freedom to slavery. The contractor, however, would not guarantee the stay of migrants for the stipulated period they were sold. In order to streamline their pockets more and more, they would send their henchmen to instigate the sold labourers to run to the contractors at night. Considering that the migrants would be thrown from frying pan to fire, they welcome this opportunity only to find that they have been sold away once again to another farmer. Quite often, those with weak links with the place of origin would send their agents to the railway stations to capture the migrant labourers like monkeys. Once brought before them they would be assaulted until they admit that Ranchi was their domicilliary place and everything else was amnesia to them. These contractors maintain account of all purchases and sale.

Bondage Under a Tyrant Landlord

The village of Talwandia Aabdar, near Bhogpur, in Jullun dur district is deeply associated with cruel treatment meted out to labourers from Bihar. It reminds one of the legecy of the recruitment of the labourers for the tea gardens in As sam towards the end of 19th century and the beginning of the 20th century. It is also a testimony to the penetration of capitalist mode of production but preserving the feudal relations of production. It was in December 1980 that a group of seven labourers from the Saharsa district of Bihar were captured at the Jalandhar railway station which they were returning from Jammu where they had worked for some time. There were two to three muselemen who lured these labourers with Rs.10 as daily wages plus food and clothes. They were to be engaged in house construction work. The wretched of the earth easily succumbed to the musclemen in the car to the village in the farm of a truant landlord. It sowed the first seed of suspicion among the labourers who asked the recruiting agent of the site of the construction work. Pat came the word "Shut up you bloody fool" accom panied with heavy blows in cheeks and back. The labourers were locked in a small room in which another group of twelve labourers were also huddled. The labourers had the freedom to urinate during night in a tin container placed in the room lest they escape. The room was locked for the whole night and a watchman was also on the wait outside. Within two to three days of their arrival the respondent's brother along with two erstwhile labourers escaped from the place. As the respondent's brother was one among the three who es caped, he had to face the brunt. The respondent was pushed to the floor and beaten mercilessly in front of other labourers to serve as lessons for others. They were engaged mainly in agricultural operations. The master would always hold a stick to beat the labourers in case he felt that the labourers were not upto the mark in their work. The respon dent still carried the scares of the healed wounds on both the hands and one of the finger nails was badly hurt. One day while the labourers were cutting some trees for fuel purpose, one of the labourers was given repeated blows on the back and flogging with the sugarcane stick on his legs for some slackness in the work. On another day five of the labourers were ordered to lift a tractor from the field and to carry it to the landlords' household. As the equipment was heavy, one of the labourers could not fully lift it which invited the master's wrath. He was beaten severely leading to the damage in the shoulder joints. Inspite of this the labourer was forced to work irrespective of his disablement. The labourers would be uncertain as to who would be the victim of the master's wrath on each day. Yet on another day a labourer almost had a providential escape. He was asked to clean the tractor but the cleaning operation was not to the satisfaction of the master. He pierced a needle (used for stitching the gunny bags) into the right eye of the labourer which missed the target and struck on his eyebrow. The respondent was full of tears while narrat ing the incident as the entire scene was vivid in his mind.

The labourers were kept under fed. They got two to three chapatis twice a day accompanied with mustard **saag** (leafy vegetable). The chapatis were made of wheat and spoiled dry peas which was not used even for the master's cattle. The entire episode was narrated by one of the labourers who could manage to escape and presently working with an employer in a nearby village. Alongwith the respondent four labourers managed to run away from the tyrant landlord on the pretext of going to the toilet during night. Each one of the labourers took different directions so that one did not know where the other escaped.

The above is just snap of the operation of the tyrant landlord. He had been involved in similar operations earlier also on a much larger scale. He has farms also in Himachal Pradesh and Mukerian in Hoshiarpur. He thus requires quite a large contingent of labourers to operate his various farms. He is generally on the hunt for cheap labourers for which he has also employed armed musclemen. This is also clear from a report which appeared in the issue of "people's Democracy" of 26th August, 1979. The report states that the armed strongman of the employer picked up 50 to 60 labourers of U.P. and Bihar from Jalandhar and Ludhiana railway stations. Heavy work was extracted from them under the supervision of armed strongman. Beating and torturing of labourers was quite common (for details please see People's Democracy, August 26, 1979 pp. 11-12).

Such incidence is not rare. The difficulty in reality is to locate and identify the cases with such severity. As the labourers are completely alienated and helpless, they meekly become the object of such "Culture of repression" and if remain alive, try to escape from such brutalities. Even such escapes are fraught with severe consequences. This would be clear from the case of a father and his two sons who were subjected to physical and brutal bondage for a period of more than over four years (for details please see Indian Express, Chandigarh Edition, May 8,1981,p.4).

Conclusions

The findings indicate that the capitalist development in agriculture in the district of Ludhiana have generated addi tional labour demand and absorbed the influx of migrant labourers. The capitalist penetration in agriculture in Lud hiana district is consistent with the capitalist modes of exploitation in the form of free wage labour. The limited development of agriculture in the district of Hoshiarpur on capitalist lines and the specific ecological, as also his torical situation, have created conditions of pre-capitalist forms of exploitation of tribal labourers. The study further questions the Ravenstenian thesis that distance deters migration of the poor people. The process of migration of the rural poor in the country in the past as also today dis prove such assertions. The observation of Connell **et at** (1976) that migration is the child and father of inequality is also substantiated from the pattern of migration analysed in this study. Such conditions are embedded in the agrarian conditions of Bihar. The study also reveals that those who migrate are drawn from agricultural labourer and poor peasant categories.

Following tentative generalization could be made based on the above analysis:

1. The subaltern classes in Bihar continue to face the severe exploitation today which they experienced during the colonial period.
2. The tribals as a subaltern class utilized their cultural ingenuities to take to the path of struggle against the hegiminic culture during the colonial period. The Scheduled Castes and the emaciated backward castes could not resist the exploitative proclivities of the dominant class due to their weak cultural roots.
3. The ethnic and caste divisions among the subaltern is a divisive force against their unity.
4. Both during the colonial and post-Independence period the development has benefitted the elite culture. The subal tern whether

tribal, Scheduled Castes, or emaciated backward classes, have experienced development of underdevelopment.

5. The cultural roots of tribals continue to be a strength for their mobilization against elites. The inculcation of proletarian culture amongst the Scheduled Castes in par ticular have activized the conscientization amongst the Scheduled Castes. Emaciated backward castes continue to wal low under 'Culture of Silence'.

6. The caste-class convergence at the lower level has acted as a necessary condition for militant mobilization. The presence of subjective factors would be the sufficient con dition to ignite.

7. The emergence of intermediate castes as dominant peasantry has accentuated the 'culture of repression' against the subaltern.

8. 'Migration' as one of the avenues to escape from the feudal-semi-feudal oppression has been the characteristic feature in the past and continues to be so today.

9. The migration of labourers from North Bihar was volun tary in nature in the past and continues to be so today; on the other hand, it was forced one for the tribals accom panied with bondage in the past and continues to be so today.

Table 1 : Wage rates of local and migrant labourers in 1980 in the village of Bassian of Ludhiana district.

(In Rs.)

Agricultural Operations	Local	Migrant
Wheat harvesting (per acre)	156	105.00
Wheat thrashing (daily wages)	15.00	11.50
Paddy transplantation	120.00	105.00
Paddy harvesting-cum thrashing	200.00	160.00

Table 2 : Daily wage rates of migrant labourers for different operations in the agricultural seasons of 1980-81 in the two villages of Ludhiana district

(In Rs.)

	Daily wage rates	
Agricultural Operations	Bassian	Udhowal
Wheat harvesting	13.00	9.35
Wheat thrashing	11.00	9.92
Paddy transplantation	10.50	11.50
Paddy harvesting cum thrashing	7.25	7.00

Table 3 : Average number of days work available and the per head savings to the migrant labourers for different operations

Agricultural Operations	Average number of days work available		per head saving (Rs.)	
	Bassian	Udhowal	Bassian	Udhowal
Wheat harvesting	17	15	195	162
Wheat thrashing	14	11	118	105
Paddy transplantation	29	32	213	324
Paddy harvesting-cum-thrashing	29	244	260	000

Table 4 : Socio-economic Characteristics of Punjab State, Ludhiana and Hoshiar pur Districts

Particulars	State Punjab	Distt. Hoshiarpur	Distt. Ludhiana
1	2	3	4
Classifications of Area (1000 hectares) in 1979-80 (P)			
a) Geographical are	5038	389	379
b) Net Area sown	4180	251	326
c) Percentage of net area sown to total area	83	64	86
Cropping intensity 1979-80	156	152	172
Percentage of net area irrigated to net area sown in 1979-80	85	45.5	92.2
No. of tractors per 1000 hectares (net area sown)	17	12	30
Number of tubewells per thousand hectares of gross cropped area in 1979-80	41.22	51.83	64.10
Fertilizer nutrients application (in kgs.) per hectare of gross cropped area in 1978-79	92.25	70.68	145.90
% Area under H.Y.V.of Principal crops in 1979-80			
Paddy	91.81	84.44	100.00
Maize	17.57	3.90	20.59
Wheat	98.65	96.15	100.00

No. of operational holdings and their percentage to total holdings (1971)				
Land size category (hects.)				
i. 0.1-2.0		777651 (56.54)	108237 (73.09)	42128 (47.18)
ii. 2.0-4.0		281103 (20.44)	22368 (15.19)	23040 (25.20)
iii. 4.0-10.0		247755 (10.02)	14128 (9.64)	21041 (23.01)
iv. 10.0-above		68856 (5.00)	3127 (12.13)	4203 (4.61)
Total		1375392	148140 (100.00)	91412 (100.00)
Percentage area under principal crops to gross cropped area of district/state(a), Production (000 tons) (P) and yield (kg/hect) (Y) during 1979-80				
Paddy	A	17.93	11.78	16.19
	P	3052	92	313
	Y	2606	2046	3443
Maize	A	6.18	20.16	12.10
	P	696	142	122
	Y	1,722	1,843	1,798
Wheat	A	43.04	4083	4679
	P	7.879	330	904
	Y	2797	2114	3436
Potato	A	0.62	3.40	0.20
	P	734.1	211.1	27.50
	Y	18.066	16.242	25.03
Percentage of Scheduled Castes population to total population (1971)		27.00	31.00	25.00
Percentage of agricultural labourers to total workers (1971)		20.11	17.92	17.95
Percentage of cultivators to total workers		42.56	43.61	32.86

Percentage of literates to total population (1971)	33.67	38.5	35.3
Percentage of scheduled castes literates 1971	16.12	29.16	20.81
Wages paid to Agricultural labourers 1980.			
Operations			
Ploughing	10.95	8.50	11.16
Sowing	11.03	8.60	10.22
Weeding	10.86	8.60	10.29
Harvesting	13.47	11.00	13.33
(for females)-cottons picking	8.25	8.00	0.0
Other agril. Operations	10.96	8.83	10.33

Source: 1 Statistical Abstracts of Punjab 1080.

Table 5 : Socio-economic characteristics of Punjab and Bihar State

Agricultural indicators

(i)	Percent net area sown	1960-61	48.40	70.50
		1966-67	42.70	76.80
		1975-76	48.87	82.61
(ii)	Percent area under major crops to gross cropped are 1977-78	Paddy	49.54	13.28
		Maize	4.21	7.14
		Wheat	17.57	41.84
(iii)	Production (Qtls/acre)-1977-78	Paddy	4.00	13.60
		Maize	4.21	6.35
		Wheat	5.10	10.28
(iv)	Net area irrigated 1974-75 (000 acres)	Canals/Wells	2191.78	3484.11
		T. Wells	2120.12	4363.79
		Total	6234.33	7865.19
(v)	Percent net area irrigated to net area sown (1976-77)		34.48	76.65

Me-chanisation of agriculture

Agricultural implements(1972)

(i)	Oil-engine pumping sets ('000)	42	248
(ii)	Electric pumps ('000)	53	79
(iii)	Tractors ('00)	56	424

Electricity

(i)	Electricity consumed in agricultural production (Million KWH) during 1976-77	449	973
(ii)	Per cent electricity consumed inirrigation 1960-61	2.00	12.60
	1969-70	2.80	14.70
(iii)	Per cent villages electrified till 313-1977	26.90	100.00
Demographic Indicators			
(i)	Population density per square K.M. (1971) **	324	269
(ii)	Rank by population with respect to other states	2	14
(iii)	Percentage of Agricultural workers to total workers (1971)	77	56
(iv)	Percentage of scheduled castes/ scheduled tribes to total population	31.61	24.71
(v)	Per capita availability of agricultural land (acres) 1970-71	0.39	0.89
Structural Indicators			
(i)	Operational holdings (acres) (Percent to total holdings)		
	Less than five	77.27	37.62
	More than ten	8.00	56.00
	More than fifteen	3.14	35.00
(ii)	Land concentration		
	(per cent to total land under cultivation)		
	77.27 per cent holdings less than 5 acres		29.30
	0.40 per cent holding above 50 acre		6.50
(ii)	Per cent area consolidated	2.00	100.00

* the figure rose to 16.11 during 1978-79.

Source: Statistical Abstracts of India.

** Pressure of Population on Bihar agriculture is more than double that of Pun jab.

Source: 1. Census Reports 1971.
2. N.S.S. Data, Report No. 159.

Source: Hazra, S(1973) "Bihar and Punjab, a study of Regional Economic Disparity", Economic and Scientific Research Foundation, New Delhi.

REFERENCES

Bose, Ashish 1973: Migration Streams in India, in Studies in India's Urbanization - 1901-71,Tata McGraw-Hill Pub lishing Company, New Delhi

Breman, J.1978: Seasonal Migration and Cooperative Capitalism: Crushing, of Cane and Labour by Sugar Fac tories of Bardoli, Economic and Political Weekly, XIII (31, 32 & 33)

Chandan, Amarjit 1979: Plight of Migrant Labourers; Economic and Political Weekly, XIV (17)

Connell, J., et. al 1976: Migration From Rural Area; Oxford University Press, Delhi.

Grewal, S.S. & Sidhu, M.S. 1979 Migrant Agricultural Labour in Punjab; Department of Economics and Sociology, Punjab Agricultural University, Ludhiana.

Guha, R. (ed.), 1982: Subaltern Studies I - Writings on South Asian History and Society; Oxford University Press, Delhi.

Jayeraman, T.K. 1979: Seasonal Migration of Tribal Labour: An Irrigation Project in Gujarat; Economic and Political Weekly, XIV (41).

Oberai, A.S. & singh, H.K.M. 1980: Migration flows in Punjab's Green Revolution Belt; Economic and Political Weekly XV (13).

Omvedt, Gail 1980: Migration in Colonial India The Journal of Peasant Studies Frank Case & Co. Lte.,London.

Premi, M.K. 1980: Aspects of Female Migration in India; Economic and Political Weekly XV (15).

Royal Commission on Labour in India 1929: Memorandum Sub mitted by the Bombay Mill owners Association, Bombay.

Saxena, D.P. 1977: Rururban Migration in India: Popular Parkashan, Bomoay.

Sen, Sukomal 1977: Working class of India; K.P. Bagchi and Co., Calcutta.

Singh, G. 1981: A study of Assess the impact of Migratory Labour upon Agricultural production on district Ludhiana; Operational and Analytical Research unit, IADP, Ludhiana.

Standing, Guy 1981: Migration and Modes of Exploitation: So cial Origins of Immobility and Mobility: The Journal of Peasant studies: Frank Case & Co., London.

Zachariah, K.C. 1964: Internal Migration in the India subcontinent; Asia Publishing House., Bombay.

SIXTEEN

P.N. Thakur

Internal Migration, Tradition & Development: A Case-Study of Unskilled Bihari Labourers in Gauhati

Ever since man learnt to stand erect and to make use of his opposable thumbs, he has wandered hither and thither in groups or in isolation in search of food, shelter, mate and comfort. This movement of human beings for the purpose of settling down which is commonly known as migration, occupies a central place in the drama of human history as well as in the growth of civilization.

At a later stage, human migration became a vehicle of dif fusion of culture - Indians settling in south east Asia; Chinese coming down more or less to the same region to join hands with them to develop a composite sino-Indian culture over the whole range of south Asia Archipelago. Similar role was played by Greece in the near East and the phoenicians in far off west in Africa, and at a later stage the Arabs over the whole of North Africa and central Asia.

But migrations have also meant the coming of the dreaded Teutonic races, the Slavs, the Magyars, the Hunas, the Mon gols and the Turks almost all over the then known civilized world of Asia and Europe. However, with the rise of new economic systems in Western Europe, migrations have changed their nature all beyond recognition. It became a symbol of new form of exploitation both of human and physical resources, worse still at the cost of the natives and their primitive economy.

Nearer home, it is one of the strangest phenomena, not yet fully analyzed, that during the decadent phase of Moghul em pire, when along with its erstwhile Rajput allies, became an easy prey to Marathas and Afghan inroads, Marwari capital spread its financial tentacles over the whole of British In dia. Only the Gujaratis, notably the Bohras and the Chet tiars of south, were their only poor second.

So it seems that the history of the world generally and the history of India in particular is replete with stories of large scale movement of people beyond the country as well as within the country with attendant consequences. This is a phenomenon which has persisted till recent times, but dif ferent from those of the ancient days.

The current trends towards the movement of people is from rural areas to the centres of growth, particularly the developing industrial and urban areas as well as areas noted for plantation economy. After the settlement of British rule, particularly all lover India, when law and order situation improved, means of communication modernized and transport facilitated, the advanturous people went to dif ferent parts of the country in search of fortune. Such for tune could easily be made in newly introduced economy of plantations mainly in North-East India and to some extent in south India.

The newly introduced economy of plantation specially in North-East India has swept the attention of fortune seekers belonging to North-Bihar mainly after the great earthquake of 1934 which altered the whole situation in North-Bihar. Due to earthquake, its rivers became the 'rivers of sorrow', soil sandy, land unfertile and further with decline of in digo industry and that of saltpetre, the area became more and more agriculture based. With the population ever on the increase and recurring floods, droughts and famines, in dustrial growth negligible transport and communication sys tem disrupted, the whole Tirhut (area lying between the Gan dak and Kosi) presents the picture of an 'area of darkness'. It is to fight against this all enveloping misery arising out of poverty and unemployment that young men, individually or collectively decided to seek their fortune in North East India. The influx of a large number of migrants, especially rural urban migrants, provided the labour force for the new plantation economy and later on they were absorbed into the new fast growing urban centres of the region doing jobs which they would be ashamed to do at home. Research in rural-urban migration in India has hitherto been mainly con cerned with destination point and no attention has been paid to the impact at the origin point. The major thrust of this paper is to remove this shortcoming.

Therefore, out of this panorama of migratory movement in North Eastern region, the present paper takes up one such sector from an anthropological point of view, the migration of a heterogenous group of people belonging to north Bihar in Gauhati a town situated on the banks of Mahabahu Brah maputra and at the feet of Goddess Kamakhya. The paper is divided into two parts, part I contains information about the socio-economic characteristics of migrants. In Part II, the paper goes on to discuss the socio-economic impact of migration at the place of origin. The discussion is mostly related to aspect such as cultivable land, status, agricul tural activities, housing pattern, indebtedness, education, remmitance and frequency of migrant's visits and material culture. In the concluding part of the paper, an attempt has been made to highlight the role of migration in strengthen ing the rural tradition. It is necessary at this stage to define "tradition". Tradition is not only a symbol of con tinuity and of looking at the present in terms of the past and at the further in terms of present but also as a gurdian of the nature and the range of the very creativity and in novativeness of the society.

50 samples were selected for village study. The data were collected from the villages of North Bihar, namely, Akaur, Chauri, Chinmiliya Ejot, Hisar and Pipraun (Madhubani district), Narenpur and Phukdoliya (Samastipur district, Surffuddinpur (Muzaffarpur district) and Kushar (Vaishali district). The paper is based on the findings of those samples from which the data has been collected on both the ends, i.e. destination and origin.

I

Socio-economic background

Out of the total 50 respondents who were interviewed 90% were in the age bracket of 15-24 at the time of migration. At the time of interview, 88% were in the age group of 25-34 years and 18% between 35-44 years. 88% of the respondents were married at the time of migration. 82% of the respon dents were illiterate and 10%

had schooling upto middle level. 70% of the respondents belonged to nuclear families.

Almost all the respondents were engaged in unskilled work. 44% were cart pullers, 21% rickshaw pullers and only 10% each were engaged in cart-driving or as coolies. 8% were en gaged in manual jobs in printing presses.

The largest single group comprises backward castes (60%) followed by scheduled castes (32%). High castes constituted only 8% of the total samples. Almost all the high caste respondents were Maithil Brahmins.

At the time of their exodus 74% possessed cultivable landed property. Only 26% were landless. 18.9% held land in between 0.00 - 0.36 acres, 45.94% were in between the 0.36 - 0.72 acres and 32.43% in between the 0.72 - 1.09 acre brack ets.

At the time of their out-migration, 86% respondents lived in mud huts with thatched roof and 10% in mud huts with tiled roof.

In a nutshell, from above observations, it can be summised that scarcity of land, illiteracy as well as increased bur den after marriage forced the migrants to enter into job market for livelihood which is not available in their own village. So, in search of appropriate jobs for livelihood they left the village in their youth. They entered into unskilled jobs to support their dependents in villages.

II

In this part of the paper, an attempt has been made to focus the attention on the socio-economic impact of migra tion in the native villages.

Cultivable land

Only 12% of the respondents were landless. 88% owned less than 1.09 acres of land and were marginal farmers.

Inquiries reveal that almost all the respondents have added to their holdings after migration of their family mem bers. Some migrant families sold their landed property to meet pressing family needs such as marriage and medical treatment.

Of 13 landless migrant families, 53.8% purchased land after the migration of one of the family members. 2% family moved up to the next higher holding bracket. The number of respondents owing land between 0.36 - 0.72 acres increased. In the case of landless 6% got land on lease whereas others remained landless as before. Only 2% respondents leased out his land. So with only a little purchase or sale of land migrants changed their land status.

Agricultural activities

It is interesting to know how the families of migrants cultivate their land or make a living after the migration. The labour used in the cultivation of land by migrant's families is shown in table 1.

Table 1 : Labour used in the cultivation of land by caste status.

Types of labour	Caste group							
	High caste		Backward castes		Scheduled castes		Total	
	No.	%	No.	%	No.	%	No.	%
By family labour	-	-	6	12.7	2	4.2	8	17.0
By hired labour	3	6.3	1	2.1	-	-	4	8.5
By family labour and hired labour	1	2.1	23	48.9	11	23.4	35	74.4

More than 74% of the families cultivate their land by a combination of family and hired labour, 17% by family labour and barely 8.5% respondents used only hired labour for the cultivation of land. A majority of the respondents belonging to Backward castes and scheduled castes used family and hired labours for cultivation. The bulk of hired labour was utilised by high castes. Out of 30 backward caste respon dents 56.6% and out of 13 scheduled castes 46.1% were work ing as agricultural labour or engage in other types of wage labour in their own village. They were mostly engaged for specificed agricultural works such as ploughing, transplan tation of paddy, weeding and harvesting etc. Only 6.6% respondent families women belonging to backward castes worked in the houses of rich farmers as domestic help.

Thus, agriculture is still the dominant occupation of the migrants family members. The attitude of members of migrant families have not changed towards agriculture.

Housing pattern

Out of total 50 respondents 52% had built new houses while remaining had repaired their old houses. Mud huts with thatched roofs usually need repairs of the thatch every other year and a major repair every five to seven years. Al most all of them received funds for construction or repair of the houses from the migrants. The number of houses with mud walls and tiled roof and brickwalls with tiled roof type of houses increased. The number of houses with mud walls and thatched roof have gone down.

It is clear that the housing pattern of migrant families has changed due to migration. The migrants invested their savings in housing which is a basic need.

Indebtedness

15 respondents were in debt. Of this 60% hailed from back ward castes and the rest were scheduled castes. Almost all the families had taken loan after the migration of their family members. The majority of the debtors belonged to the category of 0.31 - 0.59 acres of holding group. 20% landless families were also in debt.

The main sources of credit for the respondents were rich farmers and moneylenders. Two third respondents mentioned the landlord as their source for loan while the rest had taken loan from moneylender. The amount of debt varies from Rs.201 to Rs. 800. 46.6% families had taken the loan ranging between the Rs.201-400. The same percentage of respondents had taken the loan ranging between Rs. 401-600. 93.3% respondents had taken loans for consumption purposes viz. domestic needs, marriage, death-rites and medical treatment. Only 6.6% respondents belonging to higher holding group had taken loan for productive purposes.

The tendency of taking loan, however, has decreased after migration as the need for borrowing has been reduced.

Education

76% respondents considered education necessary at the present time. One of the main reasons for this positive at titude is that they believed that only through education their children would get an occupation with some status. It is also necessary to get some education for wc:king outside even as an unskilled labour and doing agricultural work. However, the children of 72% respondents were attending school. They are also provided books. slates and exercise books etc.

Thus, migration has ushered in a new type of outlook among the respondents so for as education of their children is concerned.

Remittance and Frequency of Migrants' Visits to the Village

The migrants take care of the members of their families in the village by remitting money and paying visits. Almost all the families had been receiving money every month from the migrants through money-order and sometimes through villagers/relatives who paid visits to the village. The money was utilised for domestic purpose, in performing religious ceremonies and in agriculture.

All the migrants periodically visit their native place. 74% visit their native place once a year while the others visit twice a year. All of them visit their villages on the occasion of important family events and activities. In each trip the migrants bring gifts, money and consumer items which in turn enhance their status in the neighbourhood. They participate in agricultural operations and other domes tic work during their stay at the native place.

So, it is clear that besides sending money, the frequency of a migrant's visits to his native village is an important factor in maintaining ties with the family and increasing family solidarity.

Material Culture

Almost all of the respondent families purchased household articles like stainless steel utensils and some aluminium and brass pots. They also purchased other consumer goods like lantern, transistor, radio, torch and tape recorder.

Use of soap and detergent powder was not uncommon. However, the majority of the respondents used soap to wash the clothes. Hair oil, sindur, alto, snow, powder, cream and a scent were being used by the almost all the respondent families.

Discussion

Migration acts as a source for development in a backward area. But it hardly plays against tradition. It helps the migrants in bettering their socio-economic condition as well as in maintaining their traditional norms and values.

There has been a noticeable change in the landholding of families of migrants. Those who were landless have acquired some land. Those who had land have added to their holding and have gone to the next higher holding bracket. The migrants were happy to provide funds for this or to purchase land during one of their visits. The intense desire of migrants to acquire land and increase the holding size is motivated to acquire better social status and prestige in village society. Land is a traditional value in rural India. Sale of some land by a few families for meeting expenses on marriage and medical treatment indicates that migrants are more eager to maintain their traditional values. Both the events reflect on the prestige of the head of the household.

The pattern of deployment of labour in agriculture con tinues to be the same as before. Family members continue to contribute their labour in agricultural operations as before. Some of the poor women work as maid servants.

Agriculture is still an occupation of their choice. Due to migration of some family members, attitude towards agricul tural operation has not turned negative. 75% out of 4 high caste respondent families used hired labour for the cultiva tion of their land. In absence of migrants, even women family members work as hired labour to assist in economic activities. There has been some changes in agricultural operations and these changes have helped them raise their status within the traditional economy and society.

Better financial resources have led to better housing. Even the mud houses have improved. Thatch has been replaced by tiles. The urge for better housing reflects their effort to achieve status and prestige in rural ambit. House is traditionally considered an index of status of a family.

Although, the burden of debt has been reduced. The purpose and the sources of borrowing continue to be traditional. Loans are mostly for consumption purposes and the creditors are the landlords and the moneylenders.

There is a positive attitude to education and the bulk of the respondents are sending their children to schools. They are, however, in village schools where they imbibe the traditional culture. So, the money spent on education goes for pattern maintenance rather than for social change.

The remittances are utilized for domestic purposes i.e., in performance of religious ceremonies and in agricultural improvement. It also helps in meeting kinship and familial obligations. The very idea that the migrant slogs all day only to strengthen his rural base and to revitalise his family resources helps reinforcing long-standing rural tradition.

The periodic and regular visits of the migrant to his vil lage helps not only to reunite him to his kith and kin but also to renew his bond with his traditional norms, be haviour, practices, usages etc. So, remittances, visits, gifts, assistance to new migrants may, therefore, be seen as strengthening of ethical and traditional ties with their village. Even the articles of conspicuous consumption, they bring, help in enhancing family status. This again is a means of mobility on the axis of prestige.

It could safely be stated that the changes taking place in socio-economic spheres of migrant's life at native place due to inflow of funds from outside have not ushered in the ur ban ethic but rather buttressed the rural one.

SEVENTEEN

Binod C Agrawal

Modernizing the Tradition: Closing Communication Gap Between Information Poor and Rich

The aim of this paper is to analyse whether during the Satellite Instructional Television Experiment (SITE) there was an increase in the information gap between the informa tion "poor" and the information "rich".

While planning satellite based national television for education and development in India, it is argued that the fruits of information would benefit the rich, whereas some argue that it would help to close the information gap be tween the information rich and the poor in the highly stratified, unequal, exploitative, faction ridden, and high- caste dominated villages of the country. The discussion is inconclusive; however satellite based television is being utilised to accelerate the process of development at an unprecedented scale with the help of Indian National Satel lite (INSAT) system.

In a review article Dube (1976) emphasised the positive contribution of communication development with distributive justice. Dube (1972: 156-157) earlier noted that "powerful" vested interests often tend to monopolise beneficial innova tions...such vested interests often exploit the institu tional innovations also to their advantage". Rahim (1976:158) also points out that "the general tendency of governments (in South Asia) has been to yield to pressure from the relatively prosperous class of people in the rural society". The Planning Commission in India (nd) believes that mass media is more beneficial to the rich and does in crease the information gap. Agrawal **et al.** (1977) observed that differential exposure to TV lead to differential levels of change, or gain in awareness, Knowledge, adoption and use of innovations.

In a recent book, Shingi, Kaur and Rai (1982) attempted to test the "communication effects gap" hypothesis in the con text of rural television in India. Expanding on Tichenor's "Knowledge gap" hypothesis, they argued that the same could be true for media in general, rather than a particular medium like print, which was originally tested by Tichenor **et al**(1970). Based on the findings of Shingi, Kaur and Rai (1982) Tichenor **et al.** (1970) and Agrawal **et al** (1977), it is hypothesised that other things being equal, community TV viewing would help close the information gap between those who have no access to information from other channels, in cluding developmental agencies and those who do have such access.

The Experiment[1]

The Satellite Instructional Television Experiment (SITE) was conducted in 2330 villages scattered in 20 districts in six states of India (Known as cluster) for a period of one year beginning August I, 1975. Specially pre-recorded TV programmes were telecasts using Applications Technology Statellite-6 (ATS-6) from Ahmedabad and Delhi Earth Sta tions.In this largest techno-social experiment, ever con ducted in human history, those villagers who participated had no previous TV exposure of any kind. Taking into account the relative dearth of external communication in rural In dia, SITE was a leap forward in the use of advanced technol ogy for education and rural development.

The general objectives for the social evaluation of SITE were:

i) To survey the extent to which a climate for development was created through measurement of awareness, Knowledge, adoption and use of improved practices in the field of agriculture, health, nutrition and family planning;

ii) To survey the extent to which SITE had widened horizone, raised educational aspiration, developed em pathy, increased social

1. This portion of presentation has been drawn from Agrawal, Doshi, Jesudason and Verma (1977). Hence, no specific reference has been made.

participation, and thereby ac celerated the process of development; and

iii)To explore the possibility of attitudinal and be havioural changes from a traditional to non- traditional way of life.

Social Evaluation Study Design

The Survey to evaluate social effects of SITE was designed as a "field experiment" incorporating pre-and-post observa tions in experimental and control groups. To provide an op portunity for mid-fore correction, and to predict the direc tion of change, during SITE, survey was also conducted. The study design can be represented as follows:

$O_{T\text{-}O}\ V\ O_{T\text{-}1}\ V\ O_{T\text{-}2}$ Experimental Group

$O_{T\text{-}O}\ O_{T\text{-}1}\ O_{T\text{-}2}$ Control Group

Where V represents exposure to experimental treatment (i.e., TV), the effects of which were to be determined. O's represent observations made in both the groups at pre-SITE (T-O), during SITE (T-1) and post SITE (T-2) periods. The difference of scores between two surveys indicated change (or gain) over time in the two respective groups. A com parison of the two change scores on the same dependent vari ables in experimental and control groups would indicate the treatment effect that is the impact of TV. A pre-tested com mon schedule was used in six separate languages in the respective clusters. The same pre-SITE respondents were in terviewed during and post-SITE surveys.

The Sample and Sampling Procedure

A two stage sampling procedure was followed for the selec tion of respondents. In the first stage, 12 experimental Villages, equally divided into three population categories were selected adopting Probability Proportion to Size (PPS) sampling technique in each cluster from among the SITE vil lages. Six control villages in each cluster were selected by matching the population range of the experimental villages. In the second stage, 72 respondents of 15 years and above were randomly selected from each of the 108 SITE villages (72 experimental and 36 control). The six clusters were from

Bihar, Madhya Pradesh, Rajasthan, Orissa, Andhra Pradesh and Karnataka. Totally 7,776 were expected to be interviewed. The actual number of respondents interviewed in pre-SITE survey was 7,772; during SITE survey 6,622, and in post-SITE survey 6499. There was about 14.8 per cent sample attrition between pre-and-during SITE survey, and 16.4 percent attri tion between pre-and post-SITE survey. The sample consisted of approximately equal male and female respondents.

Method of Analysis

In this survey, the independent variable was the frequency of TV viewing. The dependent variables included sex, educa tion, house type, material possession and land ownership. Various studies related to communication indicated an infor mation gap between males and females, due to unequal access to information. The existence of such a gap is accentuated by the fact that women have a lower status in rural India. Acquisition of education is associated with wealth and a higher socio-economic status. Hence, it was though that education as a dependent variable would help in testing the hypothesis. House type, material possession and land owner ship are fairly good indicators of economic status. Hence, it was thought that education as a dependent variable would help in testing the hypothesis. House type, material posses sion and land ownership are fairly good indicators of economic status. Hence, they have been used as dependent variables.

The general hypothesis that guided the analysis of the data can be stated as

$$\bar{G}_C < \bar{G}_{E1} < \bar{G}_{E2} < \bar{G}_{E3}$$

Where G is the change or gain that was observed and C (control group), E_1 (rate viewer), E_2 (occasional viewer) and E_3 (frequent viewer).

The analysis focused on the pre-and-post SITE differences in gain scores (G_2) of all clusters, separately for males and females. The respondents were classified as: control (C) no TV viewing; rare viewer (E_1)-less than one day TV viewing in a month; occasional viewer (E_2)-less than three days TV viewing in a month; and frequent viewer (E_3) four or more days of TV viewing in a month. For each of the development areas a set of items constituted a two point scale zero or one; the score G_2 can very from - 1.00 to + 1.00. The score was to be interpreted as the observed change that had oc cured during SITE, and the change in the expected direction was indicated by a positive score. 'F' and 't' values were calculated to test significance between observed values for the three experimental and control groups.

Results

Table 1 provides the composite mean or differential gain between pre-and-post SITE surveys of males and females in the area of health awareness, knowledge and adoption of in novations. The total gain score consists of 12 items (three regarding awareness, three for knowledge and six for adoption).

Table 1 : Innovations in Health : Differential Gain (or Mean Score) Between Pre and Post SITE Surveys for Males and Females.

	Control	Rate viewer	Occasional viewer	Frequent viewer
Awareness G_{-2} score				
Male	.183	.186	.271	.354
Female	.119	.97	.254	.290
Knowledge G_{-2} score				
Male	.660	.758	.834	.692
Female	.582	.653	.903	1.021
Adoption G_{-2} score				
Male	.371	.250	.477	.717
Female	.241	.287	.565	.806
Total G_{-2} score				
Male	1.423	1.466	1.799	1.938
Female	1.047	1.287	2.020	2.431
Sample (N)				
Male	1066	264	857	1089
Female	1057	917	982	288

The two most remarkable findings in the table are (a) con trol and rare viewers consistently have lower scores than the occasional and frequent viewers; the exception is the knowledge score of males

Table 2 : Family Planning : Differential Gain (or mean score) Between Pre and Post SITE Survey for Males and Females

	Control	Rate viewer	Occasional viewer	Frequent viewer
Awareness G-2 Score				
Male	.302	.098	.253	.270
Female	.265	.162	.530	.656
Interest G-2 Score				
Male	.397	.299	.458	.545
Female	.396	.031	.601	.683
Adoption G-2 Score				
Male	.054	.027	.046	.075
Female	.064	.005	.092	.106
Total G-2 Score				
Male	.754	.424	.756	.890
Female	.725	.243	1.230	1.445
Sample (N)				
Male	873	224	697	811
Female	818	742	732	218

among frequent viewers and (b) women in control and rare viewers categories have lower scores when compared with males; contrary to this the total gain in knowledge about health is higher among occasional and frequent female viewers as compared to male viewers. One observes a similar trend in case of family planning (see Table-2). Material possessions in the area of health and family planning were considered as a dependent variable. The fact that those persons who record 'no items', especially women, showed a steady gain with increased frequency of viewing TV, indicates that even those who are not 'well off' are not deprived of information and knowledge gains. Nevertheless, initial and additional levels of knowledge of a women with more material possessions are higher : this could be due to a variety of reasons, but does among females in virtually all categories of viewers. The assertion that the inferior status of women inhibits their knowledge gain and widens the information gap, is statistically proved to be unfounded in view of the date presented in Table 1 and 2. Education, housetype, material possessions, media exposure and urban contact from the perspective of education showed that illiterate women had higher score in health and family planning than illiterate men and literate women. Illiterate men also showed higher gain scores than literate men (Table not given). Further supporting the view that education is not a barrier in knowledge gain and will not widen the in formation gap provided their is an access to information.

In the light of foregoing analysis, basically it is argued that the information gap between the information poor (in this case, the women) the information rich (in this case, the men) was bridged. If information is treated as one of the forces of modernisation as indicated by Eisenstadt (1976) then the Television exposure has led in bridging the information gap contrary to the belief in India supported by empirical evidences, that women lack information much more than men. In this perspective, it would be possible to con ceive communication as modernising force of the tradition in which the information gap is consciously maintained between the men and women to have unequal position. It would be necessary to follow this line of argument to understand as to how this modernising force can be further utilised for modernising tradition.

REFERENCES

Agarwal B.C. J.K. Doshi, K.K.Verma, and Victor Jesudason 1977 SITE social Evaluation - Impact on Adults (Part I and 2); Indian Space Research Organisation, Bangalore.

Dube, S.C. 1976 Development, Change and Communication in India; In Communication and Change: The Last Ten Years - and the Next, Schramm and Lerner, (eds), The East West Centre, Honolulu.

Eisenstadt, S.N. 1976 The Changing Vision of Modernization and Development; In communication and Change : The Last Ten Years - and the Next. pp 31-44. The Univer sity Press of Hawaii, Honolulu.

Planning Commission nd Satellite Instructional ·Television Experiment : An Evaluation of its Social Impact; New Delhi.

Rahim, Syed A. 1976 Communication Approaches in Rural Development; In Communication and Change : The Last Ten Years and the Next. ed. by Wilbur Schiamm and Daniel Learner pp. 151 162. The University Press of Hawaii, Honolulu.

Shingi, Prakash, M., G Kaur and R.P. Rai 1982 Television and Knowledge - Gap Hypothesis; Indian Institute of Management, Ahmedabad.

Tichenor, P.J. et al. 1970 Mass Media Flow and Differential Growth in Knowledge; Public Opinion Quarterly, 34(2): 159 - 70.

EIGHTEEN

K.K. Verma

Role of Tradition in Rural Development: Some Observations with Reference to Bihar

The contemporary concern with the term 'development' in Third World is wide and many sided. Until the mid 1970s the dominant paradigm of development centred round the rate of economic growth. The index to measure development was the Gross National Product (GNP) or per capita income. Growth, first and equality later was often justified by trickle down theory that leading sectors once advanced would then spread their advantage to the lagging sectors (Rogers 1976 : 217). By the mid seventies people have started thinking of development not only in terms of per capita income but also in terms of improvement of quality of life.

The new definition of development concerns the human development and equitable distribution of the benefits of development to all sections of society. The focus of quan tification of development has been shifted from the 'Gross National Product' to 'Gross National Welfare'. Development in the new perspective has been referred to as an overall process of improving quality of life to a desired level. In other words, it is an overall transformation of societies to a desired social order. It connotes economic growth as well as socio-cultural change.

In recent years, increasing attention has been focussed on the significance of rural development. In India, rural development is generally equated with the development of 'rural poor'. Our experience of last three decades in the area of rural development indicates that programmes meant for the uplift of the poor generally benefit the affluent sections of the society to multiply their fortunes and thus widened the gap between the 'rich' and the 'poor' in the countryside. It also suggests that capital multiplication and technological modernisation do not necessarily lead to human development (Verma et al 1981). This has happened be cause the policy makers in India have viewed the problem of rural development from the 'top down' not 'bottom up' and as such their endeavours at rural development have remained piece-meal effort (Mehta 1984). However, the policy makers often attribute all the failures of planning to 'wretched' tradition and 'dammed' culture of the people. Thus culture and tradition have become the conventional victims of their tirade (Atal 1976 : 135).

The word tradition is derived from 'traders' which means 'to transmit'. Tradition is transmitted value and behaviour pattern of a community. The tradition - composed of religion, values and social structure - has been attributed the qualities of an unshakable colossus. However, the ideal type construct of tradition has neither historical specificity nor a realistic sociological base (Dube 1976 : 74). Traditions have shown great adaptability and resilience over time. They are not static, old traditions die and new traditions are continually being built up under the in fluence of endogenous and heterogenous factors (Sachchidananda 1973).

Development has been accepted as national goal in the perspective of directed socio-economic change. The extent of change in the socio-economic life of the people depends much on the perpetual combat of the two kinds of forces : those that seek to promote change and those that strive to main tain the status-quo (Foster 1973 : 76). The former act, through the desire for development while the latter act through the desire to preserve tradition. Development and tradition are always in interacting relationship with each other.

We may draw analogy from physical sciences in terms of screen and energy in the form of rays of light. Screen does no allow all forms of rays to pass through it. It is naturally, therefore, act as an obstruction to working of the rays operated on it. Traditional forces in the society which obstructs change in it, may be compared to screen aspect which does not permit to pass all kind of rays. On the other hand, rays which can penetrate through the screen could be compared with developmental forces. Just as some form of rays are penetrable through the screen, so certain stimulii of change could overcome the forces of tradition in the form of screen. There has always been differential and selective effect of tradition in response to different developmental packages.

The paradigm (refer to Diagram-1) given here attempts to conceptualise the situation in context of interfacing of tradition and development. The present paper attempts to ex amine the 'screen effect' of tradition in the above concep tual framework on the basis of observations in rural development in Bihar. By 'screen effect' here we mean how traditions response to various developmental packages. The observations are derived from the studies on the impact of agriculture and irrigation development programmes, introduc tion of micro-technologies, functioning of non-formal educa tion, health and family welfare measures and development communication.

Agricultural Development

Agriculture continues to be the main source of subsistence of rural people in India. Agricultural operations are guided by ideas and knowledge which people have learnt through ex perience of their elders i.e. tradition in the field. Rural development, to a great extent, in Indian context is a mat ter of agricultural development.

The study of social dimension of 'Intensive Agricultural District Programme (IADP) conducted in late sixties (Sachchidananda 1972) throws some light on the 'screen effect' of the tradition. The objective of IADP was to demonstrate the potentialities of increasing food production through multipronged concentrated and co-ordinated approach in certain area which could quickly respond to the programme. Field work was conducted in thirty villages in Shahabad district, ten each from two IADP blocks and one non-IADP block. Among the experimental block one was taken for the best performance and other for the poorest perfor mance. The study shows that the upper castes compared to the lower castes lead in adoption of agricultural innovations. Socio-economic status and adoption hold positive correla tion. The score includes caste status, landholding, occupa tion, education, social participation and level of living. Change agents also work more closely with people who belong to this section. Friends, relations and neighbours continue to be an effective traditional channel of communication. It is reported that adoption index continues to rise with the increase in the size of family and landholding and after reaching an optimal level in this respect, the adoption in dex to fall. The study indicated that it is the affluent sections of the village community which control resources and are able to increase their wealth.

Develop-ment effort	Economic Growth	Investment, Adoption of Technology, Human Resource Development, Institutional Arrangement, Development of Infrastructure	T R A D I T I O N — Change in Resultant of Development effort
	Social Change	Education, Awareness Through Communication Modification in values, norms, attitudes and socio-economic relations And provision of some opportunities and services	

Diagram-1 : Conceptual model of development process.

The adopters in terms of some indices of modernity hold significant correlation while with some other indices of adopters do not show any correlation and with a few they hold significantly negative correlation.

Those farmers who display some planning orientation, have optimal attitude to life and have tendency to save adopt agricultural innovations better. The correlation between deferred satisfaction and adoption is reported to be nega tive. The same is the case with risk taking. The correlation between desire for change and adoption is insignificant. Thus differential levels of individual modernity or tradi tion are not necessarily facilitate of or impediment to agricultural development.

The study further reveals that increase in agricultural productivity and rise in income of the people have not made any noticeable impact on their standard of living and their aspiration. The study further shows that people in the most progressive village in respect of adoption of agricultural innovation are very rigid in observance of pollution and commensal rules. The same trend is evident in regard to out look of people towards social distance between castes. The study reveals that economic development through agricultural development does not necessarily bring about improvement in quality of life of people, development in their outlook, norm and tradition.

Under 'Lab to land programme', a village in vicinity of Rajendra Agricultural University was adopted for social forestry in early 1983. Lab to Land programme aims at im proving the socio-economic condition of the rural poor by involvement of agricultural scientists themselves. Under the above programme varieties of trees were planted on the land owned by individuals both from affluent and downtrodden and community places with the objective to provide fuel-wood and promoting better ecological balance in terms of vegetation. Many varieties were uncommon in village. After the gap of six months it was observed (Verma & Sinha 1983) that trees planted on the community places and on the lands of down- trodden were left uncared or uprooted. It was also reported that some of the planted trees were sold for nominal price to affluent section or members of higher castes of the vil lage community. The villages were not familiar with the most of the varieties planted under the scheme.

At one temple site two *pipal* plants were much cared. It was because pipal was considered sacred. But in general the age old tradition to develop community place was absent. In place of community feelings individualism had grown. Among the affluent section, the planted trees were much cared. This experiment suggests that those who are economically well off take advantages more of any developmental pachage.

In a recent study on the evaluation of Kosi (Verma 1985) attempts have been made to understand some aspects of problem of a river valley project - Kosi, the development efforts in its command area and the situation in which development agencies operate. The area which suffered from flood every year is now available for cultivation round the year. The area under the command has undergone fast change over the last three decade in respect of cropping pattern. There was a proverb that people of the region used to get *desaria* (a deep water variety of paddy) and *Kewai* (a variety of fish found in mud) in abundance without much effort. Un til the construction of Koshi embankment paddy was the main crop. In general the region was characterised by mono- cropping. In low land, generally deep water paddy or jute and in levelled land paddy or jute was grown in kharif and field used to remain fellow in the Ravi season. When Kosi stopped flooding in the late fifties, maize becomes the main crop. Towards the close of the sixties, with the development of Kosi canal system for irrigation paddy again comes into prominence. Around this period, farmer started growing wheat on large scale. With the introduction of bamboo borewells in late 1960s, intensity of cultivation has greatly increased. This phase of development has changed the cropping pattern altogether. Farmers have started taking two to the three crops from the same field. Farmers now remain engaged in agriculture throughout the year. Traditions do not come in a way of agricultural development. However, upper castes con tinue to be non-cultivators of their land by themselves. They manage their farm by hiring labour.

The growth of bamboo borewell in the region much depends on tradition which acts through kinship ties. The bamboo borewell is not taken up largely by small farmers inspite of its low cost. Only one tenth of total bamboo borewells is reported to have been sunk by farmers having less than 10 acres of effective landholding. Here by effective landhold ing we mean now much land the farmer really control includ ing *benami* ownership. Some innovative farmers have sunk bam boo borewell. A few marginal farmers have been given finan cial assistance under IRDP for bamboo borings. However, the general trend is not much affected. Small farmers in general are unable to afford a pumping set. It is observed that transaction or hiring the set runs between members of same kin group on priority. Only when the set is idle, it is given on rent to others. This uncertainty has discouraged investment in bamboo borewell by small farmers who have no kinship ties with owner of a pump set.

Micro technologies

Technological innovation in the form of micro-technology such as gadget, tools, vehicle, bio-gas, etc. has far reach ing effect. Electricity, though a product of large scale technology is in nature of consumer goods. Rural people in the grid area have a choice to accept or reject the innova tion. From this point of view it falls under the category of micro technology.

The appraisal of the functioning of rural electrification project in tribal area in Bihar (Sachchidananda and Verma 1983) reveals some implications in introducing the innova tion. The study is based on the data collected from the selected rural electrification projects - two each from Ran chi and Santhal Praganas districts. The study reveals that electrification in tribal area has brought about a change in technological environment of people living in the region. This has led to a change in socio-economic life of the people. The study reveals that it is the non-tribals more than the tribals who have harnessed the new form of energy for their benefit in a much better way.

Electrification had brought about positive changes in the socio-economic life of people in qualitative terms. However, the impact in quantative terms was restricted to some in dividuals or villages. In the domestic sector, lighting was its sole utility among the tribals. Some consumers were found using other electric gadget such as fan and radio. It had influenced the life style of people. In agriculture all the cultivators who use electricity for lifting water from their well were using 3 HP motor. They claimed that they were practising intensive cultivation. Since there holdings were small, they were not in a position to make large capi tal investment for farm mechanization. However, power driven threshing and oil expeller machine are generally installed along with cereal grinding machine. At places where such facilities exist, people stopped threshing or husking paddy manually. It had influenced the cropping pattern, food habits and provided more leisure for women. These agro-processing units were becoming popular day by day. Their owners, the non-tribals, were making large profits.

In view of the small number of tribals who have got electric connection for other than domestic use there has been no substantial change in occupational pattern of the tribals. However, some rise in the level of living was evi dent in those families even which had taken electricity for domestic purposes. Similarly a change in the quality of life is also visible with more leisure for women and more study hours for children. No change in the social structure or so cial cohesiveness among tribals was in evidence even though those who got electric connections gained prestige. There have been more change in the occupational pattern, employ ment generation and income generation in the non-tribal group. Since the group was more prosperous, they took full advantage of the new oportunities.

The study of Bio-gas and its constraints in the Chandi block of Nalanda district (Prasad and Verma 1985) show that in addition to technical and financial constraints there are socio-psychological constraints. The psychological feeling producing constraints are mainly, bad odour of bio gas, in ferior quality of organic manure and unhygenic condition. The lack of cattle to energise a gobar gas plant in each household can be solved by connecting its chamber with latrine tank. But tradition comes in the way as ritual pol lution is very deeply associated with excreta.

Education

Education play vital role in manipulating tradition for development. The study of (Verma et al 1981) functioning of non-formal adult education (NAEP) indicates NAEP as change agent had percolated in the development process. Change started with the acquisition of literacy. Cases revealed that acquisition of literacy and numeracy skills had created a sense of pride and self-confidence among learners. They felt that they could now talk with official and outsiders. Cases indicated that the programme had generated a kind of chain reaction among the illiterate masses. The desire to communicate with one's own kinsmen inculcated the felt need for acquiring literacy skill especially among women.

Attempts were made through the programme to bring about the overall consciousness among the rank and file of the oppressed and weaker sections of the society. Learners were organised through the formation of chetna sangh. Cases have reveled that chetna sangh could succeed in infusing aware ness and upgrading functionality in many more ways; through chetna sanghs learners had raised their issues; at various places they succeeded in achieving their objectives; they helped villagers raise the rate of their wages; they motivated to take up community work. In many cases chetna sangh acted as a pressure group. Cases also indicated that learners had utilised the existing facilities which were earlier denied to them because of ignorance and inability for collective bargaining. The experiences confirm that education, whatever the way it may be has great potential to combat with forces of tradition in, achieving development.

Mother and child care & family welfare

The survey (Mandal 1979, Narayan 1979, Verma 1984, 1985) conducted on rural and tribal children indicates that people living in villages are facing problem of basic aminities of health. In the absence of drain, water flows through lane. In the villages, the lack of drinking water has been iden tified as one of the major causes for the spread of dis eases. Often wells in villages from which drinking water is drawn, are in unhygienic state. In summer, as many wells dry up, drinking water is drawn from ponds and wells which are also used for cattle. They are hardly aware of the useful ness of personal hygiene. Most of them do not know that dis ease like whooping cough, tuberculosis, typhoid, diphtheria, poliomyelitis and tetanus can be prevented. The situation is worse among the weaker sections. Insofar as meternal care is concerned pregnant mother seldom consult qualified medical doctors. It is partly due to non-availability of medical facilities in the area and partly because of ignorance. The studies further show that nutritional status of the people is deficient. Although poverty is the single important cause, often ignorance of the people is identified as con tributive cause. The studies also show that the rural people do not feel that children and pregnant mother need extra- food and mother's first milk is good for new born baby.

The developmental norms and tradition are found often interfac ing each other.

Children serve many functions for parents and fulfil many needs. Satisfaction and cost are therefore conceived broadly to encompass economic, social and psychological dimensions. There may be fifteen possible categories of values of children (Arnold et al 1975). These are as follows:

1. *Positive values*

   a) Emotional benefits
   b) Economic benefits and security
   c) Self enrichment development
   d) Identification with children
   e) Family cohesiveness and continuity
   f) Sibling relationships
   g) Child survival
   h) Sex preference

2. *Negative value*

   a) Emotional cost
   b) Economic cost
   c) Restriction or opportunity cost
   d) Physical demand
   e) Family cost
   f) Maternal health
   g) Societal cost

People perceive these values differently in accordance with their traditions. A value which is more emphaiszed in one society may not be considered so important in others (Verma 1984). Satisfaction and cost of children are a major motivational force in child bearing.

Developmental Communication

Evaluation (Agarwal et al 1977) of most carefully designed experiment, Satellite Instructional TV Experiment (SITE) in dicates that under 'certain conditions' the 'Communication gap' has been narrowed (for detail about the Study please see preccding pages 223-

224). The requisit conditions are the exposure of TV and TV viewing in community places. The developmental communication under this ideal sitaution helps in closing the information gap between those who have no access to information and those who have prior information. Thus development communication in this perspective can mould traditional behavior.

III

In the foregoing presentation it is evident that there had been differential "screen effect" of tradition. Tradition does not generally come in the way of agricultural develop ment. It is the financial and technical constraints which block the path of development. Economic development through agricultural development does not necessarily bring about the improvement in quality of life of people and their out look. In some areas, such as adoption of micro technologies, tradition and social norms come in the way to achieve developmental goals. Tradition in the areas of social development acts as an impediment to change. Change takes place in this area at a slower pace. In the process of com bat between development efforts and tradition, at times tradition itself be changed or modified.

REFERENCES

Agarwal, B.C., Doshi J.K. Jasudasan, Victor and Verma, K.K. 1977 Site Social Evaluation - Impact on Adult; Vol. I & II, ISRO, Bangalore.

Atal, Yogesh 1976 Asian Thinking on Development; Abhinava, New Delhi

Arnold, et al 1975 The value of children; East West Centre Honolulu, Hawaii

Foster, G. E. 1973 Traditional Societies and Technological Change; Allied Publishing House, Bombay.

Dube, S.C. 1976 Social and Cultural Factors in Development; in Atal Y. (ed.) Asian Thinking on Development; Ab hinava, Delhi.

Mandal, B.B. & Sinha, K.K. 1979 Rural Children; (Memeo), AN SISS, Patna.

Mehta, S.R. 1984 Rural Development Policies and Programmes; Sage Publications, New Delhi.

Naryayan, S. 1979 Tribal children; (Memeo), ANSISS, Patna.

Prasad, R.B. & Verma K.K. 1985 Bio-Gas Technology and its constraints; (MSS)

Rogers, E.V. 1976 Communication & Development; Communication Research, Vol. 3(2).

Sachchidananda, 1973 Tradition and Modernity; Journal of So cial and Economic Studies, Vol. 1(2).

Verma, K.K., Mishra, Rajeshwar & Lal, Manohar 1981 Adult Education for Development; (Memeo) ANSISS, Patna.

Verma, K.K. 1984 Value of Children, Family Welfare and Com munication Strategy; Journal of Social and Economic Studies, Vol. 1.3 (n.s.)

Verma, K.K. 1985 Case Studies; in Srivastava U.K. et al, (ed) Evaluation of Kosi Command Area Development Agency (Memeo): Indian Institute of Management, Ahmedabad.

Verma, K.K. 1985 Profile of Women & Children : Arki & Sher ghati ; (Memeo), ANSISS, Patna.

NINETEEN

Krishna Bala

Perception of Disease-etiology and Treatment in Perspective of Tradition and Development

Perception of any phenomenon depends on the level of so cial structure, shaped by the commulative traditions. As Dube states "tradition is to be understood as the total heritage, belief, customs and opinions transmitted from gen eration to generation" (1981). Understanding of diseases - etiology, being a life - crisis situation, is not far from the realm of tradition and development. Because, apart from a purely bilogical or pathological perspective, diseases have also been perceived in socio-cultural perspective manifesting multi-dimensional etiology. Some sociologists (Parsons 1951, Saundars 1958, Fox Renee 1968) have perceived diseases and their treatment in socio-cultural dimension and have highlighted the role of tradition and development in accepting the mode of treatment and therapeutic measures. Infact, cultural patterns envisage the manner in which ill ness or diseases are perceived, expressed and reacted upon. Disease etiology, no doubt, is determined by one's percep tion of the situation. But there may be the possibilities of gap between objective reality and subjective perception. Be cause here socialization process operates significantly which differs from culture to culture. Therefore, we per ceive the phenomenon to some extent in accordance with cul tural meanings which may not be objectively relied on.

Since the perception of disease-etiology and treatment are determined by the cultural patterns, values, and endowment of scientific knowledge, these can be analysed in the light of tradition and development.

The present paper attempts to delineate the disease etiol ogy and mode of treatment under the category of 'secular and sacred' terms as well as to see differential impact of education, health innovations and invention in the context of rural-urban exposure on socielization process.

The data incorporated in the paper were collected with the help of an interview Schedule from 300 Cardiac patients. These cases were diagnosed as cardiac patients by the com petent physicians on the basis of clinical invenstigations. Thus the data were obtained from the 300 cardiac patients admitted to the Patna Medical College Hospital and the In dira Gandhi Institute of Cardiology, Patna during 1980-82. They were asked about their perception, etiology and therapeutic measures of some common ailment like Cholera, Malaria, Jaundice, Small Pox, Tuberculosis and Chronic ill ness such as heart disease.

In order to analyse disease-etiology and mode of treat ment, Indian culture may be characterized as the 'sacred- secular' or as what parsons called 'universal - par ticularistic ascriptive' pattern. The element of rationality in it about disease-etiology was not so prominent as the sanctions, rituals, superstitions, belief in religious and supernatural powers and different types of deities were. However, in every society, irrespective of its level of development, both secular and sacred patterns coexist. This, infact, prompted Edward Shil to say "the traditional society is not by any means entirely traditional, and modern society is by no means free of tradition" (quoted from Y Singh, 1978).

In Indian Society perception of disease-etiology has varied from time to time and culture to culture. About the earliest view of diseases in India, Jolly (1958) stated," all morbid and abnormal states of body and mind for which no special reason was assignable were due to the attacks of demons". Even the Aurvedic treatise of charak and Susruta and Muslim scholar like Abul Fazal have referred to Magico- Religious causation.

Though the field is yet to be fully explored, some studies (Opler 1963, Lewis 1958, Marriot 1955, Ishwaran 1968, Hassan 1967, 1979,

Karna 1976 and Lindbery 1980) have revealed the etiology and preference for treatment in terms of 'Personalistic and Naturalistic', 'Sacred and secular' and 'Ethnomedical' versus 'Biomedical'. Under the 'sacred' or 'Personalistic' etiology, faith in God, fate, lack of har mony with the supernatural world like ghost intrusion, evil eyes, magic, sorcery etc. have been perceived as the causes of disease, whereas under the secular or 'Naturalistic physical disturbances, faulty diet, germs-infection and stress - strain are considered to be the main causative fac tors. The modes of treatment have been also perceived dif ferently. According to Foster (1976), the most powerful cures in the personalistic tradition are super natural and magical powers, and illness, religion and magic are in separable.

Prevalence of both sacred and secular orientation in the analysis of disease-etiology and mode of treatment is evi dent even to day. This is reflected from the views of the patients contacted.

It is apparant from the Table 1 that about 61% of the patients have perceived diseases in 'secular' term, whereas 39% in 'sacred' terms. The dominance of the secular over the sacred is associated with subjective and objective charac teristics. Most of the patients belonged to the urban areas. Occupationally also , they differed, as about 76% were en gaged in official works, professions, business and skilled works, while only 24% were either cultivators or unskilled workers.

Table 1 : Disease etiology as perceived by the patients

	Sacred		Secular	
Wrath of God	Magic	Fate	Irregular diet sinfection	Stress and strain
32 (10.7)	6 (2.0)	80 (26.6)	123 (41.0)	59 (19.7)
Total	118(39.3)		182(60.7)	

Note: Figures in parenthesis indicate percentage.

It is found that those living in urban areas and having better economic position were more exposed to community health programmes, modern technology and innovations regard ing health and developmental programmes like immunization, vaccination, family planning and scientific knowledge of disease-etiology.

Exposure to mass media has changed their perception. Thus the role of media in the diffusion of knowledge and technology as suggested by Learner (1958), Lewis (1958), Rao (1964) and Dubey (1976) has been demonstrated in this case too.

The perception of disease-etiology depends upon educa tional achievement of the people too, as Table 2 envisages.

Table 2 : Educational Level of the patients and Perception of disease etiology

Educational Group	Sacred			Secular		
	Wrath of God	Fate	Magic	Infection	Stress & strain	Total
Illiterate	15	39	6	34	18	112
Matric	5	20	0	20	14	59
Graduate	10	16	0	60	19	105
Post Graduate	2	5	0	10	7	24
Total	32	80	6	124	58	200
	118(39.3)					(60.7)

Note: Figures in parathesis indicate percentage.

The table suggests that the majority of the respondents availed educational facilities and obtained education. They were matriculate for above. Only 37% of them were either il literate or barely literate. This shows taht people have taken up the fruits of development. Their exposure to scien tific knowledge and to constructive health programmes has initiated process of psycholocial change. This in turn brings about a change in the perception of disease etiology. This education minimises the influence of tradition.

People's orientation and beliefs are also attributable to social milieu in which they are brought up and socialized. Socializing agencies shape value pattern of individuals and detemine their reactions towards various issues of life. Socialization is a continous process. As such only an individual's birth place does not shape his outlook, rather his stay in a particular social community for considerable length of time has important influence on him. the data reveal that with migration from rural to urban areas, prople assumed secular orientation as it is indicated in Table 3.

Tabel 3 : Birth place and migration from the native place of urban area at the dif ferent stages of life.

Place of Socialization

Birth Place		Childhood		Adolescent		Adulthood	
R	U	R	U	R	U	R	U
189	111	171	129	109	191	52	248
(63.0)	(37.0)	(57.0)	(43.0)	(36.3)	(63.7)	(17.3)	(82.7)

Note: Figures in parenthesis indicate percentage.

It is apparent from the table above that 63% of the respondents were born in rural areas, but by the time they reached adulthood they left their birth place and came to urban areas. As a result of migration, differential in fluence of socilization at different stages of life is found. Because of this, individual's exposure to the in fluence of great traditions shows secular orientation. The challenges of new environment force them to modify their at titude towards life issues and reorient values, beliefs and aspirations of life.

The made of treatment or the choice of theapeutic measures depends upon how disease-etiology is perceived. If the per ception of a disease or its cause is done in terms of sacred traditional beliefs and faith, its treatment is likely to be in the form of traditionally sanctioned way. Since disease has been perceived differently, measures suggested for treatment vary also. It displays a fusion of seculr and sacred orientation, which is reflected in Table 4

Table 4 : Preference for treatment measures of diseases. (Figures in parenthesis indicate percentage)

Disease	Only secular	Secular & sacred at a time	Only sacred
Cholera	198(66.0)	68(22.7)	34(11.3)
Malaria	230(76.7)	60(20.0)	10(3.3)
Pox & Measels	100(33.4)	40(13.3)	160(53.3)
Tuberculosis	170(56.7)	90(30.0)	40(13.3)
Jaundice	110(36.6)	50(16.7)	140(46.7)
Heart disease	165(55.0)	135(45.0)	Nil
Total	973(54)	443(24.6)	384(21.4)

Although the mode of treatment of different disease sug gests a favourable trend towards acceptance of available secular mode of treatments for different diseases, sacred from is not outrightly rejected. Rather as it is evident, people want to adopt all measures for cure. This suggests the continuance of tradition and acceptance of development side by side. The relation between the two is of mutal ajustment and not of incompatibility.

Regarding the choise of secular and sacred treatment at a time the maximum score comes for Heart disease i.e. 45 per cent, where as in other disease it is upto only 30 percent. It suggests the fact that in prolonged and terminal diseases the patients become more inclined towards secular as well as sacred treatment. Here the role of sacred beliefs in tension management and meeting crisis situations like death, distress and diseases appear to be significant in accordance with the contention of Malinowski (1954) and T. Parsons (1951).

The entire analysis of the perception of disease etiology and treatment, thus can be attributable to the previous dis cussions in the purview of variables like education and per ception of disease, rural-urban migration at the different stages of socialization and exposure to mass-media and new environment.

India has a strong religious moorings. Its traditional values, beliefs and faith are all shaped by the religion, so it can not be expected that perception of diseases and their treatment will not have the influecne of sacred tradition, rather what is expected more is that people will accept and institutionalise the secular ideas, beliefs and faith gradually along with acceptance of developmental programmes. This will in turn influence their perception of diseases and treatment no doubt in secular orientation. It is immaterial, if sacred tradition continues along with secular or develop mental norms. When the both secular and sacred orientations are mutually adopted, social and psychological tension are avoided.

REFERENCES

Dube, S.C. 1981 Traditional view of change and Development; in Absolute values and the Search for the peace of Mankin, Vol. I, the International culture Foundation Press, New York.

Foster, George M. 1976 Disease etiology in Non-Western Medi cal system, American Anthropology, Vol. 78, No. 4.

Hasan, K.A. 1967 The cultural Frontier of Health in village India; Manktals, Bombay.

_______ 1979 Medical Sociology of Rural India, Sachin Pub lication, Ajmer.

Iswaran, K. 1968 Shivpur: A south Indian village, Routledge & Kegan Panl, London.

Jaggi, O.P. 1982 Folk Medicine; Vol. III, Atma Ram & Sons Publications, Delhi.

Jolly, J. 1958 On Disease and Medicine, Encyclopedia of Religion and Ethics Vol. IV.

Karna, M.N. 1976 Health, culture and community in a North Bihar village; Indian Journal of Social work, vol. XXXVII.

Learner, Daniel 1958 The Passing of Traditional Society; Free Press, Glencoe.

Lewis, Oscar 1958 Village life in Northern India; Rendom House, New York.

Lindbergs, D.G. 1980 Pills against Poverty; A study of the Introduction of Western Medicine in A Tamil village, Mac- Millan, Comp. of India Ltd.

Malinowski, B. 1954 Magic, science and Religion and other Essays; Anchor Books, New York.

Marriott, M. 1955 Western Medicine in a village of Northern India; in B.D. Paul's (Ed.)"Health, Culture and community", Russelsage Foundation, New York.

Opler, M.E. 1963 The cultural Definition of Illness in vil lage India; Human organization, Vol. 22, No. 1, pp 32-35.

Parsons, T. 1951 The social system; Free Press, New York.

Rao, Y.L. 1964 Communication and Development; in Myron Wainer's (ed)" Modernization." Basic Books, I N C Pub lishers, New York.

Saunders, Lyle 1958 Cultural Definition and Medical care; Russelsage foundation, New York

Suchmen, A.E. 1963 Sociology and the Field of Public Health; Russelsage foundation, New York.

Singh, Yogendra 1978 Essays on Modernization in India; Manohar Publishing House, New Delhi.

TWENTY

Manohar Lal

Impact of Road Improvement in a Chotanagpur Village

Development of rural and tribal areas is linked with rapid expansion of road communication. With improvement in com munication, there is greater access to educational, health, employment, market facilities and exposure to social and political transformation that is taking place in other parts of the country. It may transform traditional norms and values governing various aspects of life and thought ways of the people. Consequently, some of these traditional norms may show visible changes; others may develop tendencies to change; while some others may resist any change. Some of the important sectors being considered for the study of road in fluence are family, kinship and marriage, economic rela tions, distribution of power, communication and outlook for the future. Such a study may reveal how old traditions be have in response to an innovation of road improvement. We may ask, whether these are yielding place to new ideas i.e. promoting growth or are impeding growth or whether these traditions are neutral to growth in the above sectors of people's life.

This paper is based on a part of data collected from Chotanagpur region for a larger study, being conducted at the A.N. Sinha Institute, with an objective to determine sociocultural, economic and political impact of road im provements in rural and tribal areas of Bihar state. Some broad generalisations are being attempted here on the basis of observations and impressions of the field area and first hand feel of the field data.

II

Bhakuadih, a village on the Sonahatu -Jamudag road in Ran chi district had been taken up for the present study. The village is situated one kilometer east of the road at the Sonahatu end. This road has been metalled in 1984 under the World Bank Project. The road is the continuation of Bundu- Sonahatu road emanating from Ranchi-Tata National Highway at Bundu. There is a regular bus service from Ranchi and Khunti to Sonahatu going up to Jamudag. Some other modes of transport carrying man and materials on this road are taxi, jeep, motor-cycle, bicycle, bullock cart and pack-animal.

Villages in the road influence area of Sonahatu-Jamudag road are populated by Kurmis, Swansis and Munda. Kurmi is the dominant caste in terms of number and landownership. Agriculture is the main occupation. Paddy, wheat, maize and pulses are important crops. Potato and other vegetables are the important cash crops. Growing of perishable crops like green vegetable must have been prompted by existence of road link with outside markets. It has been reported that fresh vegetables from this region are transported to markets in Jamshedpur and Calcutta.

Though three fourths of the land is under cultivation, only 15 percent of it is irrigated. Canal and tubewells are the main sources of irrigation. The area is electrified, but electric supply is erratic. Bhakuadih, Sonahatu, Sariyad, Dirbir and Jamudag are some of the important villages in this area.

Sonahatu is an important place. The block headquarters, police station, bank, post-office, primary health center, vetarinary hospital, bus terminus, market centre and high school are located at road side in Sonahatu. People of this area visit markets at Sonahatu, Tamar and Khunti. There is a primary school almost in each village. Ranchi, Moori and Sisai are the nearest railway stations from this area.

There are 96 households in Bhaquadih village. 90 households belong to Kurmi, 4 are from Munda tribe and 2 are Swansi respectively. Kurmi caste is dominant in terms of numerical strength, economic, social and political status. Kurmi and Swansi are Hindu and Munda profess Sarnaism as their religion. Among the Kurmi households 13 have 5 acres and more landholding, 58 have 2.5 to 5 acres and 15 have 1 to 2.5 acres of landholding each. Among the Munda 1 has 5+ acres of land and 3 have 1 to 2.5 acres. Among Swansi one household has 5+ acres of landholding and 1 has 1 to 2.5 acres of land. Thus, majority of the households comprise small farmers with 2.5 to 5 acres of land.

Total land in the village is 400 acres, of which 300 acres are cultivable. This area is single crop area and depends upon rains. Some 75 acres of land is irrigated from the nearby Kanchi river which dries up in summer. There are 15 irrigation wells in the village which irrigate about 20-25 acres of land. Latha-Kuri is used for drawing water from the well. Only one Kurmi household owns a pumping set. Paddy is the main Kharif crop. Other crops are maize, wheat, pulses, potato and other vegetables. Rabi crops and vegetables are sown in small plots of land around the location of irriga tion wells and near Kanchi river area . It was reported that villagers used high yielding varieties (HYV) of paddy e.g. Kaveri, Ratan, Mansuri etc. They also used HYV of Potato and Maize. HYV of wheat e.g. Kalyan, Sona, Sonalika etc. are also used by them.

III

Impact of Road Improvement

As mentioned earlier location of Bhakuadih village was such that it had partial exposure to road communication through Bundu-Sonahatu metalled road for number of years before Sonahatu-Jamudag road was taken up for improvement in 1983 under the World Bank project. In addition to this, num ber of other factors of change such as education, urbanisa tion, industrialisation, community-development projects, democratic processes and administrative machinary etc. have been operative in this area. Efforts to isolate the effects or changes brought out by different factors may not always prove successful. It is rather hazardous to analyse the cause and effect relationship in a dynamic process. In the larger study, of which the present paper is a small part, the problem of isolating effect of road improvement has been solved by adopting quasi-experimental - pre-post-control group design. While the data is awaiting statistical treat ment, an attempt is made here to hint at the type of qualitative changes supposed to be occuring predominantly due to road improvement. However, it will be difficult to assess the actual contribution of road improvement in the spheres of change.

Family, Kinship and marriage

Average size of a family in the village is five persons and renges between 3 to 8 persons. Nuclear family, compris ing husband, wife and unmarried children, is thc most common form of family. 6 out of every 10 families are nuclear in nature. 3 out of every 10 are nuclear with dependent father or mother. One out of every 10 families is of patrilineal extended type where members belonging to three generations with at least two lineally united couples with their children live together. Majority of the heads of households possess modern attitude towards ideal family size. 5 out of every ten heads consider two children ideal for a couple. 3 out of every 10 and 2 of the 10 consider 3 children and 4 children respectively ideal for a couple. Those considering 2 or 4 children as ideal have equal preference for sons and daughters. While those thinking 3 children to be ideal prefer 2 sons and one daughter. Most of those who prefer 2 children as ideal are also in favour of family planning practices. Most of them who favour family planning also practice some family planning method. Incidently those con sidering two as the ideal number of children also possess less than three children. Sachchidananda (1979) have found that people in a road side village (Amlesa) have lower family size (5.4) than in a remote village (Gutuhatu, having 7.3). Similarly, while two-thirds of the families in Amlesa were nuclear, only one third of the families in Gutuhatu were nuclear in nature.

The same study (Sachchidananda, 1979) has revealed that age at marriage in Amlesa was higher than that in Gutuhatu. Age at marriage for males was 25 years in Amlesa and 23 years in Gutuhatu. Similarly for females it was 20 years in Amlesa and less than 20 in Gutuhatu respectively.

With the improvement in road situation, villagers get access to distant places for establishing marital alliances. It was observed that of the 20 marriages taking place in the village during the last 5 years, 5 marriages each took place at distance of less than 5 Km. and less than 10 Km. respec tively. 10 marriages i.e. half of the total marriages were performed in distant villages located at 20 Km. and more. Similarly in Amlesa (Sachchidananda, ibid) 17%, 27% and 47% marriages took place within 5 Km., 10 Km., and 11-20 Km. respectively. In Gutuhatu (remote village) 29%, 35% and 25% marriages took place within 5 Km., within 10 Km. and between 11-20 Km. respectively. Thus, in most of the cases the dis tance of marital alliance is more in the road side village than in the remote village.

Economic relations

Most of the villagers are owner-cultivators. Agriculture is a family occupation where women and children of the house assist the menfolk in various agricultural operations. The educated among the villagers are being drawn into service sector. There were forty matriculates, fifteen intermediates and six graduates in the village. Sixteen of them were en gaged in different types of service occupations such as school teacher, technician in HEC, TELCO, ECL at Hatia, Tata and Gomia respectively. One of them is police constable at Daltonganj, and another person is a practising lawyer at Khunti court. One person has opened a fertilizer shop. As many as 20 persons own bullock carts. In addition to serving personal requirement, they transport goods for others as well.

This shows that though agriculture still remains the primary occupation and main source of income among them, the more enterprising have always ventured into non-traditional ways of augmenting their income such as service, business, industry, trade etc. For instance, the villagers grow vegetables and sell in the weekly markets for profit. Women trade in rice. They purchase paddy from the market, husk it and sell in the market for a small margin of profit. Income from the sale of rice is used as a revolving fund to con tinue their business.

The functional relationship between tribes and castes in this village is similar to jajmani system. Under this system each caste is expected to give certain standardised services to the families of other castes. They are paid in cash, grain on a daily, monthly or yearly basis. With the diver sification of occupation, this socio-economic relationship is decreasing. Individual labourers are employed in dif ferent families as servants who work all the year round. They are paid annually Rs. 350/- or 10 mounds of paddy.In addition, they get daily meals and clothes occasionally. They also work on daily wages on farms during cropping season. During construction of Sonahatu-Jamudag road they got wage employment for number of months.

Thus with opening up of markets, monitisation, and employ ment in non-agricultural occupations, the earlier system of reciprocal exchange of services and commodities has given way to cash transactions. The functional relationship is moving towards the contractual one, devoid of any social obligation towards each other.

Opening up of road has also provided the villagers an access to employment outside the village. They go up to Bundu (13 Km), Tamar (20 Km) etc. for employment as well as for trade to important markets. Cycle and bus service are the important modes of transport for personal mobility and to carry goods.

The Bank of India has opened a branch at Sonahatu. It has acted as an alternate source of loan and minimised the role of traditional moneylenders. Though for paddy loan for con sumption they still depend upon rich villagers, Bank has helped many of them under IRDP to purchase draft animal, and fertilizer, or start a petty business. One of the villagers has also got loan from the Bank for his daughter's marriage. One of the Swansi family engaged in its traditional caste occupation of weaving also got loan from BOI for making im provement in his occupation. Thus, existence of institu tional source of credit has helped to alter the traditional relationship between moneylenders and villagers. They have come in contact with new set of people, procedures and value system through banking system which is bound to influence the traditional economic relations in the village.

Distribution of Power

The power structure in the village is undergoing change under the impact of modern forces of change. Opening of road has exposed the village people to political changes taking place in the region. Participation in democratic processes has helped in the emergence of new elite. These elite are taking up leadership roles in transforming their own society as well as integration with the wider Indian society. They have organised a socio-political organisation in the village named as Hind Majdoor Kisan Panchayat. The functions of this panchayat include solution of disputes in the village and to act as facilitator to help the people in getting them serv ices and facilities from the block, cooperative society, Bank, health centre etc. located in Sonahatu. The office bearers of this panchayat wield influence inside the village as well as outside.

Communication

With the opening of roads, personal mobility of the vil lagers increased considerably. Majority of them made local trips within the road influence area. Large number of them also made trips to destinations up to 20 Kms. Important places frequented by them are local villages for social visits to relations, Sonahatu for market purpose, earn wage labour, attend school, work in the bank & block and to get medicine from the health centre. Other places visited by them are Bundu for shopping and schooling, Tamar for meeting relations or teaching in a school, Khunti for Official work, Chaibasa for appearing in school examination. They also visited the district town Ranchi quite often for various purposes such as treatment of a patient, shoping, meeting a relative, to seek employment or do service, registration of land etc. The mode of transport for visiting various places were cycle and bus service. The improvement of road and plying of buses have enabled them to move out more frequently because of reduction in cost and time for each trip.

Perception of Villagers about impact of road improvement

The villagers gave multiple responses showing impact of improved roads in more than one way. Majority of them per ceived that improved roads held a promise of betterment in travelling and communication facilities for their families. Large number of them felt that improved road has helped in improving employment opportunities for them outside the vil lage. Some of them also opined that improvement in road meant better scope for doing petty business. Other benefits from road improvement included easy access to institutional facilities like bank, block, hospital, school, market etc. It also reduced trip time and trip cost thus making people and commodities move faster and timely. It resulted in faster distribution of inputs and marketing of farm products. It produced a change in cropping pattern towards more perishable crops like vegetables and led to promotion of participation of rural labourers in non-agricultural oc cupations. It also encouraged growth of small business and commercial establishment. It facilitated the spread of rural electrification. They also felt that with improvement in roads villagers get more exposure (through travel) to educa tional, political and social changes taking place in other areas.

Outlook for the Future

Most of the villagers felt that happiness in life would be the ideal condition for future. Some of them aspired for more education. Some others considered economic improvement as their ideal in life. For their village, they aspired that best possible situation will come through improved road transport and communication, all round happiness in villager's life, improvement in education, religious har mony, better housing conditions and finally overall develop ment of the village. For the nation, the best possible fu ture was perceived as economic development, national security, overall development, educational improvement, clean administration, improvement in educational facilities etc.

Villagers' fears about future of family life centred around situation like poverty, loss of health and prestige, famine and flood, God's mercy, litigation and Indebtedness and lack of employment and education opportunities. Similarly their fears about future of community life centred around items like caste exploitation, flood and famine, loss of education and employment opportunities, corruption and voilence etc. About the nation's future their fears were about corruption in public life, communalism, decline in socio-economic progress, flood and famine, disease and caste exploitation.

It was observed that most of them were optimistic about future of their families, community and nation respectively. In all the cases they perceived moderate level of socio- economic standing at the present time. They felt that the condition at present was certainly better than what it was 5 to 7 years back and would improve (though moderately) in the coming 5 to 7 years.

With regard to reckoning of time most of the villagers still reckoned it through movement of the sun. Some of them also keep time by watch. In the same way majority of them measured distance through the unit of mile. Some of them also reckoned space with kilometers. Villagers'aspirations for education of their children are moderate. Most of them wanted their children to complete high school and become school teachers earning upto one thousand rupees per month.

IV

Direct or indirect impact of roal improvement was felt in almost all spheres of villagers' life and norms and values governing these aspects. In most of the cases the tradi tional norms and values existed side by side with the new ones. Road improvements have exposed the villagers to so cial, economic, psychological and political changes taking place in the region and their influence is being felt in the changing social and economic relations, attitudes and aspirations of the village people. Thus, road improvement has proved to be a crucial input in the development process. Roads seem to be a must to promote social, cultural, economic and political development of rural and tribal areas.

REFERENCES

Lal,Manohar, 1983: The Munda Elite; Amar Prakashan, Delhi.

— 1983: A Pilot Study Report of Socio-Economic Conditions and Mobility Pattern in Usri-Bihta road Influence Area; Report No. 1, (mimeographed) ANSISS, Patna.

— 1985: Patterns of Rural Mobility in Bihar; Paper presented at the 72nd session of I S C A at Lucknow Univer sity, Lucknow.

— 1984: socio-Economic conditions and Mobility Pattern in Some Road Influence Areas: Baseline Survey; Report No. 2 (mimeographed) ANSISS, Patna.

Sachchidananda, 1979: The Changing Munda; Concept Publishing House, New Delhi.

TWENTY ONE

Samita Mann

Tradition and Modernity of a Small Town

Tradition and modernity are two important concepts for as sessing the entire social situation, because all societies are constantly in the process of change in different de grees. The conflict between the old and the new is very com mon in all times and in all societies. Many scholars have tried to interprete this everchanging phenomenon in terms of two distinct poles-changed and unchanged, modernity and tradition. But, in reality, these two terms are relative (Tripathi 1976 : 181). What is modern in one situation might be traditional in another context; again, within the same country to-day one thing appears to be modern, but tomorrow it will become traditional. Tradition and modernity include certain traits which are crystalised, deeply embedded in culture and are related to time-space dimension.

But tradition and modernity cannot be viewed as discrete polarities, because modern societies may have a latent un dertone of traditional elements and the traditional societies also have the potentiality for modernisation (Rudolph and Rudolph : 1967). Considering all these factors, it can be stated that no society is fully traditional, nor fully modern (Srinivas 1976:206). Change is continuous, but in certain aspects it is more repaid.

According to Bottomore (1971:286), the term 'development' has been used in quite different way. First, it is used to differentiate two broad types of society - on one side the prosperous industrial societies and on the other side all those societies (very diverse in other respects) which are predominently rural, agricultural and poor. Secondly it is used to describe the process of industrialization or modern ization.

Etymologically, the work 'tradition' means 'handing over'. It is derived from 'traders', which means 'transmit'. Singh (1965:52) defines tradition as "the cumulative heritage of a Society which permeats through all levels of social organisation; for example, the value system, the Social structure and the structure of personality".

Indian traditionalism was continued for a long time, reflected in clear occupational guild, through its prepon derance of caste system, compact and more or less self- sufficient village life. But such type of rigidness of the society began to alter due to the forces of historicity, coupled with economic changes through new occupation and modern education. From time to time, with different histori cal upheavals, the outsiders came, interacted and these caused changes in the so-called traditional aspects of life and, in this way, traditionalism melted slowly with a change through modernity which is relevant to the situation in terms of need, sentiment and emotion.

Modernisation roots from the Latin work "modo" meaning modern. However, some scholars explain it in different ways when they corroborate facts in support of their views.

Singh states (1973:121)

"Modernization as a process, in fact, has more elasticity of form than tradition. It implies, an open world - view which like science undergoes perpetual self-falsification and self transcendence in its value structure and postulates".

In this context it can be said that rural societies in most of the cases are more traditional due to lack of ex position to any external situation. But urban societies are almost a transformed society through historical processes, due to more contact and interaction, through varied ways of life.

II

Historically, Mahishdal is a very famous place inthe dis trict of Midnapore, West Bengal, as it was once the king's Headquarters. The growth of this area actually started slowly sometimes in sixteenth century. But only in 1961, Census Department declared it as a small town. In the year 1951 its population was 5,210 and in 1981 it was 11,913. Mahishadal stands at a distance of 16 Km from Sub-divisional headquarters Tamluk and 88 Km from the district headquarters of Midnapore. This is 90 Km away from Calcutta which can be reached by railway, roadway and riverine routes.

The present habitational area of Mahisadal comprises six villages (1) Garkamalpur (404 acres), (2) Rangibasan (251 acres), (3) Teropekhia (114 acres), (4) Jagannathpur (112 acres), (5) Ghagra (147 acres) and (6) Basulia (509 acreas). A representative number of respondents was contacted and in terviewed in each village for data collection. Basulia was left out, as this village was situated far away from the herb of the town. The five villages comprised 1449 households. Out of these one sixth or 240 households were drawn as sample. The list of households was collected from Panchayat offices and ration shops. Table I shows the total number of households and the sample size.

Table 1 : Sample Households

Sl. No	Village	Total No. of Households	Sample
1.	Garkamalpur	772	127
2.	Rangibasan	227	38
3.	Teropekhia	180	30
4.	Jagannathpur	149	25
5.	Ghagra	121	20
	Total	1449	240

A set of four important socio-psychological variables was selected for the study. Respondents' answers to different statements were recorded mostly on Likert type point scales. Likert's 4-point scale indicated one's degree of agreement or disagreement with the statement:

1. Anomie : 9 items
2. Political Ideology : 6 items
3. Achievement Motivation : 3 items
4. Overall Modernity scale : 13 items

Anomie Scale

This scale was constructed by McClosky and Sehaar (1965). It consisted of 9 statements all of which are positive in nature. The method of scoring was as suggested by Likert. Mallick (1977) found 0.67 correlation between Bengali ver sion and original English one.

Political Ideology Scale

Alexander's (1973) scale consisted of 6 statements. Four positive representing communistic ideas, slogans etc. and two negative representing traditional views, to measure one's orientation to the communistic ideology. Likert's method of scoring was followed. The correlation between original English and modified Bengali versions of this scale was 0.86 (Mallick : 1977).

Achievement Motivation Scale

This scale was constructed by Kivlin **et al.**, (1971) con sisted of 3 positive items. The authors found this to be a reliable and valid instrument for measuring achievement motivation. English and Bengali versions of this scale correlated to the extent of 0.79 (Mallick, 1977). The method of scoring was as suggested by Likert.

Overall Modernity Scale

The scale was originally developed by Inkeles and Smith (1966) for a cross-cultural study over six nations and sub sequently adapted to the Indian condition as a dependable measuring instrument of overall modernity (Pareek and Rao : 1974).

Out of thirteen items, for I item there were three alter natives, for 6 items two alternatives, for 4 items four al ternatives and for 1 item 5 alternatives and there was one open ended question. Likert type scoring pattern as sug gested by the authors was followed.

All the respondents were interviewed by following the In terview method. The field work began in the early part of October, 1980, and it continued for more than a year.

After completing the collection of data items of scales of the schedule were scored according to the scoring pattern as suggested by different authors.

After scoring and coding the figures they were tabulated in the master table. The summated scores were calculated as and when necessary. Percentage distribution, means, standard deviations 't' test and analysis of variance had been used for the purpose of analysis of the data; level of sig nificance for 't' test and analysis of variance had been used for the purpose of analysis of the data; level of sig nificance for 't' test and analysis of variance are fixed at 0.01 level.

The style of life at Mahishadal, should exhibit, as is ex pected, some mixed traits where ruralism is in the process of omission, though it has emerged out of its rural back ground two decades ago. On the other hand, urban characters or traits are slowly in the process of incorporation into the matrix of the rural core through time and space. People living therein may share both rural as well as urban charac teristics. The psychological aspects of the people may also swing from rural to urban, hinging on an accommodative and assimilative cushion. With this view, anomie, political ideology, achievement motivation and overall modernity have been examined.

III

The term 'Anomie' was first used by the French Sociologist, Durkheim, to denote several aspects of social participation where the conditions necessary for man to ful fil himself and to attain happiness were not present. Any state, where there are unclear, confilicting and unin tegrated norms, in which the individual has no morally sig nificant relation with others or in which there are no limits set to the attainment of pleasure, is called a state of 'Anomie' (Mitchell : 1968).

McClosky and Scharr (1965) place emphasis on "feelings of normlessness and deregulation" and included bewilderment, pessimism, alienation and sense of futility.

No. of items -9. Possible score ranges from 9 to 36. Ob jective Mid-point (OM) 22.50. Actual score ranges from 19 to 35. High score indicates presence of anomie.

Table 2 depicts that the lowest mean score (27.53) has been obtained by the villagers of Teropekhia and the highest mean score (29.13) by the villagers of Rangibasan. These two mean scores together with those for other villages, viz., Garkamapur (28.52), Ghagra (28.15) and Jagannathpur (27.96) lie on the positive side of the objective mid-point.

Table 2 : Test of significance of inter-village differences in mean scores on Anomie (general)

Sl. No.	Villages	Scores M	Scores SD	F
1.	Garkamalpur (GK) (N=127)	28.52	1.54	
2.	Rangibasan (R) (N=38)	29.13	1.54	
3.	Teropekhia (T) (N=30)	27.53	3.03	0.150 (not significant)
4.	Jagennathpur (J) (N / 25)	27.96	1.80	
5.	Gaghra (G) (N=20)	28.15	2.1042	

The scores indicate that the people of all the five vil lages of Mahishadal town suffer from anomie. The differences among the mean scores of different villages, however, are not significant, as is evident from the value of F,. 150 (Table 2). The combined mean score (28.41) lies on the right hand side of the objective mid- point. So there is homogeneity among the residents of Mahishadal town regarding the feeling of normlessness.

The life, nowadays, is full of uncertainty, discomfort and pain. Naturally, one has little faith in people. Social in stitutions are changing so fast that stable social life is also hampered. People are always in dilemma and doldrums.

In simple society or in rural society, the people face less problems as compared to those of the complex society or the urban society. Tensions and conflicts are synonymous to urban life which is characterised by more competition and higher aspiration levels. Anomie is chiefly the result of social class and perhaps economic frustration (Greer : 1972). In conclusion, it can be said that the town people of Mahishadual suffer from anomie like the people of the com plex urban area. So, they are not traditional minded in this respect.

Political Ideology

According to Tracy (Baradot, 1979) ideology is a study of the process of forming ideas, a "science of ideas". Ideas, Tracy believes, are stimulated by the physcial environment.

Ideologies are based on the value systems of various societies (Sargent, 1972). Modern societies are complex and often contradictory. Naturally, individuals within a society may not accept a single ideology; they may appropriate parts of several ideologies.

No. of items - 6. Possible score ranges from 6 to 24. Ob jective mid-point (OM) 15.00. Actual score ranges from 10 to 23. High score indicates one's political ideology towards communism.

It is revealed from the Table 3 that the highest mean score (19.20) has been obtained by the people of Jagannath pur and the lowest (17.21) by those of Rangibasan. Besides these, mean socres for other villages, viz., Ghagra (17.40), Teropekhia (17.30) and Garkamalpur (17.24) lie on the posi tive side of the objective mid-point. Considering these mean values, it can be inferred that the people of four villages are like-minded and have slight inclination to a communist ideology.

The differences among the mean scores of different vil lages are significant at .01 level. The significant group differences are observed between the responses of Jagannath pur and those of other villages, viz., Garkamalpur (t = 4.26), Rangibasan (t = 3.95), Teropekhia (t = 3.51) and Ghagra (t = 3.46), all t's being significant at .01 levels.

Table 3 : Test of significance of inter-village differences in household mean scores on political ideology

Sl. No.	Villages		Scores M	SD	Difference Between	T	F
1.	Garkamalpur (N=127)	(GK)	17.24	2.52	GK & R	.08	
2.	Rangibasan (N=38)	(R)	17.21	1.88	R & J	3.95*	
					R & G	.56	
3.	Teropekhia (N=30)	(T)	17.30	2.04	T & GK	.14	
					T & R	1.87	
4.	Jagannathpur (N=25)	(J)	19.20	2.00	J & G	3.46*	4.101**
					J & T	3.51*	
5.	Gaghra (N=20)	(G)	17.40	1.53	G & T	.19	
					G & GK	.39	

** F : Significant at .01 level
* t : Significant at .01 level

The results indicate that the respondents of Jagannathpur support the communist ideology more than the those of other four villages. The probable cause may be that the respon dents of Jagannathpur belong to the low socio-economic status.

The people of Mahishadal think that without exploiting the poor it is not possible for a rich person to become richer. They feel that poor-man's Penury is rich man's power. They hold the view that there is nothing wrong in taking away some portion of the wealth of the rich and that equality may be brought about only through revolution. The people of Mahisadal have orientation towards communism. It is also evident from the Panchayat election. In that elec tion, most of the seats were won by the leftist parties. The people of Mahishadal possess some left orientation which is considered to be modern attitude.

Achievement Motivation

Human beings have many needs of which achievement need has been given top priority in modern society because it helps economic and social growth.

In the opinion of McClelland (1963) high need for achieve ment makes a man modern, low need for achievement makes a man non modern. He has defined achievement motivation as "a special value that emphasises a desire for excellence in or der to attain a sense of personal accomplishment" (p.76).

The goal of achievement activity is to succeed,to perform well in relation to a standard of excellence or in com parison with others who are competitors.

According to Atkinson (1968:27) , achievement motivation is an important determinant of aspiration effect and per sistance.

Need for achievement varies from person to person because of different factors, such as, cultural background to which a person belongs, the social class of which he is a member and the family setting in which he grows up. Attitude towards work, success in occupation and determination for achieving one's goal in the face of heavy odds indicate one's achievement motivation.

No. of item - 3. Possible score ranges from 3 to 12. Ob jective Mid-point (OM) 7.5. Actual score ranges from 5 to 11. High scores indicate high level of achievement.

Table 4 depicts that the highest mean score (9.10) has been obtained by the people of village Ghagra and the lowest mean score (8.28) by those of Jagannathpur. The mean scores for other villages -- Rangibasan (8.89), Teropekhia (8.87) and Garkamalpur (8.50) lie on the positive side of the objectixve mid-point.

These mean values indicate that the people of all the five villages show more or less similar degree of achievement motivation. The differences among the mean scores of dif ferent villages are not significant.

The combined mean score (8.64) lies on the righthand side of the objective mid-point, but not too far from the objec tive mid point. It reflects that all the people of this area have some amount of achievement motivation, though not remarkable.

They do not have strong achievement motivation which is an urban characteristics. Observation in respect of achievement-motivation indicates that the ιown people here have little inclination towards modernity.

Table 4 : Test of significance of inter-village difference in households mean scores on achievement motivation.

Sl. No.	Villages		Scores M	Scores SD	F
1.	Garkamalpur (N=125)	(GK)	1.50	1.65	
2.	Rangibasan (N=38)	(R)	8.89	1.41	
3.	Teropekhia (N=30)	(T)	8.87	1.23	.545
4.	Jagannathpur (N=25)	(J)	8.28	1.37	
5.	Gaghra (N=20)	(G)	9.10	1.34	

Combined Mean - 8.64
F : not significant.

Over Modernity Scope

When a man has undergone a change in spirit and has ac quired certain new ways of thinking, feeling and acting, he may be considered as truly modern (Inkeles, 1966 : 140). Ac cording to Lerner (1965), a modern man is urbanised, literate and participant, while a non-modern is less edu cated.

The characteristics that make man modern have been class ified by Inkeles (1966) into external and internal factors. In the former category, he puts environmental factors (i.e., attributes of one's life space), such as, urbanisation, education, mass-communication, industrialisation and politicialisation. In the latter case, he includes per sonality traits, such as, attitudes, values and beliefs peculiar to modern man.

Inkeles and Smith (1966:353) developed the Overall Mod ernity (OM) scale for the measurement of the level of in dividual modernization. They define individual modernity as "a set of attitudes, values, and ways of feeling and acting presumably of the sort either generated by or required for effective participation in a modern society".

Number of items are 13. Possible score ranges from 12 to 38. Objective Midpoint (M) 25.00 Actual score ranges from 20 to 34. High score declares a man to be modern.

It has been observed from Table 5 that the highest mean score (28.25) has been obtained by the people of village Garkamalpur and the lowest (27.16) by those of Rangibasan. But actually the difference between the highest score and the lowest score is very small. Since the scores of other villages lie in between these two scores, naturally, the scores vary very little among themselves. But all the scores lie on the positive side of the objective mid-point. The difference among the mean scores of individual villages is not significant.

Table 5 : Test of significance of inter-village differences in households mean scores on overall modernity scale.

Sl. No.	Villages		Scores M	Scores SD	F
1.	Garkamalpur (N=127)	(GK)	28.2520	3.14	
2.	Rangibasan (N=38)	(R)	27.2579	3.05	
3.	Teropekhia (N=30)	(T)	27.9000	3.22	.889
4.	Jagannathpur (N=25)	(J)	27.8400	2.80	
5.	Ghagra (N=20)	(G)	28.000	3.46	

Combine mean : 27.97,
F : Not significant.

The combined mean score (27.97) lies on the right hand side of the objective mid-point, but it is very close to it. It clearly indicates that the people of Mahishadal are not traditional minded, but they are modern to a limited extent. Their modernity has been expressed in terms of their ex posure to radio, liking for small family, higher education aspiration for their childern and acceptance of new technol ogy, secular ideas and also acquaintance with varied problems of the modern society.

IV

By way of conclusion it can be said that this small town of Mahishadal is in the process of gradual transformation. Its people suffer from anomie, have political awareness with an inclination to communism, show achievement motivation and want to move ahead with the characteristics of modern man. They are exposed to mass media, like small family, aspire higher education for their children, accept new technology and secular ideas and are aware of varied problems that a developing country like India faces.

REFERENCES

Alexander, K.C. 1973 Agrarian unrest in Kuttanad, Karala; Behavioral Science and Community Development, 7; 1-16.

Atkinson, J.W. 1968 Achievement Motivation; in International Encyclopeedia of Social Sciences, 1 : 27-33,Macmillan Pub lishing Co. New York.

Baradat, L.P. 1973 Political Ideologies; Prentice Hall In ternational, London.

Bottomore, T.B. 1962 Sociology; George Allen and Unwin, Lon don.

Greer, S. 1972 The Urbane view; Oxford University Press, London.

Inkeles, A. 1966 The Modernization of Man; in Modernization(ed); H. Weiner; Basic Book, New York.

Inkeles, A., and Smith, D. 1966 The O.M. Scale : A compara tive Socio psychological Measure of Individual modernity; Sociometry, 29 ; 353-377.

Kivlin, J.C.Fliegel, F.C.Roy, P. and San, L.K. 1971 Innova tion in Rural India; Bowling Grean University Press, Ohio.

Lerner, D. 1965 Passing of Traditional Society: Free Press, New York.

Mallick, A.K. 1977 Becoming Democratic Minded (unpublished manuscript).

McClelland, D.C. 1963 Methods of Measuring Human Motivation; in Motives in Fantacy Action and Society (ed) J.W. Atkinson, D.Von Nostrand, Princeton.

McClosky, H., and Schaar, J.H. 1965 Psychological Dimensions of Anomy; American Sociological Review,30 ; 14-49.

Mitchell, O.D. 1968 A Dictionary of Sociology; Routledge and Kegan Paul, London.

Pareek, U., and Rao, T.V. 1974 Handbook of Psychological and Social Instruments; Indian Institute of Management, Samasthi;

Rudloph L.I., and Rudolph, S.H. 1967 The Modernity of Tradition; University of Chicago Press, Chicago.

Sargent, L.T. 1972 Contemporary Political Ideologies, Dorsey Press; Home Wood.

Singh, Y. 1965 Traditional, Culture Pattern of India and In dustrial Change; in Tradition and Modernity in India (ed) : A.H. Shah, Manktatas: Bombay.

Singh, Y. 1973 Modernization of Indian Tradition; Thompson Press; Delhi.

Tripathi, S. 1976 Role of Elites in Modernization in context to value and Ideology; in Tradition and Modernization (ed) S.K. Srivastava, Indian International: Allahabad.

Index